Communications
in Computer and Information Science 1360

More information about this series at http://www.springer.com/series/7899

Christian Zirpins · Iraklis Paraskakis et al. (Eds.)

Advances in Service-Oriented and Cloud Computing

International Workshops of ESOCC 2020
Heraklion, Crete, Greece, September 28–30, 2020
Revised Selected Papers

 Springer

Editors
Christian Zirpins (ID)
Karlsruhe University of Applied Sciences
Karlsruhe, Germany

Iraklis Paraskakis
CITY College
Thessaloniki, Greece

Workshop Editors *see next page*

ISSN 1865-0929   ISSN 1865-0937   (electronic)
Communications in Computer and Information Science
ISBN 978-3-030-71905-0   ISBN 978-3-030-71906-7   (eBook)
https://doi.org/10.1007/978-3-030-71906-7

This Springer imprint is published by the registered company Springer Nature Switzerland AG
The registered company address is: Gewerbestrasse 11, 6330 Cham, Switzerland

Workshop Editors

EdgeWays

Vasilios Andrikopoulos ⓘ
University of Groningen
Groningen, The Netherlands

Claus Pahl ⓘ
Free University of Bolzano
Bolzano, Italy

Nane Kratzke ⓘ
University of Applied Sciences Lübeck
Lübeck, Germany

Nabil El Ioini ⓘ
Free University of Bolzano
Bolzano, Italy

WESOACS

Andreas S. Andreou ⓘ
Cyprus University of Technology
Limassol, Cyprus

Guadalupe Ortiz ⓘ
University of Cádiz
Cádiz, Spain

George Feuerlicht ⓘ
Unicorn University
Prague, Czech Republic

Willem-Jan Van den Heuvel
Tilburg University
Tilburg, The Netherlands

Winfried Lamersdorf ⓘ
University of Hamburg
Hamburg, Germany

Christian Zirpins ⓘ
Karlsruhe University of Applied Sciences
Karlsruhe, Germany

PhD Symposium

Jacopo Soldani ⓘ
University of Pisa
Pisa, Italy

Massimo Villari ⓘ
University of Messina
Messina, Italy

EU Projects Track

Giuliano Casale ⓘ
Imperial College London
London, UK

Pierluigi Plebani ⓘ
Politecnico di Milano
Milano, Italy

Preface

The European Conference on Service-Oriented and Cloud Computing (ESOCC) is among the leading events on advancing the state of the art in services and cloud technologies. It serves as an important venue for scientists as well as practitioners from academia and industry. The main objective of the event is to provide a broad forum for the exchange of ideas. In this respect, workshops are an important part of the conference. They contribute to an intensive exchange in special fields of service-oriented and cloud computing. In addition, ESOCC includes a PhD symposium where PhD students can present their ideas and results, ranging from early ideas to almost-completed work. Another part of ESOCC is the EU projects track, which discusses recent developments from European Projects. The workshop proceedings of ESOCC 2020 contains contributions from the following workshops and events:

- First International Workshop on Edge Migration and Architecture (EdgeWays 2020)
- Sixteenth International Workshop on Engineering Service-Oriented Applications and Cloud Services (WESOACS 2020)
- ESOCC 2020 PhD Symposium
- EU Projects Track of ESOCC 2020

We are grateful to Kyriakos Kritikos and his team for the excellent organization. They made it possible to successfully hold the conference in a virtual form despite all worries and restrictions of the 2020 pandemic situation. We also thank the organizers and program committee members of the workshops. Their efforts enabled an attractive program. Finally, we thank the authors who submitted their contributions to the workshops, the presenters, and the attendees. Without their support, active and fruitful workshops would not be possible.

January 2021

Christian Zirpins
Iraklis Paraskakis

Organization

General Chair

Kyriakos Kritikos   FORTH-ICS and University of the Aegean, Greece

Program Chairs

Antonio Brogi   University of Pisa, Italy
Wolf Zimmermann   Martin Luther University Halle-Wittenberg, Germany

Workshop Chairs

Christian Zirpins   University of Applied Sciences Karlsruhe, Germany
Iraklis Paraskakis   CITY College, Greece

Steering Committee

Antonio Brogi   University of Pisa, Italy
Schahram Dustdar   TU Wien, Austria
Paul Grefen   Eindhoven University of Technology, The Netherlands
Winfried Lamersdorf   University of Hamburg, Germany
Frank Leymann   University of Stuttgart, Germany
Flavio De Paoli   University of Milano-Bicocca, Italy
Cesare Pautasso   University of Lugano, Switzerland
Ernesto Pimentel   University of Malaga, Spain
Pierluigi Plebani   Politecnico di Milano, Italy
Ulf Schreier   Hochschule Furtwangen University, Germany
Massimo Villari   University of Messina, Italy
John Erik Wittern   IBM T.J. Watson Research Center, USA
Olaf Zimmermann   HSR FHO Rapperswil, Switzerland
Wolf Zimmermann   Martin Luther University Halle-Wittenberg, Germany

Contents

ESOCC 2020 PhD Symposium

ESOCC 2020 EU Projects Track

1st International Workshop
on Edge Migration and Architecture
(EdgeWays 2020)

Preface to the First International Workshop on Edge Migration and Architecture

The first International Workshop on Edge Migration and Architecture (EdgeWays 2020) aimed to bring together cloud and edge computing experts from academia and industry from different IT communities, e.g., edge computing, cloud computing, IoT, software engineering, services computing, big data, information systems, etc. Its main goals were to promote discussions and collaboration amongst participants, to help disseminate novel edge computing practices and solutions, and to identify future edge computing challenges and dimensions.

The first edition of the workshop focused on edge adoption and applications. Edge computing introduces a new architecture and deployment model that extends the cloud infrastructure. It has huge potential in scenarios where the traditional cloud fails to meet certain quality requirements. Many of the major IT companies and start-ups envision edge computing as i) a key enabler for IoT infrastructures and services, by providing the needed processing and storage capacities often limited in IoT devices ii) allowing cloud resources to be closer to data sources, which allows higher performance and context aware services, iii) increasing security and privacy by placing security checks closer to the data sources. From a business point of view, organizations can benefit from the distributed nature of edge computing to deploy dedicated services on a context or time basis to serve certain areas. From a technological perspective, the scalability, interoperability, and efficient (de-)allocation of resources at the edge can enable a whole new set of scenarios in the context of IoT.

Six papers were presented in the workshop dealing with different aspects of Edge computing, including applications architecture, deployment, modeling, and simulation. The participants had the chance to share their research and results as well as receive feedback from experts from different research areas. All the participants were given the possibility to include additional content based on the received comments to improve the quality of their papers.

November 2020

Vasilios Andrikopoulos
Nane Kratzke
Claus Pahl
Nabil El Ioini

Organization

Program Committee Chairs

Vasilios Andrikopoulos	University of Groningen, the Netherlands
Nane Kratzke	Technical University of Applied Sciences Lübeck, Germany
Claus Pahl	Free University of Bozen-Bolzano, Italy
Nabil El Ioini	Free University of Bozen-Bolzano, Italy

Program Committee

Paulo Henrique Maia	Ceará State University, Brazil
Dana Petcu	West University of Timisoara, Romania
Américo Sampaio	University of Fortaleza, Brazil
Claudio Ardagna	University of Milan, Italy
Hamid Reza Barzegar	Free University of Bozen-Bolzano, Italy
Mohammad Al-Zinati	Jordan University of Science and Technology, Jordan
Sören Frey	Daimler TSS, Germany
Wilhelm Hasselbring	Kiel University, Germany
Ali Khajeh-Hosseini	Infracost, UK
Xiaodong Liu	Edinburgh Napier University, UK
Lylia Alouache	CY Cergy Paris University, France

Finding Feasible Application Deployments in Edge Clusters, with Limited Resources

Jacopo Soldani$^{(\boxtimes)}$

University of Pisa, Pisa, Italy
soldani@di.unipi.it

Abstract. Edge computing brings the service and utilities of cloud computing closer to end users. At the same time, the devices forming edge clusters are limited in featured computing resources, e.g., memory and storage. Running multi-component applications on edge clusters hence requires suitably selecting the nodes where to deploy the software stacks forming an application, so that they get actually hosted on cluster nodes featuring enough computing resources. In this paper, we illustrate a solution allowing to automatically determine feasible application deployments in edge clusters, i.e., automatically associating the software stacks forming an application to the nodes in a cluster that feature enough memory and storage for running them. Our solution is based on an existing graph transformation-based algorithm, with the main aim of demonstrating its potentials when applied to edge-related problems. Finally, we also illustrate an open-source prototype implementation of our solution.

Keywords: Application topology · Deployment · Edge cluster

1 Introduction

Edge computing brings the service and utilities of cloud computing closer to end users, by providing low latency, mobility and location awareness to support delay-sensitive applications [9]. At the same time, edge clusters are built up by physical devices, which are limited in available computing resources, hence differing from the elastic, virtual computing environments characterising cloud infrastructures and platforms [11,13].

Being limited in available computing resources (e.g., featured memory and storage), the nodes in an edge cluster cannot be used for running any possible software stack. It is rather needed to suitably distribute the various components forming an application across the nodes forming an edge cluster, so that each component or software stack is placed in a cluster node featuring enough computing resources for allowing to run the components it hosts [9,12].

Consider, for instance, the application deployment modelled in Fig. 1(a), which we shall exploit as running example in this paper. The figure displays the topology (i.e., the structure) of a web-based application, given as a typed

© Springer Nature Switzerland AG 2021
C. Zirpins et al. (Eds.): ESOCC 2020 Workshops, CCIS 1360, pp. 5–17, 2021.
https://doi.org/10.1007/978-3-030-71906-7_1

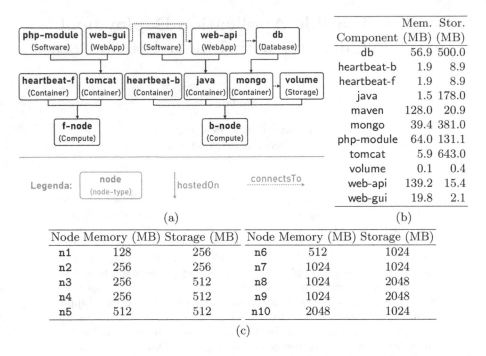

		Mem.	Stor.
Component		(MB)	(MB)
db		56.9	500.0
heartbeat-b		1.9	8.9
heartbeat-f		1.9	8.9
java		1.5	178.0
maven		128.0	20.9
mongo		39.4	381.0
php-module		64.0	131.1
tomcat		5.9	643.0
volume		0.1	0.4
web-api		139.2	15.4
web-gui		19.8	2.1

(a)   (b)

Node	Memory (MB)	Storage (MB)	Node	Memory (MB)	Storage (MB)
n1	128	256	n6	512	1024
n2	256	256	n7	1024	1024
n3	256	512	n8	1024	2048
n4	256	512	n9	1024	2048
n5	512	512	n10	2048	1024

(c)

Fig. 1. Example of multi-component application to be deployed on a edge cluster, with (a) depicting the application topology according to the TOSCA graphical notation [10], (b) listing the memory and storage consumption of the components forming the application, and (c) listing the nodes forming the edge cluster, i.e., their labels **n1...n10** and the amounts of memory and storage they feature.

directed graph. Topology nodes model application components, while arcs model horizontal and vertical dependencies occurring among components (i.e., which components a component connects to, and which component is used to host another component). As per Fig. 1(a), the components forming the considered application have to be deployed on two different compute nodes, i.e., two different nodes in the target edge cluster. Suppose now that the application components experience memory and storage consumption listed in Fig. 1(b), and that the considered edge cluster is formed by the nodes in Fig. 1(c). A question naturally arises: Which are the "feasible" deployments for such application on the target edge cluster? More precisely, which nodes in the cluster feature enough memory and storage for actually being used as compute nodes in our application?

Even if simple, the application in our running example makes it not easy to come to an answer to the above question. This holds especially since, when composing the memory and storage consumption of application components, we should consider the inter-dependencies occurring among them [5]. If project-ing the same question to realistic scenaria involving more complex applications and clusters, it becomes clearer that we need some machinery for automatically determining the cluster nodes featuring enough computing resources for running the components forming a to-be-deployed software stack, as also outlined in [9].

The first contribution of this paper is precisely to propose one such machinery, by illustrating a solution enabling to automatically determine feasible application deployments in edge clusters. Our solution first determines the overall resource requirements of the various stacks forming an application (such as those rooted on f-node and b-node in Fig. 1(a)), and it then identifies the nodes in a cluster that can be used to host such software stacks. We also illustrate a prototype implementation of our solution, called *ShipTo*. With our solution (and *ShipTo*), application administrators are only required to indicate deployment-specific information, i.e., the topology of the application to be deployed, the memory and storage consumption of application components, and the list of nodes forming the edge cluster, together with the memory and storage they feature. Our solution then automatically associates the root of each software stack in an application with the cluster nodes featuring enough memory and storage to host the application components forming the software stack.

Our solution is based on an existing graph transformation-based algorithm for solving general purpose estimation problems on application topologies, i.e., *EvalTo* [5]. We indeed show how a suitable configuration of *EvalTo* allows us to solve the aforementioned placement problem by taking into account memory and storage. Changing or refining the placement problem to solve (e.g., for taking into account also network consumption and bandwidth) just requires to accordingly change the illustrated configuration of *EvalTo*. The main contribution of this paper is indeed to demonstrate the potentials and applicability of *EvalTo* (and, in general, of graph transformation-based algorithms) to support the deployment of multi-component application topologies on edge infrastructures.

The rest of the paper is organised as follows. Section 2 sets the stage for presenting our solution. Sections 3 and 4 illustrate our solution and its prototype implementation. Finally, Sects. 5 and 6 discuss related work and draw concluding remarks.

2   Setting the Stage

EvalTo [5] is a graph transformation algorithm for solving general purpose cost estimation problems on multi-component applications. Given the topology of an application, and the costs associated to the nodes forming such application, *EvalTo* can automatically compose the costs of the nodes forming the application to estimate the overall cost of the application. Notably, different types of costs can be associated with different types of nodes, and costs associated with two nodes can be composed differently based on whether they horizontally or vertically depend one on the other. This gives room for solving various different problems, from checking installation conflicts in multi-component application to estimating the minimum and maximum costs that would be paid if distributing a multi-component application across various heterogeneous cloud offerings.

Fig. 2. Graph transformation rules iteratively employed by *EvalTo*.

We hereafter sketch the *EvalTo* algorithm[1], by providing the necessary background for setting our solution for automatically determining feasible deployments for multi-component applications on edge clusters. In this perspective, we first retake the definition of *topology* for a multi-component application, which is formalised as a typed directed graph in [5]. The nodes of the graph represent the components forming an application, and node sorts are used to distinguish component types, e.g., to distinguish a container from a web application. Arcs instead represent inter-component dependencies, and their types allow distinguishing vertical and horizontal dependencies. A vertical dependency from a node u to a node v indicates that u is contained in v (e.g., because u is hosted on v). A horizontal dependency from u to v instead means that u uses (at run-time) functionalities provided by v, hence requiring u and v to run simultaneously.

Definition 1 (Topology). *The* topology *of an application is a typed and directed graph $T = \langle N, S, \mathsf{s}, D_h, D_v \rangle$, where*

- *N is a finite set of nodes, representing the application components,*
- *S is a set of node sorts, i.e., the possible types of components,*
- *$\mathsf{s} : N \to S$ is a function associating each node with its sort,*
- *$D_h \subseteq N \times N$ is the set of arcs representing horizontal dependencies, and*
- *$D_v \subseteq N \times N$ is the set of arcs representing vertical dependencies.*

EvalTo [5] estimates of the overall cost of a topology $T = \langle N, S, \mathsf{s}, D_h, D_v \rangle$, by suitably composing the costs associated with its components. Note that the overall cost of a topology is unclear when looking at it, as the costs of the nodes forming a topology must be composed by properly taking into account all vertical and horizontal dependencies occurring among them. Instead, when looking at the two simple sub-cases shown in Fig. 2 the cost composition is much clearer.

In the lefthand case, we can directly compose the cost of u with that of v for obtaining their overall cost. This intuitively means that u and v can be seen as a *collapsed* node w, which cost is obtained by composing those of u and v, and which ingoing/outgoing dependencies are obtained by preserving those of u and v. In the righthand case, we instead first compose the cost of u and v, and we then compose the resulting cost with that of z. Intuitively, this also means that u and v can be seen as a *collapsed* node w, which cost is obtained by composing those of u and v, and which ingoing/outgoing dependencies are obtained by preserving those of u and v. The overall cost can then be obtained by composing that of w and z by re-applying case the lefthand case.

---

[1] Interested readers can find a detailed, self-contained presentation of *EvalTo* in [5].

The algorithm *EvalTo* precisely realises the above explained intuition, by realising the machinery for automatically deriving the cost of an overall application, by iteratively applying the collapsing rules in Fig. 2. The machinery of *EvalTo* is proved to be terminating and confluent, and to result in reducing the initial topology to a single node, which associated cost is unique and corresponds to the composition of the costs of the initial nodes in the application topology [5]. To do so, *EvalTo* needs to be provided with the topology T of an application, and with the *cost estimation problem* P to be solved on T.

Definition 2 (Cost estimation problem). *Let $T = \langle N, S, \mathsf{s}, D_h, D_v \rangle$ be a topology, and let N_s denote the nodes of sort s, i.e., $N_s = \{u \in N \mid \mathsf{s}(u) = s\}$. A cost estimation problem on T is defined by a tuple $P = \langle T, C, U, \mathsf{c}, \mathsf{v}, \mathsf{h} \rangle$, where:*

- *$C = \{C_s \mid s \in S\}$ contains the sets of admissible costs for each sort (i.e., C_s is the set of all possible costs that can be associated with nodes of a sort s),*
- *$U = \{U_s \mid s \in S\}$ contains the set of admissible upper costs for each sort (i.e., U_s is the set of all possible costs that can be associated with nodes directly contained in a node of sort s),*
- *$\mathsf{c} = \{\mathsf{c}_s : N_s \to C_s \mid s \in S\}$ is the set of functions associating the nodes in N with a cost,*
- *$\mathsf{v} = \{\mathsf{v}_s : U_s \times C_s \to C_s \mid s \in S\}$ is the set of vertical cost compositors, and*
- *$\mathsf{h} = \{\mathsf{h}_s : U_s \times U_s \to U_s \mid s \in S\}$ is the set of horizontal cost compositors.*

An example of cost estimation problem is available in Sect. 3, while the rationale of its definition is the following. As different types of costs may be associated with different sorts of nodes, the admissible costs for nodes of sort s are constrained by defining a set C_s. A function c_s then associates each node of sort s with its actual cost, and the set of all such functions is denoted by c.

The costs associated with the nodes forming a topology must then be composed to derive the overall cost of the application. The composition of the costs of two nodes u and v connected by a vertical dependency is represented by a set v of vertical cost compositors. Each function $\mathsf{v}_s \in \mathsf{v}$ indicates how to combine the cost of a node v of sort s with that of a node u contained in v (such as those in Fig. 2(a)). Each function $\mathsf{h}_s \in \mathsf{h}$ instead indicates how to combine the cost of a node v with that of a node u horizontally depending on v, in the context given by the node w of sort s in which both u and v are contained (such as those in Fig. 2(b)). In both v and h, the set U_s constrains the admissible "upper" costs for nodes of sort s, i.e., the type of costs that can be associated with the nodes directly contained in a node of sort s.

Finally, to succeed in reducing an application topology to a single node, *EvalTo* needs the initial topology to be "rooted", i.e., to contain only one node with no outgoing vertical dependencies. As shown in [5], this can be easily obtained on any topology T, by simply adding a new "bottom" node $\bot$, and by adding a vertical dependency targeting $\bot$ from each node in T with no outgoing vertical dependency. In our running example, this would mean adding a new node $\bot$, and two vertical dependencies from f-node and b-node to $\bot$. To avoid changing the overall cost of the topology, the cost compositors associated with $\bot$ have to be functions suitably aggregating the costs of each original stack (e.g., with set unions), and the cost associated with $\perp$ should be the neutral element for such functions (e.g., the empty set).

3 Computing Feasible Deployments, with *EvalTo*

Following our main aim of demonstrating the potentials and applicability of *Eval-To* (and of graph transformation-based algorithms) to support the deployment of multi-component applications on edge infrastructures, we hereby show how *Eval-To* can be used to automatically solve the problem of finding feasible application deployments in an edge cluster, i.e., determining the nodes of the edge cluster that can actually be used to host each software stack forming the application. More precisely, given that the graph transformation machinery is fully automated by *EvalTo*, what we hereafter show is how to set up a class of cost estimation problems, which enables *EvalTo* to solve the aforementioned problem.

Firstly, the topology $T = \langle N, S, \mathsf{s}, D_h, D_v \rangle$ of an application is constrained by setting its nodes to be either software components or compute resources, i.e., $S = \{sw, com\}$. In accordance with the TOSCA standard [1], this enables to distinguish the topology nodes forming the multiple software stacks in an application from those representing the compute nodes in edge clusters used to host such stacks. To set up cost estimation problems on such a kind of topologies, we hereafter suitably set costs and cost compositors. We also show the rationale behind our setting, by showing it applied to our running example.

Cost and Cost Compositors for Software Components. We set the possible costs for software components to be pairs of real numbers, which elements represent the memory and storage consumption of a node, and we set their cost function accordingly, i.e., $C_{sw} = \mathbb{R} \times \mathbb{R}$ and $U_{sw} = \mathbb{R} \times \mathbb{R}$. To enable the composition of the costs of software components interconnected by vertical or horizontal dependencies, we define the cost compositors v_{sw} and h_{sw} to pairwise sums, i.e., $\mathsf{v}_{sw}(\langle m, s \rangle, \langle m', s' \rangle) = \langle m+m', s+s' \rangle$ and $\mathsf{h}_{sw}(\langle m, s \rangle, \langle m', s' \rangle) = \langle m+m', s+s' \rangle$ (where m, m' denote values of memory consumption, while s, s' denote values of storage consumption). The rationale behind this choice is the following: If two software components u and v are connected by a vertical or horizontal dependency, they must run simultaneously since u is actually exploiting v to run (either as hosting node, or by consuming some of its functionalities). This means that the memory and storage required by u and v are consumed simultaneously, hence somehow requiring to "pay both".

The above setting already allows to partly run *EvalTo*. As *EvalTo* starts from "topmost" nodes (i.e., nodes without ingoing vertical dependencies), it can already be used to reduce stacked software component to single nodes, which associated costs are stacks' overall memory and storage consumption.

Example. Consider the application in our running example, and the memory and storage consumption of its components (Fig. 1). By applying all possible initial iterations of *EvalTo*, i.e., all iterations involving the cost compositors v_{sw}

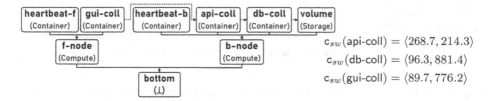

Fig. 3. Application topology and costs obtained after collapsing software components.

and h_{sw}, the corresponding cost estimation problem is reduced to that in Fig. 3. Beyond observing the addition of the bottom node, we can observe that software stacks have been reduced to single nodes, which associated memory and storage consumption are obtained by summing those of the components forming the stacks. For instance, the nodes php-module, web-gui and tomcat in the original application have been collapsed into the node gui-coll, which associated memory and storage consumption is given by the sum of those of the collapsed nodes.

To allow *EvalTo* further reducing the topology and progress solving the desired cost estimation problem, we need to define how costs of nodes directly hosted in compute nodes have to be composed together (if horizontally inter-depending), or with that of the compute node hosting them.   □

Cost and Cost Compositors for Compute Nodes. Our aim is to compute the memory and storage requirements needed by the (possibly multiple) software stacks hosted on each compute node, and to determine cluster nodes offering enough memory and storage to satisfy such requirements. We hence set the possible costs for compute nodes to tuples, each including a reference to the compute node itself, the maximum memory and total storage needed to run the software stacks it hosts, and the set of cluster nodes providing enough memory and storage for hosting the above software stacks. For compositionality reasons (which will become clear after discussing cost and cost compositors associated with $\bot$), we actually set the costs for compute nodes to set of tuples. Upper costs are instead obviously those of software components.

Formally, let E be the labels of available cluster nodes (e.g., n1...n10 in our running example), and let $\hat{E} \subseteq E \times \mathbb{R} \times \mathbb{R}$ be the triples associating each $e \in E$ to the memory and storage featured by the corresponding cluster node. We set $C_{com} = \mathcal{P}(N \times \mathbb{R} \times \mathbb{R} \times \mathcal{P}(\hat{E}))$, where $\mathcal{P}(X)$ is used to denote the power set of a set X, and $U_{com} = \mathbb{R} \times \mathbb{R}$. The function c_{com} then takes each compute node u and associates it with the initial cost $c_{com}(u) = \{\langle u, 0, 0, \hat{E} \rangle\}$. The latter models that u may be on any cluster nodes, as initially requiring no memory or storage.

Memory and storage requirements of the software stacks hosted on a compute node are derived only after suitably composing their memory and storage consumption. Our idea is to exploit the initial cost of each compute node (given by c_{com}) as starting point. We then increase memory and storage requirements of each compute node by composing its initial cost with the memory and storage consumption of hosted software stacks, and we restrict the set of cluster nodes where such component can be hosted accordingly. We indeed define the vertical

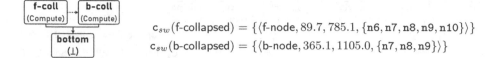

$$c_{sw}(\text{f-collapsed}) = \{\langle \text{f-node}, 89.7, 785.1, \{\text{n6}, \text{n7}, \text{n8}, \text{n9}, \text{n10}\}\rangle\}$$
$$c_{sw}(\text{b-collapsed}) = \{\langle \text{b-node}, 365.1, 1105.0, \{\text{n7}, \text{n8}, \text{n9}\}\rangle\}$$

Fig. 4. Application topology and costs obtained after collapsing compute nodes with the software stacks they host.

cost compositor v_{com} to keep the maximum memory required by hosted software stacks, to sum all storage requirements of such stacks, and to accordingly keep only those cluster nodes featuring enough memory and storage, i.e.,

$$v_{com}(\langle m, s\rangle, \{\langle n, mm, ts, A\rangle\})$$
$$= \{\langle n, \mathsf{max}(m, mm), s + ts, \{\langle e, m_e, s_e\rangle \in A \mid m_e \geq m \wedge s_e \geq s + ts\}\rangle\},$$

(where mm and ts are used to denote the required maximum memory and total storage, and A denotes the set of available cluster nodes satisfying such requirements). We instead define the cost compositor for combining the costs of two horizontally inter-dependent software stacks hosted on the same compute node as the sum of their memory and storage consumption. Being horizontally depending one another indeed inherently means that they must simultaneously run (Sect. 2), i.e., $\mathsf{h}_{com}(\langle m, s\rangle, \langle m', s'\rangle) = \langle m + m', s + s'\rangle$.

The above allows to continue iterating with *EvalTo* to collapse nodes representing software stacks and compute nodes. This allows associating each compute node with its overall memory and storage requirements, and with the cluster nodes satisfying such requirements. The following example shows this, by also clarifying the rationale of using max to compute overall memory requirements.

Example (cont.). Consider the situation shown in Fig. 3, and suppose we proceed with the iterations of *EvalTo*, by applying the iterations collapsing nodes and composing costs with the newly introduced v_{com} and h_{com}. The resulting situation would be that all software stacks are collapsed with their hosting compute nodes. Figure 4 shows this, with f-coll and b-coll obtained by collapsing the software stacks originally hosted on f-node and b-node, respectively.

The figure also shows the costs associated with f-stack and b-stack, computed by *EvalTo* and denoting the overall memory and storage consumption of the stacks originally hosted on f-node and b-node, together with the cluster nodes featuring enough memory to satisfy such memory and storage requirements. For instance, the memory requirements associated with f-coll are obtained as the maximum among the memory consumed by hearbeat-f and gui-coll, since (according to the application specification) the corresponding software components do not depend one on the other, hence not necessarily needing to simultaneously run. In this way, we keep only those compute nodes that can run hearbeat-f and gui-coll, at least alternatively. The storage requirements associated with f-coll are instead obtained by summing the storage consumption of such nodes. Finally, f-coll is also associated with the set of nodes in the cluster satisfying such memory and storage requirements. □

Cost and Cost Compositors for $\perp$. The bottom node is finally used for collecting all tuples associating compute nodes with their memory and storage requirements, and with the cluster nodes satisfying such requirements. Given that costs associated to compute nodes are singleton sets of tuples, it is enough to set the cost compositors for $\perp$ to be set unions, and to associate the node $\perp$ with a cost being the neutral element for such compositors, i.e., the empty set. Formally, this corresponds to setting $C_\perp = \mathcal{P}(N \times \mathbb{R} \times \mathbb{R} \times \mathcal{P}(\hat{E}))$, $U_\perp = \mathcal{P}(N \times \mathbb{R} \times \mathbb{R} \times \mathcal{P}(\hat{E}))$ and $c_\perp(\perp) = \emptyset$, as well as to set both $v_\perp$ and $h_\perp$ to be the set union $\cup$.

The above allows completing the iterations of *EvalTo*. Remaining nodes can indeed be reduced to a single node, which associated cost represents the feasible deployments for the original application. The obtained cost is a set of tuples, each associating a compute node in the original application with the memory and storage required to host its above software stacks, and with the cluster nodes featuring enough memory and storage to satisfy such requirements.

Example (cont.). The above introduced cost and cost compositors allows to collapse all nodes in Fig. 4 into a single node (app-coll), which associated cost is the union of the costs of f-coll and b-coll, i.e., $c_\perp(\text{app-coll}) = \{\langle \text{f-node}, 89.7, 785.1, \{\text{n6, n7, n8, n9, n10}\}\rangle, \langle \text{b-node}, 365.1, 1105.0, \{\text{n7, n8, n9}\}\rangle\}$. Please note that the obtained "overall cost" indicates the memory and storage requirements for both compute nodes of the original application (i.e., f-node and b-node), and the cluster nodes that can actually implement them.   □

Discussion. The outcomes produced by our solution can be exploited to develop ad-hoc policies for placing software stacks on cluster nodes. The output produced by *EvalTo* indeed associates the software stacks to be hosted on a compute node with their memory and storage requirements, and with the cluster nodes that can satisfy such requirements. Such information can then be combined with the memory and storage featured by cluster nodes to devise placement policies, e.g., for shipping/migrating software stacks to/across cluster nodes.

It is also worth noting that our setting of *EvalTo* defines a class of placement problems, which can be instantiated into a concrete problem by only requiring application administrators to provide application- and cluster-specific information. Everything needed by *EvalTo* to solve placement problems is indeed already set, but for (i) the application topology, (ii) the memory and storage consumption of software components, and (iii) the set of physical entities forming the edge/fog cluster where to deploy the application should not be considered a restriction. This is obviously not a restriction of our solution, but rather defining the *deployment-specific* information, which is known only by the administrator of an application, hence defining the input she has to provide to our solution.

Changing the problem to solve, or including additional metrics for refining that illustrated in this section (e.g., for taking into account also network consumption and bandwidth) only requires to update the illustrated configuration of *EvalTo*. It can indeed be obtained by changing/extending the tuples defining the resources required by software components and those featured by edge nodes, and to update the cost compositors accordingly. A guiding example on how to do this (even if for a different application domain) can be found in [5].

4   Open-Source Prototype Toolchain

We developed an open-source prototype implementation of our approach, called *ShipTo*. *ShipTo* is implemented in Python 3.7, and it provides a command-line interface allowing to run an instance of the existing *EvalTo* prototype, which is pre-configured to solve the class of cost estimation problems described in Sect. 3.

Application administrators only need to provide *ShipTo* with the TOSCA specification of an application and a YAML file composed by two objects, i.e., `consumption`, which associates each application component with its memory and storage consumption, and `clusterNodes`, which lists the nodes forming the cluster where to deploy the application together with the memory and storage they feature. *ShipTo* then exploits its first module (i.e., `Loader`) to process the given input and generate the input file needed to instantiate *EvalTo* to solve the desired estimation problem, i.e., to return a file listing the actual memory and storage requirements for each compute node, and the cluster nodes that can satisfy such requirements (Fig. 5). The output of *EvalTo* is then processed by the `Exporter` module, which serialises it in a human-readable YAML file[2].

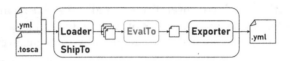

Fig. 5. Architecture of the prototype implementation of our approach, i.e., *ShipTo*.

5   Related Work

Despite there already exist applications that can be deployed on edge clusters (e.g., for big data stream processing [15]), the problem of planning their actual deployment over edge cluster is still open [9]. Solution tackling such a planning problem have been proposed, with FogTorch [3] and FogTorchPi [4] perhaps being the closest approaches to ours. They both indeed determine feasible application deployments in infrastructures with limited computing resources, by mapping the components forming an application to nodes satisfying their deployment requirements (including needed memory and storage), while at the same trying to optimise the QoS of the overall application. FogTorch and FogTorchPi do so by considering flattened application topologies, i.e., only modelling horizontal "connects to" relationships. We instead also enable modelling vertical dependencies for stacking application components, and we differently process vertical and horizontal dependencies to derive the overall memory and storage consumption for the software stacks forming an application.

---

[2] Further details on the implementation of *ShipTo* can be found in its GitHub repository (i.e., https://github.com/jsoldani/ship-to). The repository also provide a concrete example of input to be provided to *ShipTo*, based on our running example.

Similar considerations apply to other approaches for enacting QoS-optimal edge application deployments, e.g., [8,14,16,17]. Our approach could serve as a pre-processing step for all such approaches, as it allows deriving the resource required by each software stack, and the cluster nodes that can satisfy such requirements. Software stacks could then be considered as singleton components to flatten the topology, and mappings to cluster nodes could be used to reduce the search space where to look for QoS-optimal (feasible) deployments.

Other approaches worth mentioning are Zephyrus [2,7] and TosKeriser [6], both allowing to plan the deployment of multi-component applications in cloud-based virtual environments, so that each component is deployed in an environment offering what the component needs to run. Zephyrus consider computing resources actually available in cloud offerings, and computes cost-optimal, feasible application deployments. Similarly to the other approaches discussed above, it does so by relying on flat description of application topologies, involving only horizontal inter-component dependencies. TosKeriser instead also considers stacked topologies, as we do in our approach, but it focus on finding runtime environments offering needed software support, rather than on determining the overall computing resources required by each stack in an application and on identifying environments satisfying such requirements.

In summary, to the best of our knowledge, ours is the first approach for computing feasible application deployments in edge clusters that enables dealing with stacked application topologies, and which determine the overall amount of computing resources needed by the stacks forming an application by suitably combining those needed by the components forming such stacks (based on the horizontal/vertical dependencies occurring among components). It is also the first work showing potentials of *EvalTo* [5] (and of graph transformations, in general) to support the planning of application deployments.

6   Conclusions

We presented a solution for automatically determining feasible deployments for multi-component applications in edge clusters, for which we also provided an open source prototype implementation. With our solution, application administrators are only required to provide *deployment-specific* information, i.e., the application topology, the memory and storage consumption of application components, and the nodes forming the target edge cluster. Our solution then automatically computes the overall memory and storage requirements of each software stack forming the application, and it associates such stacks with the cluster nodes featuring enough memory and storage for running them. It does so by relying on the automated machinery provided by *EvalTo* [5], hence demonstrating its potentials and applicability to tackle problems related to edge deployment.

For future work, we plan to extend the set of considered metrics (e.g., by including network consumption and bandwidth), to refine our approach for finding suitable deployments of multi-component applications on edge cluster. We also plan to integrate our approach with existing solutions for planning QoS-optimal application deployments in edge/fog infrastructures (such as [3,4]), e.g., as a pre-processing step enabling them to also consider stacked topologies.

References

1. TOSCA Simple Profile in YAML, Version 1.2. OASIS Standard (2019)
2. Ábrahám, E., Corzilius, F., Johnsen, E.B., Kremer, G., Mauro, J.: Zephyrus2: on the fly deployment optimization using SMT and CP technologies. In: Fränzle, M., Kapur, D., Zhan, N. (eds.) SETTA 2016. LNCS, vol. 9984, pp. 229–245. Springer, Cham (2016). https://doi.org/10.1007/978-3-319-47677-3_15
3. Brogi, A., Forti, S.: QoS-aware deployment of IoT applications through the fog. IEEE Internet Things J. 4(5), 1185–1192 (2017)
4. Brogi, A., Forti, S., Ibrahim, A.: How to best deploy your fog applications, probably. In: Proceedings of the IEEE 1st International Conference on Fog and Edge Computing (ICFEC 2017), pp. 105–114 (2017)
5. Brogi, A., Corradini, A., Soldani, J.: Estimating costs of multi-component enterprise applications. Formal Aspects Comput. 31(4), 421–451 (2019)
6. Brogi, A., Neri, D., Rinaldi, L., Soldani, J.: Orchestrating incomplete TOSCA applications with Docker. Sci. Comput. Program. 166, 194–213 (2018)
7. Di Cosmo, R., Lienhardt, M., Treinen, R., Zacchiroli, S., Zwolakowski, J., Eiche, A., Agahi, A.: Automated synthesis and deployment of cloud applications. In: Proceedings of the 29th ACM/IEEE International Conference on Automated Software Engineering (ASE), pp. 211–222. ACM (2014)
8. Gupta, H., Vahid Dastjerdi, A., Ghosh, S.K., Buyya, R.: iFogSim: a toolkit for modeling and simulation of resource management techniques in the internet of things, edge and fog computing environments. Softw. Pract. Experience 47(9), 1275–1296 (2017)
9. Khan, W.Z., Ahmed, E., Hakak, S., Yaqoob, I., Ahmed, A.: Edge computing: a survey. Future Gener. Comput. Syst. 97, 219–235 (2019)
10. Kopp, O., Binz, T., Breitenbücher, U., Leymann, F.: Winery – a modeling tool for TOSCA-based cloud applications. In: Basu, S., Pautasso, C., Zhang, L., Fu, X. (eds.) ICSOC 2013. LNCS, vol. 8274, pp. 700–704. Springer, Heidelberg (2013). https://doi.org/10.1007/978-3-642-45005-1_64
11. von Leon, D., Miori, L., Sanin, J., El Ioini, N., Helmer, S., Pahl, C.: A lightweight container middleware for edge cloud architectures. In: Fog and Edge Computing, pp. 145–170. John Wiley & Sons, Ltd. (2019)
12. Pahl, C., Helmer, S., Miori, L., Sanin, J., Lee, B.: A container-based edge cloud PaaS architecture based on Raspberry Pi clusters. In: Proceedings of the IEEE 4th International Conference on Future Internet of Things and Cloud Workshops (FiCloudW 2016), pp. 117–124 (2016)
13. Pahl, C., Lee, B.: Containers and clusters for edge cloud architectures - a technology review. In: Proceedings of the 3rd International Conference on Future Internet of Things and Cloud (FiCloud 2015), pp. 379–386 (2015)
14. Saurez, E., Hong, K., Lillethun, D., Ramachandran, U., Ottenwälder, B.: Incremental deployment and migration of geo-distributed situation awareness applications in the fog. In: Proceedings of the 10th ACM International Conference on Distributed and Event-Based Systems (DEBS), pp. 258–269. ACM (2016)

15. Scolati, R., Fronza, I., Ioini, N.E., Samir, A., Pahl, C.: A containerized big data streaming architecture for edge cloud computing on clustered single-board devices. In: Proceedings of the 9th International Conference on Cloud Computing and Services Science (CLOSER), pp. 68–80. SciTePress (2019)
16. Shahid, H.F., Pahl, C.: Enhanced particle swarm optimisation and multi objective optimization for the orchestration of edge cloud clusters. In: Proceedings of the 11th International Joint Conference on Computational Intelligence (IJCCI), pp. 155–162. ScitePress (2019)
17. Wöbker, C., Seitz, A., Mueller, H., Bruegge, B.: Fogernetes: deployment and management of fog computing applications. In: IEEE/IFIP Network Operations and Management Symposium (NOMS 2018), pp. 1–7 (2018)

Edge Computing Simulation Platforms: A Technology Survey

Thanh Van Le$^{(\boxtimes)}$, Nabil El Ioini, Claus Pahl, and Hamid R. Barzegar

Free University of Bolzano, Piazza Domenicani 3, Bolzano, Italy
{vanle,nabil.elioini,claus.pahl,hamid.barzegar}@unibz.it

Abstract. As the interest in Edge Computing (EC) increases, the need for platforms to support building and evaluating EC based systems becomes more evident. EC has been defined as an extension of the cloud, an architecture that consists of moving part of the cloud resources to the edge of the network. EC does not pose any technological limitations on how it needs to be implemented, however, to be considered EC, a set of features need to be supported. Given the scale, heterogeneity, and complexity of the EC environment (e.g., hardware and software), being able to perform real experiments would require substantial investments, without being able to capture all the possible scenarios. In the cloud space, simulation has been used extensively to study and evaluate architectural and quality variations. Simulation platforms have been developed to reduce costs and speed up the design and evaluation phases. However, in many cases, they can be limited to specific properties or application domains. In this paper, we provide an overview of EC simulation platforms, looking first at the main EC features, then comparing the platforms in terms of the features they support.

Keywords: Edge computing · Internet of Things · Simulation platforms · Technology review

1 Introduction

Edge Computing (EC) has been defined as a model for supporting cloud resources (e.g., computing, storage, networking) at the edge of the network, at close proximity to data sources [12]. While the European Telecommunications Standards Institute (ETSI) provides a reference architecture for EC systems, there are still many conflicting views on how to implement them [10]. The heterogeneity of EC technologies makes it hard to offer commercial off-the-shelf solutions that fit all use cases. In the EC space, different platforms are being developed, some of them have a clear focus on specific features (e.g., Virtual Machine (VM)/container migration), while others target specific use cases (e.g., IoT devices, moving devices). Recently, as the demand for ultra-Reliable and Low-Latency (uRLLC) systems to serve mission-critical systems such as autonomous and assisted driving increases, the need for flexible environments

© Springer Nature Switzerland AG 2021
C. Zirpins et al. (Eds.): ESOCC 2020 Workshops, CCIS 1360, pp. 18–28, 2021.
https://doi.org/10.1007/978-3-030-71906-7_2

that allow fast and highly configurable settings become of paramount importance. Simulation environments have played for decades an important role in modeling complex systems by providing full control over all experiment variables, in order to evaluate an EC simulation platform, we will first define the requirements that make any given simulator interesting for the community.

As part of our effort to identify the main EC requirements that simulators need to support, we have considered the requirements of the different flavors of EC implementations, namely fog computing, mobile edge computing, and cloudlet computing [9]. Based on a literature review done on existing applications and approaches using these implementations, eight technical requirements have emerged.

The remainder of this paper is organized as follows. Section 2 describes related works which review EC simulators, Sect. 3 demonstrates technical requirements for EC platforms, Sect. 4 shows nine simulator tools studied, and the last section is about our conclusion and future work.

2   Related Work

The close connection between the cloud and the edge makes it relevant to discuss some of the predominant cloud simulators. CloudSim [8] is one of the most used simulation environments for the cloud, it provides a rich environment with more than 30 extensions. CloudSim toolkit supports both system and behavior modeling of cloud system components like data centers, VMs, and resource provisioning policies.

Since this paper focuses on EC simulator requirements, we investigated surveys related to both EC platforms and EC simulators. We found that there are many studies comparing EC architectures and platforms, however, only a few of them touch EC simulation platforms. Abreu et al. [20] analyses EC simulator architectures such as IFogSim [11], CloudSimSDN [22], YAFS [15], EmuFog [18], FoxTorch [7], EdgeCloudSim [23]. They compare these tools with diverse metrics including CPU and memory usage, network consumption as bandwidth, and latency. Their work is comprehensive with comparative diversity, only with metrics but also application models and other in-depth analysis. Their work was used as a starting point for our analysis. Mach et al. [16] present several usage cases and examples of comparison where the EC is relevant. Additionally, they have identified emerging concepts that integrate EC functionalities into mobile networks and discussed current progress in EC standardization. [1] presents a comprehensive survey of EC, concentrating on its general overview and its advantages, architectures, security and privacy issues, as well as application areas. Comparison among other implementations of edge computing such as fog computing, cloudlet, and EC has been studied in [9].

Sonmez et al. in [24] studied one of the new simulators called Edge-CloudSim. EdgeCloudSim builds on CloudSim to meet the specific requirements of edge computing research and supports the required features. Modeling and simulation of fog and edge computing environments based on iFogSim toolkit with different examples, configuration and installation of this simulator are presented in [17].

3   EC Key Characteristics

In this section, we list the main EC characteristics that simulators need to implement. We have identified 11 requirements.

3.1   Visualization Support

Visualization is an essential requirement for EC, which allows building an isolated environment for applications. *Hypervisors* and *containers* are the two common techniques [6] to implement virtualization. Hypervisors provide the guest operating systems with a virtual operating platform while still sharing the same physical hardware, containers provide only the basic services to all containerized applications using virtual-memory support for isolation. Containers are a better fit for EC with limited resources. Visualization is essential for an EC simulators since we can evaluate nodes performance when we run multiple services and examine the flexibility of the system.

3.2   Network Support

This characteristic is mainly related to simulation platforms, since we assume that **network generation** could affect the design of EC simulation (1G to 5G, 2.4 Kbps to 10 Gbps [13]). In the case of 1G or 2G, we do not need an EC platform since mostly these are radio based generations and do not support high data rate links, but with 4G and later, an EC node can control flows of big data [3]. Particularly, in 5G network, it should support low latency edge servers close to the towers to 10–20 ms. Besides this, a network controller also enables route tracking, so we can evaluate how requests are allocated in the network. Roaming is a clear example of the demand for network simulator when the requests do not go to EC, rather, they are re-routed to their home network. Moreover, bandwidth consumption also should be considered, similar traffic aggregation will reduce bandwidth between EC and the main server [4], so instead of sending requests one by one to the cloud, channels will be created for similar routes.

3.3   Orchestrator Support

Orchestrator [19] is a controller of EC, it takes a responsibility to collaborate with local controller based on its metric status as CPU or RAM, and decides when EC needs to offload or join its computation with other ECs.

3.4   Local Controller

Since EC is closer to the user, it needs to manage data locally as well as implement a level of smart behaviour. In particular, three main requirements are considered:

Local Analysis. EC needs to pre-process the data locally before sending it to the main cloud, for example, data from IoT devices or wearable devices should be analyzed and cleaned in advance and only send reports to the cloud or make local decisions (e.g., gas consumption alert to clients).

Edge Content Delivery. Shifting computation resources including service contents from the main cloud to edge will reduce a massive amount of requests to the remote servers. EC could respond to requested content to user applications with low latency. Content moving to EC can be executed using content caching techniques [29] for instance.

Machine State. EC nodes need to control their resources by themselves to report power consumption, CPU, and RAM utilization. Since the deployment of VM or containers could lead to an overload condition of EC, so these metrics should be under the control of both EC and the orchestrator.

3.5   Offloading

Offloading is the process of moving the computationally intensive tasks to a dedicated processing unit. In EC offloading has two main purposes:

Offloading from User Equipment. EC could reduce power intensive tasks executed by users' applications by moving them to EC (e.g., data encryption).

Offloading to Cloud System. Another goal for offloading is to increase the response time of services, which are deployed in EC, not in remote servers, so requests from users' applications are not routed to the main server.

3.6   Mobility Support

Mobility support concerns mainly two aspects, i) mobility simulation, and ii) mobility management. Mobility simulation refers to the ability to create simulations where users can communicate with EC nodes while they are on the move. For mobility management, EC can only access a coverage range of its deployed Base Transceiver Station (BTS), when user requests arrive, EC has to follow and response in time, but the traffic could be affected by distance from users or even when users move out of the coverage range. Mobility management should be set to estimate users' movements and make decisions to support other tasks.

3.7   Migration Support

Service migration [2] is one of the main requirements of mobility management which is a process that occurs during handover events, services are deployed in a visualized and encapsulated environment with virtual machines or containers.

The migration process will transfer the states of the service (i.e. file system, RAM, CPU) from the current EC node to the next, and redirect network traffic to reconnect with it.

3.8   Security

Moving a part of resources and computation from cloud to edge could lead to security issues. Cloud servers are generally protected by the cloud perimeter, firewalls and IDSs, while EC nodes might not meet the computational requirements to run any malicious detection software, thus, each EC device can represent a potentially vulnerable endpoint. A simulation platform that allows the definition and enforcement of security policies could help avert many of the security threats before real deployment.

4   EC Simulator Platforms

In this section, we will describe each of the EC simulation platforms. In total nine platforms have been identified.

4.1   IoTSim-Edge

IoTSim-Edge[1] is an IoT and edge computing testbed, which allows users to test IoT infrastructure and framework in an easy and configurable manner, this simulator is based on CloudSim [8]. IoTSim-Edge architecture inherits from CloudSim with additional edge controller modules as edge data center, edge broker, edge device. EdgeDataCenter manages the core edge infrastructure, intercepts all incoming events to submit mobile edge let (MEL) requests, this module also model location-awareness mechanism for IoT and edge devices, support power-awareness technique to track battery lifetime of EC. EdgeBroker generates user requests and sends them to MEL and EC. EdgeDevice presents for a real edge device, hosts MEL, and facilitates state control policies. This platform also simulates IoT devices to generate, send data and perform specific sensors like light, voice, etc.

4.2   EdgeCloudSim

EdgeCloudSim[2] is also built on top of CloudSim. The platform addresses specific demands of edge computing and supports the functionality in terms of computation and networking abilities. EdgeCloudSim provides a modular architecture for modules. The core simulator module loads scenarios from a configuration file and logs results into CSV file format. The network module solves transmission delay of Wireless LAN(WLAN) and WAN in both up/download link. The edge orchestrator module is a decision-maker that decides when and how a request should be handled. The mobility module only offers simple coordination with x and y of clients and edge nodes.

---

[1] https://github.com/DNJha/IoTSim-Edge.
[2] https://github.com/CagataySonmez/EdgeCloudSi.

4.3   ECSim++

ECSim++[3] is a fork from OMNetpp simulator [26] version 5.1.1, the tool is designed to simulate edge services, edge devices. ECSim++ framework is also based on INET [25] with extensions to build an edge cloud computing (ECC) environment. EdgeNode is the main module of ECC, extends from module Router of INET to present an EC node. Service table stores all current cloud services which are run on EdgeNode, each cloud service is presented by an IPv4 address. ServiceAware manages incoming requests and decides which services from the service table could handle them. EdgeService simulates a running service, the developers only focus on User Datagram Protocol (UDP) applications. Edge Node Management (Enoma) is located in the cloud core and control services on all edge nodes. The power module instead, is a simple power control for the edge, which calculates energy consumption on each network node to manage data caching at the edge.

4.4   IFogSim

IFogSim[4] is a toolkit that models IoT and Fog environments and measures cloud and network metrics. This tool is also inherited from CloudSim. IFogSim architecture starts with IoT sensors and actuators, which receive and response data to the real world, respectively, received data will be analyzed in upper layers. Fog devices act as gateways for a parent-child pair communication in the hierarchy topology. Resource management manages resources in the fog device layer, its policies allow component migration, dynamic changes in device resources. The application model simulates data processing components used for transferring data among dependent modules. Besides that, this tool also supports cost, energy model, and VM resource migration that is reused from CloudSim.

4.5   CloudSimSDN

CloudSimSDN[5] is another simulation framework based on CloudSim but focuses mainly on Software Defined Network (SDN). This platform has some additional components to control SDN behavior. The framework design is closer to telecommunication infrastructure, which contains cloud resources (host, switch, link), workload control (request, processing, transmission), and also virtual channel. The virtual channel is created to separate dataflows, their idea is to allow priority traffic to consume more bandwidth than normal traffic, and enables common routes to use the same channel.

---

[3] https://github.com/LarryNguyen/ECSimpp.
[4] https://github.com/Cloudslab/iFogSim.
[5] https://github.com/Cloudslab/cloudsimsdn.

4.6   YAFS

YAFS[6] stands for Yet Another Fog Simulator. The goal of YAFS is to analyze the design and deployment of applications via customized and dynamical strategies. Metrics reported by YAFS are network utilization, network delay, response time, waiting time, which are all stored in CSV format. The YAFS architecture is defined by six main classes: Topology, Core, Application, Selection, Placement, and Population. Core integrates other components, while topology prepares a set of note graph interconnected via network links. The other classes provide orchestration and allocation of resources in entities of the structure. Dynamic movement is described as a scenario for YAFS evaluation, but mainly focus on resource allocation, and service migration is not mentioned.

4.7   EmuFog

EmuFog[7] is an emulation framework for fog computing that enables researchers to design different network topologies and run Docker-based applications on nodes connected by a simulated network. It is an extensible emulation framework built on top of MaxiNet [30], which is also an extension of the popular network emulator Mininet [14]. The architecture of EmuFog is presented by a four-step workflow. *1)* topology generation: generates a network topology or load configuration from files. *2)* topology transformation: translates an undirected graph of a network to topology model by EmuFog. *3)* topology enhancement: identifies and combines edge and fog configuration policies to build a fog node placement, which shows fog nodes and their computational power. *4)* deployment and execution: emulates fog nodes from step *3*, where services running in Docker containers are being deployed on the nodes to test their performance. A new contribution of EmuFog is to load and deploy configurations with real applications in Docker. Nevertheless, all services have to run in a physical machine so performances could be limited because of restricted hardware and mobility support is not mentioned.

4.8   FogTorch

FogTorch[8] exploits Monte Carlo simulations to deploy applications and components in a fog infrastructure. The simulator uses an agriculture scenario to investigate remote monitoring and irrigation of crops.

FogTorch contains three main components. *ThingsController* interacts with IoT sensors and actuators such as fire sensors, electronic water valves, or video cameras. *DataStorage* stores all collected information from IoT devices. The *Dashboard* takes the responsibility of visualizing, monitoring, and controlling data from the sensors, along with historical data and machine learning engine rules.

---

[6] https://github.com/acsicuib/YAFS.
[7] https://github.com/emufog/emufog.
[8] https://github.com/di-unipi-socc/FogTorch.

Monte Carlo simulators are used to account for probabilities when assigning QoS profiles to communication hyperlinks. With each communication link, Fog-Torch generates and runs with input for fog infrastructure. In the end, a result shows two aggregated metrics of QoS-assurance (percentage of runs for generated deployment) and fog resource consumption (aggregated average percentage of consumed RAM and storage in fog nodes).

4.9 BEC

We proposed a blockchain-based EC management system (BEC) [28] with the goal to efficiently guarantee service continuity. Our work is built on top of the OMNetpp simulator [26] version 5.1.1, and mobility simulator inherits from SimuLTE [27], Veins [21], and Sumo [5]. The system architecture contains three main modules which are the mobility module, orchestrator module, and authentication module. Mobility module is built on Sumo and Veins and runs a simulated TCP application to forwards requests. The orchestrator receives requests and makes decisions to deploy a suitable Docker-based application into the nearest node, nodes are deployed in independent physical machines to enable a scalability and flexibility of testing environment. The authentication module is a standout component in our system which controls requests and decision flows of all modules, service information is stored in a blockchain network and requires access rights to receive. Blockchain also builds a secure channel for services and infrastructure vendors communication. However, the system does not support resource control in the edge node and the simulated network is outdated, only support 3GPP.

5 Simulator Tool Comparisons

A general overview of the identified platforms is shown in Table 1. A more detailed comparison is described in regard to the different requirements.

Visualization Support: Since EC is an extension of cloud computing, when it comes to simulators we have found that many projects are essentially forks come from CloudSim, which means that they inherit some of its core features such as virtualization simulation. Only EmuFog and BEC support real services packed in Docker. All nodes and Docker containers have to run in a single physical machine in EmuFog, which leads to a lack of scalability, while BEC separates EC nodes in different computers.

Network Support: when it comes to networking support, almost all platforms do not specify possible network generation, CloudSim extensions provide network environments as WAN, LAN, 3g, 4G and Bluetooth. Only ClouSimSDN offers traffic aggregation to build channels for common routes.

Table 1. Platforms comparison in terms of EC requirements.

Requirement/ Simulator	Visualization	Network	Orchestrator	Local controller	Offload	Mobility	Security
IoTSim-Edge	Yes, simulated VM	Up to 4G	No	Basic	Basic	Yes	No
EdgeCloudSim	Yes, simulated VM	Up to 4G	Yes	Basic	Basic	Yes	No
ECSim++	No	No	Yes	Basic	Basic	No	No
iFogSim	Yes, simulated VM	Up to 4G	No	Basic	Basic	No	No
CloudSimSDN	Yes, simulated VM	Up to 4G	No	Basic	Basic	No	No
YAFS	No	No	No	Basic	Basic	Yes	No
EmuFog	Yes, Docker	Common	No	Basic	Basic	No	No
FogTorch	No	Common	No	Basic	Basic	No	No
BEC	Yes, Docker	Up to 3G	Yes	Basic, no machine state	Basic	Yes	With blockchain

Orchestrator Support: EdgeCloudSim, ECSim++ and BEC include an orchestrator module (EdgeOrchestror, Enoma, Orchestrator respectively). while in the other platforms, orchestration needs to be managed by external modules (e.g., add-ons or third party orchestrator).

Local Controller: Only BEC does not control machine states as CPU or RAM, all other platforms on the other hand include some level of support to manage the local analysis.

Offloading: since it is considered one of the most important features for EC, all platforms support basic controls and try to reduce bandwidth to the main cloud, however regarding the computation merging with other EC to support the entire system, no simulation environment supports this feature by default.

Mobility Support: the network topology is given as an input and then the platform configures the network as in the case of FogTourchPi, EmuFog. CloudSimSDN focuses more on network infrastructure and ECSim++ works mainly on resource usages, does do not support mobility or service migration. Only BEC proposes a service migration but solely for stateless services.

Security Support: BEC supports secure authentication using EChanism based blockchain. All the other platforms instead rely on external components to handle security.

6   Conclusion and Future Work

In this survey, we investigated the importance of simulation platforms to support the design and evaluation of EC based systems. We looked at the features and characteristics of the major EC simulation platforms and compare them based on a set of requirements we collected from the existing literature. Our research has reviled that most of the platforms have focused primarily on the main functionality of EC, which is computation offloading and virtualization, while they support the other requirements at different degrees. One of the main reasons is to allow simulation environments to support multiple scenarios and be easily extendable. As future work, we intend to implement different scenarios using the different simulation environments to assess the maturity and non-functional properties of each platform.

Acknowledgment. This work has been performed in the framework of the EU Horizon 2020 project 5G-CARMEN co-funded by the EU under grant agreement No. 825012. The views expressed are those of the authors and do not necessarily represent the project.

References

1. Abbas, N., Zhang, Y., Taherkordi, A., Skeie, T.: Mobile edge computing: a survey. IEEE Internet Things J. **5**(1), 450–465 (2017)
2. Abdah, H., Barraca, J.P., Aguiar, R.L.: QoS-aware service continuity in the virtualized edge. IEEE Access **7**, 51570–51588 (2019)
3. Barzegar, H.R., Le, V.T., Pahl, C., Ioini, N.E.: Service continuity for CCAM platform in 5G-CARMEN. In: 16th International Wireless Communications and Mobile Computing Conference (IWCMC 2020) (2020)
4. Beck, M.T., Werner, M., Feld, S., Schimper, S.: Mobile edge computing: a taxonomy. In: Proceedings of the Sixth International Conference on Advances in Future Internet, pp. 48–55. Citeseer (2014)
5. Behrisch, M., Bieker, L., Erdmann, J., Krajzewicz, D.: SUMO - simulation of urban mobility - an overview. In: Proceedings of the 3rd International Conference on Advances in System Simulation (SIMUL 2011), pp. 63–68, October 2011
6. Bernstein, D.: Containers and cloud: from LXC to docker to kubernetes. IEEE Cloud Comput. **1**(3), 81–84 (2014)
7. Brogi, A., Forti, S., Ibrahim, A.: How to best deploy your fog applications, probably. In: 2017 IEEE 1st International Conference on Fog and Edge Computing (ICFEC), pp. 105–114, May 2017
8. Calheiros, R.N., Ranjan, R., Beloglazov, A., De Rose, C.A.F., Buyya, R.: CloudSim: a toolkit for modeling and simulation of cloud computing environments and evaluation of resource provisioning algorithms. Softw. Pract. Exp. **41**(1), 23–50 (2011)
9. Dolui, K., Datta, S.K.: Comparison of edge computing implementations: fog computing, cloudlet and mobile edge computing. In: 2017 Global Internet of Things Summit (GIoTS), pp. 1–6. IEEE (2017)
10. ETSI. Multi-access Edge Computing (MEC) (2018). https://www.etsi.org/technologies/multi-access-edge-computing. Accessed 17 Feb 2020
11. Gupta, H., Vahid Dastjerdi, A., Ghosh, S.K., Buyya, R.: iFogSim: a toolkit for modeling and simulation of resource management techniques in the Internet of Things, edge and fog computing environments. Softw. Pract. Exp. **47**(9), 1275–1296 (2017)
12. Hu, Y.C., Patel, M., Sabella, D., Sprecher, N., Young, V.: Mobile edge computing-a key technology towards 5G. ETSI White Paper **11**(11), 1–16 (2015)

13. Javed, M., Siddiqui, A.T.: Transformation of mobile communication network from 1G to 4G and 5G. Int. J. Adv. Res. Comput. Sci. **8**(3), 193–197 (2017)
14. Lantz, B., Heller, B., McKeown, N.: A network in a laptop: rapid prototyping for software-defined networks. In: Proceedings of the 9th ACM SIGCOMM Workshop on Hot Topics in Networks, Hotnets-IX, New York. Association for Computing Machinery (2010)
15. Lera, I., Guerrero, C., Juiz, C.: YAFS: a simulator for IoT scenarios in fog computing. IEEE Access **7**, 91745–91758 (2019)
16. Mach, P., Becvar, Z.: Mobile edge computing: a survey on architecture and computation offloading. IEEE Commun. Surv. Tutorials **19**(3), 1628–1656 (2017)
17. Mahmud, R., Buyya, R: Modelling and simulation of fog and edge computing environments using iFogSim toolkit. In: Fog Edge Computing: Principles and Paradigms, pp. 1–35 (2019)
18. Mayer, R., Graser, L., Gupta, H., Saurez, E., Ramachandran, U.: EmuFog: extensible and scalable emulation of large-scale fog computing infrastructures. In: 2017 IEEE Fog World Congress (FWC), pp. 1–6, October 2017
19. Pahl, C., Ioini, N.E., Helmer, S., Lee, B.: An architecture pattern for trusted orchestration in IoT edge clouds. In: 2018 Third International Conference on Fog and Mobile Edge Computing (FMEC), pp. 63–70, April 2018
20. Perez Abreu, D., Velasquez, K., Curado, M., Monteiro, E.: A comparative analysis of simulators for the cloud to fog continuum. Simul. Model. Pract. Theory **101**, 102029 (2019)
21. Sommer, C., Yao, Z., German, R., Dressler, F.: Simulating the influence of IVC on road traffic using bidirectionally coupled simulators. In: Proceedings - IEEE INFOCOM (2008). 00(c)
22. Son, J., Dastjerdi, A.V., Calheiros, R.N., Ji, X., Yoon, Y., Buyya, R.: CloudSimSDN: modeling and simulation of software-defined cloud data centers. In: 2015 15th IEEE/ACM International Symposium on Cluster, Cloud and Grid Computing, pp. 475–484, May 2015
23. Sonmez, C., Ozgovde, A., Ersoy, C.: EdgeCloudSim: an environment for performance evaluation of edge computing systems. In: 2017 Second International Conference on Fog and Mobile Edge Computing (FMEC), pp. 39–44, May 2017
24. Sonmez, C., Ozgovde, A., Ersoy, C.: EdgeCloudSim: an environment for performance evaluation of edge computing systems. Trans. Emerg. Telecommun. Technol. **29**(11), e3493 (2018)
25. Varga, A.: INETFramework - GitHub Repository (2020). https://github.com/inet-framework/inet. Accessed 22 Feb 2020
26. Varga, A., Hornig, R.: An overview of the OMNeT++ simulation environment. In: Proceedings of the 1st International Conference on Simulation Tools and Techniques for Communications, Networks and Systems & Workshops, ICST, p. 60 (2008)
27. Virdis, A., Stea, G., Nardini, G.: SimuLTE - a modular system-level simulator for LTE/LTE-A networks based on OMNeT++, pp. 59–70 (2014)
28. Le, V.T., Pahl, C., Ioini, N.E.: Blockchain based service continuity in mobile edge computing. In: 2019 Sixth International Conference on Internet of Things: Systems, Management and Security (IOTSMS), pp. 136–141, October 2019
29. Wang, S., Zhang, X., Zhang, Y., Wang, L., Yang, J., Wang, W.: A survey on mobile edge networks: convergence of computing, caching and communications. IEEE Access **PP**, 1 (2017)
30. Wette, P., Draxler, M., Schwabe, A., Wallaschek, F., Zahraee, M., Karl, H.: MaxiNet: distributed emulation of software-defined networks, pp. 1–9 (2014)

Platforms for Serverless at the Edge: A Review

Nabil El Ioini[1](✉), David Hästbacka[2], Claus Pahl[1], and Davide Taibi[2]

[1] Free University of Bozen-Bolzano, Bolzano, Italy
{nabil.elioini,claus.pahl}@unibz.it
[2] Tampere University, Tampere, Finland
{david.hastbacka,davide.taibi}@tuni.fi

Abstract. The continuous demand for low latency, high reliability, and context-aware content has pushed the existing computational models to their limit. The cloud with its infinite resources can accommodate many of the existing scenarios, however, as new scenarios emerge in the IoT area, the cloud falls short. In this context, the Edge Computing model emerged as an extension to the cloud in support of low latency and high-performance applications, by placing part of cloud resources at the edge of the network, in close proximity to the data sources and applications. The goal of Edge Computing is to provide the same level of abstraction at the cloud but in a local context. However, since Edge Computing inherits many of the benefits provided by the cloud, it also inherits some of its drawbacks. One such limitation is the management overhead needed to set-up and continuously configure the Edge Computing applications. In the cloud space, this problem has been addressed using a new paradigm called serverless technology. Similarly, in the Edge Computing, few attempts are being developed to bring the concept of Serverless Computing at the edge. In this paper, we survey the main edge computing platforms that provide support for serverless computing comparing their characteristics and identifying issues and research directions.

Keywords: Serverless · Edge computing · FaaS · Function-as-a-Service · Technology review

1 Introduction

Edge computing, the new buzzword, has been gaining a lot of traction from developers and the industry. Companies are mainly interested in improving the performance of their systems and reducing the operational costs, by moving part of the cloud resources closer to the data sources. One major use case of edge computing is IoT applications [5,9]. In industrial settings, there are many scenarios such as condition monitoring and general production monitoring that would benefit from processing the often huge amounts of sensor data closer to the source [6]. Similarly in multi media applications, receiving data from nearby edge computing units [7] can have a huge impact on latency and the user experience.

© Springer Nature Switzerland AG 2021
C. Zirpins et al. (Eds.): ESOCC 2020 Workshops, CCIS 1360, pp. 29–40, 2021.
https://doi.org/10.1007/978-3-030-71906-7_3

Together with Edge computing, serverless computing (also known as Function-as-a-Service or FaaS) is now gaining more and more interest from companies. Cloud vendors such as AWS and Microsoft have hyped serverless almost everywhere, from practitioners' conferences to local events, to blog posts. They are promoting the idea of allowing companies to focus only on their business logic, while delegating all the operational tasks to the cloud provider. However, serverless is not just about the hype but has several benefits that enable companies to reduce costs and to focus more on the business logic of applications. Since the main goal of edge computing is to locate cloud resources closer to the end user, and serverless technology is one of these resources, it is legitimate to investigate how these two technologies can be combined and what are the benefits and limitations of such integration.

Different companies have started already combining the power of edge with the operational easiness of serverless providing edge platforms for deploying serverless functions. The adoption of serverless computing on edge nodes might help to reduce the computational time, and reduce network-related costs [2,3,8,11,13]. However, in this fast-growing market, it is still not clear how to benefit from the serverless capabilities on edge platforms, and especially how the available solutions on the market allow us to abstract from the hardware used at the edge using containers or serverless functions at the edge.

In order to help practitioners, and stimulate the discussion on this topic, we aim at comparing the most common edge platforms that provide serverless support, discussing pros, cons and highlighting open issues and research directions. Therefore, the main contributions of this work are:

- A list of the most common edge platforms that support serverless functions
- Comparison of the main characteristics of the platforms
- Identification of open issues and research directions

The results can be useful to the research community and to practitioners that can easily compare the different features of the platforms and understand how to better select edge platforms that support serverless.

The remainder of this paper is structured as follows. Section 2 introduces the background of Serverless and Edge Computing. Section 3 describes and compares the selected edge-computing platforms. Section 4 discusses the results and identify open issues and research directions. Finally, Sect. 5 draws conclusions and highlight future works.

2   Background

In this section, we introduce the two main technologies subject of this review, namely Serverless technology and Edge Computing.

2.1   Serverless

A few years ago, most companies were entirely responsible for the operations of their server-side applications, then the cloud enabled companies to outsource part of the operations, renting virtual machines by the hour and paying as much concern to how much electricity our systems require as to how to use a mobile phone. However, the software systems remain as servers–discrete components that require allocation, provisioning, setting up, deploying, shutting down, ... In 2012 [10], developers started thinking about operating their systems instead of operating their servers, considering applications as workflows, distributed logic, and externally managed data stores. This way of working can be considered "serverless", not because no servers are running, but because developers do not need to think about them anymore.

In serverless, the cloud provider dynamically allocates and provisions servers. The code is executed in almost-stateless containers that are event-triggered, and ephemeral (may last for one invocation), and fully managed by the cloud provider [10].

However, the term serverless can be misleading. Serverless covers a wide range of technologies, that can be grouped into two categories: Backend-as-a-Service (BaaS) and Functions-as-a-Service (FaaS).

Backend-as-a-Service enables to replace server-side components with off-the-shelf services. BaaS enables developers to outsource all the aspects behind a scene of an application so that developers can choose to write and maintain all application logic in the frontend. Examples are remote authentication systems, database management, cloud storage, and hosting.

An example of BaaS can be Google Firebase, a fully managed database that can be directly used from an application. In this case, Firebase (the BaaS services) manages data components on our behalf.

Function-as-a-Service is an environment within which is possible to run the software. Serverless applications are event-driven cloud-based systems where application development relies solely on a combination of third-party services, client-side logic, and cloud-hosted remote procedure calls [1].

FaaS allows developers to deploy code that, upon being triggered, is executed in an isolated environment. Each function typically describes a small part of an entire application. The execution time of functions is typically limited (e.g. 15 min for AWS Lambda). Functions are not constantly active. Instead, the FaaS platforms listen for events that instantiate the functions. Therefore, functions must be triggered by events, such as client requests, events produced by any external systems, data streams, or others. The FaaS provider is then responsible to horizontally scale function executions in response to the number of incoming events.

Serverless applications can be developed in several contexts while, because of its limitations, it might have some issues in other contexts. As an example, long-running functions, such as machine learning training or long-running algorithms might have timeout problems, while constant workloads might result in higher costs compared to indefinitely running on-demand compute services like virtual machines or container run-times. Even if serverless is a very recent topic, researchers already investigated several aspects, such as patterns [12] anti-patterns [10], problems and issues [1].

2.2 Edge Computing

The increasing demand for computation, storage, and network resources are some of the most evident challenges for cloud providers and mobile network operators. Optimizing data traffic has a direct effect on the reliability and quality of services. The cloud has served this purpose for years, however, when it comes to IoT, the cloud falls short. The high number of IoT devices plugged in day induces a high traffic load, which can have a negative effect on the whole network. As a result, Edge Computing has emerged to address these issues, by placing part of the cloud resources (e.g., computation, storage, logic) closer to the edge of the network, which allows faster and more context-dependent data analysis and storage.

In terms of implementation, Edge Computing is composed of a set of nodes, each supports different computation, storage, and network requirements. Different flavors of Edge Computing networks exist, which are similar to what the cloud provides already. Private Edge Computing consists of a private network of Edge Computing nodes managed by a single organization. Public Edge Computing, allows customers to deploy their services on top of a managed infrastructure, and Hybrid Edge Computing, which combines the two previous types.

3 The Serverless Edge Computing Platform

As of today, several edge computing platforms have emerged. Some platforms have been developed for specific purposes, such as increasing the performance of HTTP requests and web content delivery, while others are generic and can be used in different context. In our survey, two main groups of platforms have been identified (Fig. 1). The first group focuses on using serverless functions to customize content at the edge before delivering it to the user, while the second group focuses on executing serverless functions on the data collected at the edge, before either pushing it to the cloud or sending the result back to the user. We have named the first group of platforms *Content Delivery Network platforms*, since they deal mostly with content delivery, while we named the second group *IoT platforms*, since they fit mostly IoT scenarios.

3.1 Content Delivery Network Platforms

Content Delivery Network or Content Distribution Network (CDN) is a network of servers geographically distributed, with the goal of providing high availability and performance by distributing the service closer to the users. CDNs is a very old approach, introduced in the late 1990s to reduce internet bottlenecks [4]. CDN is now frequently adopted by media companies and e-commerce to increase the performances of different services such as video streaming, software downloads, web, and many other systems. Several CDN providers recently saw the potential benefits of providing serverless support in their nodes, enabling not only the caching of the web content on their nodes, but also providing computational capabilities in their nodes, with the serverless technology. In this Section,

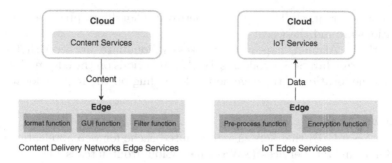

Fig. 1. Serverless at edge platforms categorization

we compare six CDN platforms that allow developing serverless functions on their edge nodes (Table 1).

Akamai Edge

Akamai[1] is one of the leading content delivery network (CDN) providers worldwide. Akamai provides a distributed platform consisting of more than 60,000 servers deployed over 70 countries. Akamai manages more than 15% of the web content. As part of the provided services, a dedicated edge platform called Edgeworkers has been developed. The main goal of edge workers is to allow cloud platforms to provide personalized business logic at the edge to support context aware services and at the same time reduce services latency. In this context, serverless functions can be customized and deployed closer to the customer infrastructure. Developers can take advantage of the wide network managed by Akamai to have control over where the functions are needed and what type of customization is needed to improve user experience in terms of performance and content.

IBM Edge Functions
Edge Functions on IBM Cloud Internet Services (CIS)[2] supports serverless computing at the edge closer to end-users across 180+ global network points of presence. As an example, it is designed to be able to pre-process HTTP requests and post-process responses e.g. for personalized user experience or improved API responsiveness. It is based on "isolates" that run on the V8 engine thus limiting the development to JavaScript.

Cloudflare
Cloudflare[3] is a CDN provider, with the main focus on performances. Cloudflare handles nearly 10% of the Internet HTTP requests, with peaks of more than 25

---

[1] https://www.akamai.com/us/en/products/performance/serverless-computing-edgeworkers.jsp.

[2] https://cloud.ibm.com/docs/infrastructure/cis?topic=cis-edge-functions.

[3] https://www.cloudflare.com/learning/serverless/glossary/what-is-edge-computing.

trillion monthly requests through their network. Cloudflare provides servers in 154 locations around the world.

Similarly to Akamai, it provides workers (Cloudflare workers) that enable developers to run JavaScript code as serverless functions on the edge nodes, while it controls the location of the edge nodes depending on the request locations.

Cloudfront

Cloudfront[4] is a CDN that acts as a distributed cache for web applications, part of the Amazon Web Services (AWS) offer. Cloudfront fetches files from their source location ("origin" in CloudFront terms) and places the copies of the files in different edge locations across the Americas, Europe, Asia, Africa, and Oceania. It enables to deploy serverless functions in its edge nodes, using the AWS "Lambda@Edge" functions enabling to run business logic, implemented in the functions. Differently from Akamai and Cloudflare, it supports the deployment of functions in several languages.

Edjx

Edjx[5] is a distributed edge computing platform. Combining packed as small microservers, container technology, and blockchain, Edjx can deliver a rich environment for developers to write, test and deploy serverless functions at the edge. The main target of Edjx is IoT applications with high bandwidth and low latency requirements. Using blockchain, Edjx provides a Pay as you go model for resources provisioning. Two main components make up the Edjx infrastructure:

– EDJX Nanoserver Infrastructure: it represents the hardware back-end of the system. It is composed of a set of lightweight servers that can be deployed as edge nodes. The servers are packed as small form factor with an Intel i7 CPU, 16 GB of RAM and 1 TB of storage.
– EDJX Serverless Edge: it represents the software component to manage the serverless functions lifecycle and orchestration. Since Edge Computing nodes need to collaborate in order to deliver services, the platform creates a peer-to-peer network among all the participating nodes.

Edjx promise is to make the deployment process transparent to the developers. The platform handles the process of locating the closest node to the user and deploy the serverless functions. To securely access services and data records, Edjx relies on Chainyard[6] to deliver blockchain based distributed serverless applications.

---

[4] https://aws.amazon.com/cloudfront/.
[5] https://edjx.io.
[6] https://chainyard.com/.

Stackpath

Stackpath[7] is a general-purpose cloud-based CDN with edge nodes in the whole world except Canada, Russia and Africa. The Stackpath serverless scripting engine is built on the Chrome V8 JavaScript Engine providing support for JavaScript. However, it enables also us to use WebAssembly supporting additional language support such as PHP, C, C++, Go, Python, Perl, Rust, and more.

Table 1. Comparison of the CDN platforms

Features	CDN platforms with serverless support						
	Akamai	Cloudflare	Stackpath	CloudFront	Edjx	IBM edge functions	Nuclio
Support of AI on the edge				✓	✓		✓
Availability	Globally	Globally	Limited	Globally	Limited	Globally	Limited
Supported platforms (edge hardware)	Akamai nodes	Cloudflare nodes	Stackpath nodes	AWS nodes	Nanoservers	IBM centers	Portable across constrained devices
Supported languages	JavaScript	JavaScript	Multi-lang	Multi-lang	Multi-lang	JavaScript	Multi-lang
Cost model	Pay as you go						Hosting cost
License	Proprietary						Open source

3.2   IoT Platforms

Internet of Things (IoT) platforms include connectivity, management, and programming mean for running various devices or things as part of Internet applications. In their simplest form, IoT devices transmit some sensor readings but as more advanced they include various functionalities such as preprocessing of sensor data or actuating with the physical world. These advanced IoT devices can thus be seen as an extension of the Internet-based application system including application software connecting with both cloud and edge components.

AWS IoT Greengrass

AWS IoT Greengrass[8] is Amazon's extension of the cloud to the edge of the network and physical devices. Greengrass has been designed from the beginning for use in the user's own hardware while using the same cloud management mechanisms, analytics, and durable storage. Regarding serverless Greengrass is well known for its capability to execute AWS Lambda functions and in most cases, they can be the same as those run in the cloud. The Lambdas that can be run on Greengrass edge devices can be implemented in several programming languages and the edge software platform can be installed on platforms including x86-64, ARMv8, ARMv7 and also as Docker containers.

---

[7] https://www.stackpath.com/products/edge-computing/serverless-scripting/.

[8] https://aws.amazon.com/greengrass/.

Azure IoT Edge

Azure IoT Edge[9] is Microsoft's edge computing and IoT Hub cloud extension for the physical devices of the user. IoT Edge supports several Linux versions and Windows 10 or Windows Server 2019 on their Tier 1 level and multiple other operating systems including virtual machines as Tier 2 level supported. X86-64 as well as 32-bit and 64-bit ARM architectures are supported. In terms of serverless functionality, it allows the containerization of Azure Functions developed in multiple programming languages to be deployed on IoT Edge devices. It is worth noting that IoT Edge software is free and open source.

Fogflow

Fogflow[10] is an edge computing framework designed to automate and optimize IoT services orchestration. It leverages three types of context to provide unique context-driven feature, *i)* System context: it relies on geo-distributed services to make sure that resources are available where needed, *ii)* Data context: it uses a unified data model to detect relations between tasks in order to optimize task flows, and *iii)* Usage context: orchestration decisions can be based on user-specific rules and thresholds. In Fogflow, the flow of execution can span across multiple Edge Computing nodes depending on the different combinations of aforementioned types of context (e.g., two services located in different areas and the second service relies on the first service output). To facilitate services migration, Docker containers are used to package services logic and all its dependencies. On top of Fogflow, serverless functions can be deployed. Fogflow support serverless function by:

- invoking serverless function once the input data are available
- automatically managing scalability of instances (e.g., create new instances)
- automatically locating the best Edge Computing node (i.e., closer to the data producer or data consumer) to deploy serverless functions.

Nuclio

Nuclio[11] is a serverless framework focusing on high data, I/O and compute intensive workloads. The framework supports a wide range of data sources and supports CPU and GPU execution modes. One of the main goals of Nuclio is to provide an open environment that allows easy portability and rapid deployment time. It supports most popular data science tools such as Jupyter and kubeflow, which increases deployment automation. Nuclio has been used predominantly in IoT scenarios where IoT data can be analysed closer to the data sources.

---

[9] https://docs.microsoft.com/en-us/azure/iot-edge/.
[10] https://github.com/smartfog/fogflow.
[11] https://nuclio.io.

OpenWhisk-Light

The standard OpenWhisk[12] is an open-source initiative for distributed server-less execution of functions in response to various events. OpenWhisk-Light[13] is a runtime with the standard OpenWhisk API for local or edge execution also supporting resource-constrained devices while maintaining a centralized OpenWhisk cloud instance as a master repository and catalog of its actions (i.e. functions). It supports the execution of OpenWhisk actions developed using multiple programming languages and can be deployed on the edge as Docker containers. It has also been demonstrated working on devices as constrained as a Raspberry Pi which makes it a candidate for IoT edge devices. It is based on an open source licensing similar to the original OpenWhisk (Table 2).

Table 2. Comparison of the IoT platforms

Features	IoT platforms with serverless support				
	AWS GreenGrass	Azure IoT	FogFlow	OpenWhisk-Light	Nuclio
Support of AI on the edge	✓	✓	✓	✓	✓
Availability	Globally	Globally	Limited	Limited	Limited
Edge hardware	Docker support	Tier 1: containers support. Tier 2: Virtual machines support	Docker support	containers support. Demonstrated for limited operation also in Raspberry Pi	Portable across constrained devices
Supported languages	Multi-lang	Multi-lang	Multi-lang	Multi-lang	Multi-lang
Cost model	Pay as you go		Private setting		Private or hosting cost
License	Proprietary	Open source			

4 Discussion

The initial comparison suggests that the existing platforms in the two categories have clearly specific goals. While the CDN category focuses more on taking advantage of serverless technology to increase availability and reduce costs, the IoT category points more towards portability, AI and multi-language support (Fig. 2).

Even-though serverless on the edge is still at its infancy, the first proofs of its potential usage can already be seen in the proposed solutions and platforms. On one side, existing Edge providers are extending their offers providing serverless support on their edge nodes. On the other side, new serverless-specific edge platforms have been introduced in the last years.

---

[12] https://openwhisk.apache.org.
[13] https://github.com/kpavel/openwhisk-light.

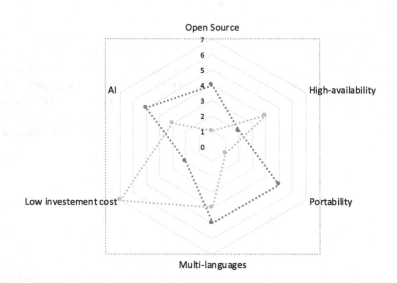

Fig. 2. Serverless at edge categories comparison

Existing edge platforms often enable only to deploy functions written with a limited set of languages. As an example, the traditional CDN platforms enable to write Javascript code on their edge nodes, while new platforms enable developers to use different languages.

IoT applications with more advanced processing on the edge device or edge of the network could significantly benefit from the serverless paradigm and especially the management and deployment of versions across fleets of devices. In addition to traditional sensor data processing, video or image-based processing as well as distributed AI-based inference are expected to be application areas of interest.

For IoT targeted solutions it seems that Microsoft with its IoT Edge is striving for a more open platform compared to AWS Greengrass. Both platforms support different hardware and installation on own equipment but the biggest difference is in Microsoft IoT Edge open source licensing that enables companies to use and extend their open source components on local hardware. Microsoft also supports an open ecosystem through the Azure Marketplace, e.g. acquiring solutions developed by others and deploying on the edge. Both of the platforms, however, rely heavily on their cloud service counterparts increasing the vendor lock-in. The OpenWhisk-Light is a fully open source alternative that offers similar features but with less tooling and support. As a consequence, however, it requires management of the OpenWhisk cloud counterpart to which the edge component is an extension of.

4.1   Open Issues

This work enabled us to identify a set of open issues:

- *Vendor Lock-In.* Commercial serverless platforms require to write functions that use the infrastructure provided, increasing vendor lock-in. As an example, an application developed with Greengrass would require a major effort to be deployed in Azure IoT. Currently, no frameworks allow to use hybrid clouds and to write generic functions that could be deployed in different ecosystems.
- Lack of decision frameworks to understand when is beneficial or not to use serverless on edge
- Lack of best practices, patterns and anti-patterns for creating serverless applications on the edge.

We believe that the research community should help practitioners to understand how to create serverless functions on the edge that could be deployed everywhere, and provide guidelines, including validated patterns and anti-patterns for creating serverless applications on the edge.

5   Conclusion

In this paper, we described the most common platforms for Serverless in Mobile Edge Computing.

Some of the selected platforms are targeted to specific purposes such as IoT, while others are specifically targeting Content Delivery Network (CDN). Moreover, it is interesting to note that several CDN providers that offered edge support for increasing the performances of web systems recently introduced the possibility to deploy code as serverless functions, enabling to compose dynamic web pages on the edge, but also to run part of the business logic.

As future work, we are planning to investigate the usefulness of serverless on edge computing, with a special focus on the identification of benefits and issues in this context and supporting companies to understand when it is beneficial to adopt it, and when it would be better to use different solutions.

References

1. Baldini, I., et al.: Serverless computing: current trends and open problems. In: Chaudhary, S., Somani, G., Buyya, R. (eds.) Research Advances in Cloud Computing, pp. 1–20. Springer, Singapore (2017). https://doi.org/10.1007/978-981-10-5026-8_1
2. Baresi, L., Mendonça, D.F.: Towards a serverless platform for edge computing. In: Proceedings of the IEEE International Conference on Fog Computing (ICFC 2019), pp. 1–10. IEEE (2019)
3. Cheng, B., Fuerst, J., Solmaz, G., Sanada, T.: Fog function: serverless fog computing for data intensive IoT services. In: Proceedings of the IEEE International Conference on Services Computing (SCC 2019). pp. 28–35. IEEE (2019)

4. Dilley, J., Maggs, B., Parikh, J., Prokop, H., Sitaraman, R., Weihl, B.: Globally distributed content delivery. IEEE Internet Comput. **6**(5), 50–58 (2002). https://doi.org/10.1109/MIC.2002.1036038

5. Hassan, N., Gillani, S., Ahmed, E., Yaqoob, I., Imran, M.: The role of edge computing in internet of things. IEEE Commun. Mag. **56**(11), 110–115 (2018). https://doi.org/10.1109/MCOM.2018.1700906

6. Hästbacka, D., et al.: Dynamic and flexible data acquisition and data analytics system software architecture. In: 2019 IEEE SENSORS, pp. 1–4 (2019). https://doi.org/10.1109/SENSORS43011.2019.8956662

7. Liu, M., Yu, F.R., Teng, Y., Leung, V.C.M., Song, M.: Distributed resource allocation in blockchain-based video streaming systems with mobile edge computing. IEEE Trans. Wirel. Commun. **18**(1), 695–708 (2019). https://doi.org/10.1109/TWC.2018.2885266

8. Nastic, S., et al.: A serverless real-time data analytics platform for edge computing. IEEE Internet Comput. **21**(4), 64–71 (2017). https://doi.org/10.1109/MIC.2017.2911430

9. Ning, H., Li, Y., Shi, F., Yang, L.T.: Heterogeneous edge computing open platforms and tools for internet of things. Future Gener. Comput. Syst. **106**, 67–76 (2020). https://doi.org/10.1016/j.future.2019.12.036

10. Nupponen, J., Taibi, D.: Serverless: what it is, what to do and what not to do. In: IEEE International Conference on Software Architecture (ICSA 2020) (2020)

11. Palade, A., Kazmi, A., Clarke, S.: An evaluation of open source serverless computing frameworks support at the edge. In: Proceedings of the IEEE World Congress on Services (SERVICES 2019), vol. 2642–939X, pp. 206–211 (2019). https://doi.org/10.1109/SERVICES.2019.00057

12. Taibi, D., El Ioini, N., Pahl, C., Schmid Niederklfler, J.R.: Serverless cloud computing (function-as-a-service) patterns: a multivocal literature review. In: International Conference on Cloud Computing and Services Science (CLOSER 2020) (2020)

13. White, G., Cabrera, C., Palade, A., Clarke, S.: Augmented reality in IoT. In: Liu, X., et al. (eds.) ICSOC 2018. LNCS, vol. 11434, pp. 149–160. Springer, Cham (2019). https://doi.org/10.1007/978-3-030-17642-6_13

Formal Modeling and Simulation
of Collaborative Intelligent Robots

Abdelhakim Baouya[1]([⊠]), Salim Chehida[1], Miquel Cantero[2], Marta Millet[2],
Saddek Bensalem[1], and Marius Bozga[1]

[1] Verimag Lab, CNRS, University Grenoble Alpes, Grenoble, France
{abdelhakim.baouya,salim.chehida,saddek.bensalem,
marius.bozga}@univ-grenoble-alpes.fr
[2] Robotnik Automation S.L.L, Valencia, Spain
{mcantero,mmillet}@robotnik.es

Abstract. Internet of Things consists of several interconnected physical
devices through the internet, whereas fog and cloud technologies are
hosting tasks responsible for device controlling and management. Such
an environment is significantly scalable, and its capacity to handle a large
volume of data is proven. For this reason, we propose an IoT architecture
featuring necessary technologies to cope with robot orchestration and
monitoring. At the fog level, an IoT platform is deployed with all required
features to monitor robots remotely. The modeled system in BIP has been
wholly instantiated in a real infrastructure after formally checking and
simulation against requirements by applying classical code simulation
and statistical model checking.

Keywords: Robotics · IoT · Fog computing · Statistical model
checking

1 Introduction

New trends in robotic systems seek quasi-optimal parameters that industrials
in delivery and electronic commerce need to improve performance. There is an
increasing interest in autonomous systems that do not require human interven-
tion, which can manage the robots locally or remotely. In literature, the use
of autonomous robots leads to three issues: smart management, locating, and
evolution.

In terms of location and navigation, Global Positioning Systems (GPS) [23]
are widely used. Although GPS has a reasonable degree of precision, it is more
efficient in an outside environment. In warehouses, the robot movement surface
is represented by a grid, and each square of the grid has two coordinates in 2D
space. Some other solutions have a drawback at the level of computation, such
as image recognition [14].

Deploying fog computing may represent a solution that handles a dynamic
growing or diminishing number of robots on the surface [27] and also when the

© Springer Nature Switzerland AG 2021
C. Zirpins et al. (Eds.): ESOCC 2020 Workshops, CCIS 1360, pp. 41–52, 2021.
https://doi.org/10.1007/978-3-030-71906-7_4

latency is the main challenge that must be addressed since such environment is mostly delay-sensitive. Experiences stemming from some technology leaders that provide services over the internet, such as Google, Amazon, and Microsoft, indicate that application infrastructures in the cloud context should be highly scalable. The need to host scalable systems has necessitated the emergence of large scale data centers comprising hundreds of thousands of compute nodes [17]. So, technology leaders provide frameworks such as Amazin's AWS, Google's AppEngine, and Microsoft Azure for hosting third-party applications in their data-center infrastructures.

In terms of smart management, the software orchestrating the robot's movement shall be efficient in managing the load fluctuations occurring daily, weekly, and over longer periods. Researchers have focused on two types of orchestration: centralized and decentralized orchestration [8]. In decentralized orchestration [9,31], robots are collaborating through an orchestrator distributed over different servers within fog nodes, whereas activity and misbehavior log is recorded over the cloud as efficiency is proven in [18] to handle scalability. In the case of centralized orchestration [22], robots communicate among themselves directly through a master controller. The advantages and drawbacks of both configurations are detailed in [18]. The paper mainly relies on decentralized architecture based on a fog model in charge of robot orchestration.

This paper describes the use of a master controller deployed over fog nodes that performs robot orchestration, whereas data storage and analysis are performed over the cloud. First, required IoT concepts and reference architecture are highlighted to model the system accurately. Second, classical code simulation and statistical model checking tools like SMC-BIP [20] are used to check whether the modeled system satisfies requirements expressing collision avoidance and service delivery. The results will lead designers to judge the quality of deployment.

This paper is organized as follows: Sect. 2 presents the architecture highlighting the main concepts related to the IoT system with a projection into the cloud infrastructure. Section 3 describes the use case related to the robotic system. The analysis is portrayed in Sect. 4. To sum up, Sect. 5 identifies the existing work in the area of a cloud-based IoT system, and we draw our conclusions and also perspectives in Sect. 6.

2   IoT Concepts and Architecture

The definition of IoT concepts and relationships are made available for stakeholders by refining models found in the literature [5,6]. *Virtual entities* are synchronized representations of a given set of aspects of the *device* entity. *Resources* are executable code for accessing and storing information. Resources are made available on the cloud, the fog, or the end devices depending on the partitioning guide. A *service* provides a standardized interface for interacting with such devices. Figure 1 depicts the relationship between services, resources, and devices for a specific deployment option. Network-based resources are not shown, as they can be regarded as being hidden behind fog/cloud-based entity. In this kind of architecture, a fog smart gateway (FSG) [1] is a gateway made smarter with functionalities related to robots orchestration.

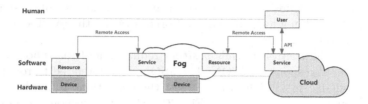

Fig. 1. Fog/Cloud-based IoT system.

Starting from the concepts defined earlier, the IoT reference architecture is depicted in Fig. 2 based on [10,16]. Five layers are highlighted for the IoT architecture: Application, Orchestration and virtual entity, services, communication, and devices. The *application layer* describes the functionalities provided by the applications that are built on the top of the implementation of the IoT in the Fog/Cloud. *Orchestration* resolves the appropriate services that are capable of handling the IoT user's request. *Virtual entity* searches for *services*, exposing resources related to the virtual entity by means of REST API. *Communication* component provides connectivity for the transport of IoT service and application-specific data. In the paper, we highlight sensinact controller [12] as a smart gateway endowed with southbound and northbound connectors. The northbound allows the software/software interaction, whereas the southbound allows communication with the outside world based on different protocols such as MQTT and CoAP.

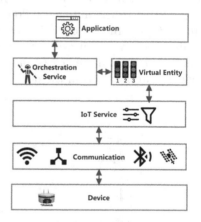

Fig. 2. IoT reference architecture.

3 Robots Orchestration: A Case Study

A private company owns a warehouse containing thousands of carts filled with two or three products. Robots manufactured by Robotnik[1] are programmed to

---

[1] Robotnik is a company specialized in robot product development and commercialization (mobile robots, robot arms, robotic hands, and humanoids).

travel in four cardinal directions to reach their destination (See Fig. 3). Once at the desired cart, the devices make a corkscrew motion to lift the cart off the ground and transport the entire unit to the storage area ② as depicted in Fig. 3 where humans pack the appropriate items. The robot then travels back into the unload area ③ and finds a new cart in an area with densely filled shelves. A brain controller within a fog is in charge of orchestrating the robot's movements within the 2D surface.

Every 0.5 s, the controller sends *position* requests, and the robots will send back a structured response in JSON. The JSON scripts related to robots interactions is available in [3]. The robots read their positions from the QR-code tag placed on the square grid (see Fig. 3). Also, the response contains the actual robot state, such as "stopped" or "running". The robots are endowed with motion sensors in the front to switch to "stopped" state if obstacles were detected, so the robot response includes, also, an integer attribute "detect" taking values from 0 to 2. If it is 0, then no obstacle is detected else, the obstacle could be a door or robot. When the robot detects a door, the orchestrator will send a request to the automatic door to open, and then the robot could enter the unload area. In case of collision shall be avoided, the controller will execute a "collision resolve" that orders the robots to update their positions. When the robots collect the required carts and drop them in the storage area, they return to their initial positions in the docking area.

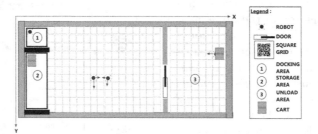

Fig. 3. 2D map surface of the warehouse.

The company in charge of the deployment of such a system would ensure that the operation of loading and unloading are correctly working and collision avoidance is also correctly executed. So, two requirements shall be satisfied by the orchestrator deployed over the fog:

- **REQ-1**: If a cart is detected with densely filled shelves, then, the robot does a corkscrew motion to lift the cart off the ground and transport the entire unit to the storage area.
- **REQ-2**: If a robot in front is detected then the collision avoidance shall be resolved and the robot continues until its destination.

To satisfy such requirements we have to build a corresponding model in a formal language called BIP to apply statistical model checking by using tools developed around it.

4   Modeling and Verification Environment

4.1   Modeling in BIP

We have chosen to use the BIP (Behavior, interaction, priorities) framework for its component-based formalism and its statistical model checking engine for systems verification [20].

BIP [4] allows building systems in the hierarchy structure starting from atomic components characterised by a behaviour expressed in automaton fashion and their interfaces (i.e. ports) to convey data to/from components. Moreover, BIP has a stochastic semantics and efficient tools for analysis based on statistical model checking techniques.

The architectural assembly of our system is pictured in Fig. 4, where the internal behavior is portrayed in the form of automata for robots ⑤, door ⑥ and orchestrator ⑦. Robots and door are considered as virtual entities since we try to extract precisely the behavior of the system based on the services exposed on the cloud. These services are functions used to build automata. The orchestrator ⑦ is developed to manage the robots on the surface. We have to note that the "orchestration" service is abstracted from the BIP model.

Ports are action names that can be associated with data and used for interactions with other components. For instance, component ① notifies the component ⑦ by sending the robot ID through the port "stop". So, the orchestrator could proceed to the identification of the obstacle if it is a door or another robot. This decision is made by the orchestrator based on the incoming notifications from component ②.

States denote control locations where components wait for interactions. A transition is an execution step, labeled by a port, from one control location to another. Each transition has an associated guard (i.e. object detection function in component ②) and action. If the robot is detected, then a collision resolve is initiated by the same robot discovering that obstacle and transition in component ③ is triggered. In case of door detected then, a transition in component ⑥ labeled "open" is triggered. Transition steaming from S_1 triggers the door closing operation after 5 s. In the case where the orchestrator detects that the robot is in the docking area, then it triggers successive transitions from S_3 to S_0 based on the load charge. So, if the unloading area is not empty, then the orchestrator asks the robot to move that area (i.e., transition from S_5 to S_0). Also, the resulting action is the update of the variable *load* (i.e., load := load-1).

Moreover, in BIP, complex data and their transformation are written in C/C++. Composite components called *Compound* are defined by assembling constituent components using connectors or by exporting their atomic internal ports (i.e., delegation) such as component ⑤.

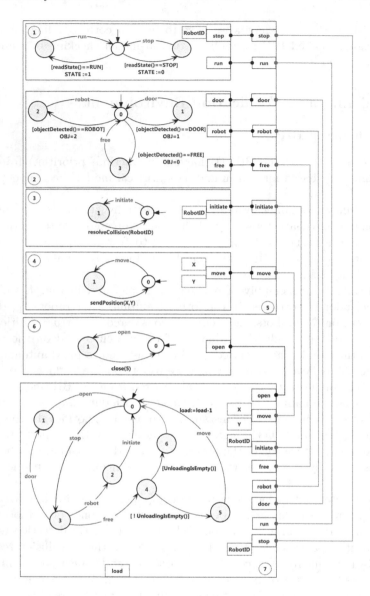

Fig. 4. Virtual entities and orchestrator in BIP.

Connectors define relationships between ports of interacting components. For instance, we identify eight connectors in Fig. 4 linking the atomic/composite components. The involved ports in the connectors are ready to participate (i.e., strong synchronization). It means that connectors fulfill their roles only if the involved ports are available.

4.2   Verification Using SMC-BIP

SMC-BIP tool[2] checks the stochastic BIP models, it takes as input the executable model of the system of interest and a requirement given in some logic to verify. Using the tool, it is possible to estimate qualitatively and quantitatively the probability that the system satisfies the requirement. To check such requirements, the SMC engine relies on probability estimation techniques [15] and hypothesis testing [30] algorithms to determine the number of simulations to reach a verdict. Also, the tool offers an integrated development environment including a graphical user-interface permitting to edit, compile, simulate models, and plotting graphs for parametric requirements.

The properties specification language over stochastic systems is a probabilistic variant bounded Linear-time Temporal Logic (LTL). Using this language, it is possible to formulate two kinds of queries on the given system:

- Qualitative queries: $P_{\geq\theta}[\varphi]$, where $\theta \in [0, 1]$ is a probability threshold and φ is a bounded LTL formula.
- Quantitative queries: $P_{=?}[\varphi]$ where φ is a bounded LTL formula.

Table 1. Requirements expressed in LTL

ID	LTL property
REQ-1	$P_{=?}[(c7.load = 5 \ \& \ c7.RobotID = 1 \ \& \ c4.x = doc_x \ \& \ c4.y = doc_y) \ \cup^{100}$ $(c7.load < 5 \ \& \ c7.robotID = 1 \ \& \ c4.x = stor_x \ \& \ c4.y = stor_y)];$
REQ-2	$P_{=?}[F^{100} \ (c2.obj = Z0 \ \& \ c7.RobotID = 1 \ \& \ c1.state = z1)]; \quad z0 = 0 : 2 :$ $1 \ z1 = 1 : 2 : 1;$

Table 2. Symbols used in Table 1

Symbol	Definition
doc_X	The x coordinate in Cartesian coordinates of docking area;
doc_Y	The y coordinate in Cartesian coordinates of docking area;
$stor_X$	The x coordinate in Cartesian coordinates of storage area;
$stor_Y$	The y coordinate in Cartesian coordinates of storage area;
$c1... c7$	The id of the component in Fig. 4;

Path formulas are defined using four bounded temporal operators namely, Next ($N\psi_1$), Until ($\psi_1 \cup^k \psi_2$), Eventually ($F^k\psi_1$), and Always ($G^k\psi_1$), where k is an integer value that specifies the length of the considered system execution

---

[2] https://www-verimag.imag.fr/BIP-SMC-A-Statistical-Model-Checking.html?
lang=en.

trace and ψ_1, ψ_2 are called state formulas, which is a Boolean predicate evaluated on the system states. Interpretation of requirements in Sect. 3 are reported in Table 1 and related abbreviation are detailed in Table 2. For instance, the first query REQ-1 in Table 1 checks if the robot lifts the cart or not from the docking area and put it in the storage area. The query is satisfied, and the returned probability is 0.95. So, considering this probability, the robot cart movement is ensured.

Concerning the second requirement REQ-2, the property returns a probability on the state of the robot (running or stopping). Moreover, we encode the values in a graphical chart as in Fig. 5, and we could identify manually from the simulation traces the case where possible collision is detected. We highlighted the collision resolve with a red box and door detection with a green box. As observed, one collision is detected on the trace since we simulate only two robots. The time elapsed between the door and robot detection is approximately 10 time units.

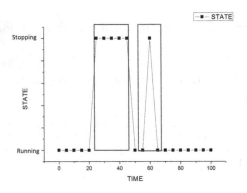

Fig. 5. Graphical interpretation of the LTL requirement REQ-2.

4.3   Validation

Although our proposed approach based on statistical model checking can provide an estimation while satisfying requirements, the behavior could also be radically different at a low level. So, we generate a code from the BIP model (i.e., the code generator and source code are available in [3]) and we deployed it over fog clusters with Ubuntu-16.04 desktop Intel core i7-950@3.07 GHz and ROS Kinetic with STAGE [25] and "rviz GUI" [24]. Also, we use sensinact controllers [12] that implements the mechanic to communicate with the simulation platform called ROS-REST API. We use "rviz" to plan the intelligent robot's movement within a 3D movement area and STAGE to capture a robot's movement into a 2D plan. This simulation is done to validate the requirement REQ-2.

The sequence of robots movements is portrayed in Fig. 6, Fig. 7 and Fig. 8. Figure 6 represents the initial state of the robots in the docking area. Figure 7 represents the state of the blue robot in front of the door, so the door is not visible on the figure. Figure 8 portrays the carts and robots in the unload area. Through the simulation, no collision was observed; this is due to the random execution of the scenario and competitive access to the unload area. However, we could observe that the door reacts to the robot's demand to open it. These observations help the designer to place judgment on the correctness of the modeled system

Moreover, we update the fog architecture (i.e., managed by virtual machines) by orchestrating three clusters loading three robots within the fog entity. The simulation is done by computing the time elapsed from the event triggering the robots until the last cluster response to the cloud entity. As observed in Fig. 9, the time differences between the number of orchestrated robots are not significant, and it is only counted in terms of seconds, thanks to the architecture deployed in [18].

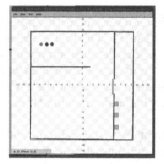   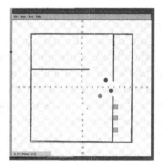

Fig. 6. Robots in docking area   **Fig. 7.** Robots in front of the door

5   Related Works

In this section, we provide an overview of different existing solutions for cloud computing and IoT integration. These solutions cover research projects, commercial and open source products. OpenIoT [21] is an open-source middleware, co-funded by European Union Programme for getting information about devices over a cloud platform. Also, it provides interoperability between external systems based on a semantic structure using ontologies. Moreover, it includes visualization, monitoring, and configuration over the connected devices. Xively [29] is considered as "IoT platform as a service" for the management of connected things through a Web UI using different communication methods, like REST API or MQTT supporting different data formats such as JSON and XML. Now, Xively is part of the Google Cloud Platform product family. SensorCloud [26] leverages the cloud computing technologies for data storage and management platform. To link the platform to the IoT devices, a specific gateway provided by MicroStrain [19], which collects data from different sources based on REST API. Besides, a collection of tools is provided for plotting graphs and analyzing data. thethings.io [28] provides a back end solution for IoT application developers

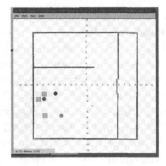

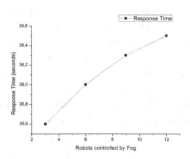

Fig. 8. Robots in storage area　　　　　**Fig. 9.** Response time/robots

through an easy and flexible API. The platform is hardware agnostic and could connect any device through any protocol MQTT, CoAP, HTTP. The development of the cloud is presently made on top of AWS. A detailed survey on the existing platforms is provided by [7] and [11]. Current projects such as Seriot project [13] draws great attention. It focuses on security aspects of the IoT systems by providing a means to understand the existing and emerging threats at the communication and device layers.

In the literature, a few papers shine a spotlight over the IoT concepts to give a comprehensive view of the IoT architecture and how it is deployed on a local or a distributed environment. Authors in [6] give the main IoT concepts and their relationships serving as a common lexicon and taxonomy and thus as a basis for the development of IoT. So, inspiring by that document, we build our architecture based on the technologies supported by our industrial partners. Our contribution leverages the verification based statistical model checking to improve the quality of the Fog/Cloud-based IoT system with complex behavior. Using SMC than the traditional model checker is mainly due to its advantages related to scalability. BIP SMC is known to be far less memory and time-intensive than exhaustive ones [2].

6　Conclusion

A part of the IoT concepts is presented in this paper to highlight the IoT's formal terms. These terms are used to define the reference architecture and a projection over the fog/cloud where communication and devices are hidden from users. Also, we were able to build a formal model of the robotic system in BIP language and then to check if the functional requirements expressed in LTL format are satisfied. Meanwhile, fog and cloud infrastructure are sensitive to external attacks, and failures may have a negative impact on the robot's movement and company business sustainability. Thus, in the future works, we intend to integrate this transversal concern mainly at orchestration service of the reference architecture to manage the network transactions.

Acknowledgement. The research leading to the presented results has been undertaken within the research profile Brain-IoT - model-Based fRamework for dependable sensing and Actuation in INtelligent decentralized IoT systems, funded by the European Union, grant number: 780089.

References

1. Aazam, M., Huh, E.: Fog computing and smart gateway based communication for cloud of things, pp. 464–470 (2014)
2. Agha, G., Palmskog, K.: A survey of statistical model checking. ACM Trans. Model. Comput. Simul. **28**(1), 6:1–6:39 (2018). https://doi.org/10.1145/3158668
3. Baouya, A.: Code generator - JSON files (2020). https://github.com/hakimuga/Resulted_Robots_Orchestration_Bundles
4. Basu, A.: Rigorous component-based system design using the BIP framework. IEEE Softw. **28**(3), 41–48 (2011)
5. Bauer, M., et al.: IoT reference model. In: Bassi, A., et al. (eds.) Enabling Things to Talk, pp. 113–162. Springer, Heidelberg (2013). https://doi.org/10.1007/978-3-642-40403-0_7
6. Ben Hassine, T., Khayati, O., Ben Ghezala, H.: An IoT domain meta-model and an approach to software development of IoT solutions. In: 2017 International Conference on Internet of Things, Embedded Systems and Communications (IINTEC), pp. 32–37 (2017)
7. Botta, A., de Donato, W., Persico, V., Pescapé, A.: Integration of cloud computing and internet of things: a survey. Future Gener. Comput. Syst. **56**, 684–700 (2016)
8. Chowdhary, R.R., Chattopadhyay, M.K., Kamal, R.: Comparative study of orchestrated, centralised and decentralised approaches for orchestrator based task allocation and collision avoidance using network controlled robots. J. King Saud Univ. Comput. Inf. Sci. (2018)
9. Correll, N., Bachrach, J., Vickery, D., Rus, D.: Ad-hoc wireless network coverage with networked robots that cannot localize. In: Proceedings of the 2009 IEEE International Conference on Robotics and Automation. ICRA'09, pp. 3554–3561. IEEE Press, Piscataway, NJ, USA (2009)
10. da Cruz, M.A.A., Rodrigues, J.J.P.C., Al-Muhtadi, J., Korotaev, V.V., de Albuquerque, V.H.C.: A reference model for internet of things middleware. IEEE Internet Things J. **5**(2), 871–883 (2018)
11. Díaz, M., Martín, C., Rubio, B.: State-of-the-art, challenges, and open issues in the integration of internet of things and cloud computing. J. Netw. Comput. Appl. **67**, 99–117 (2016)
12. Gandrille, E.: CEA LIST: sensinact gateway. Accessed on Jan 17 2020 (2019). https://wiki.eclipse.org/SensiNact
13. Gelenbe, E., Domanska, J., Czàchorski, T., Drosou, A., Tzovaras, D.: Security for internet of things: The seriot project. In: 2018 International Symposium on Networks, Computers and Communications (ISNCC), pp. 1–5 (2018). https://doi.org/10.1109/ISNCC.2018.8531004
14. Gomes, S., et al.: Embedded real-time speed limit sign recognition using image processing and machine learning techniques. Neural Comput. Appl. **28**, 573–584 (2017)
15. Hérault, T., Lassaigne, R., Magniette, F., Peyronnet, S.: Approximate probabilistic model checking. In: Steffen, B., Levi, G. (eds.) VMCAI 2004. LNCS, vol. 2937, pp. 73–84. Springer, Heidelberg (2004). https://doi.org/10.1007/978-3-540-24622-0_8

16. International Telecommunication Union: Y.2060: Overview of the internet of things. Recommendation y.4000/y.2060. Accessed on Jan 17 2020 (2012)
17. Li, X., Liu, Y., Kang, R., Xiao, L.: Service reliability modeling and evaluation of active-active cloud data center based on the it infrastructure. Microelectron. Reliab. **75**, 271–282 (2017)
18. Maiti, P., Apat, H.K., Sahoo, B., Turuk, A.K.: An effective approach of latency-aware fog smart gateways deployment for IoT services. Internet of Things **8**, 100091 (2019)
19. MicrosStrain: Accessed Jan 17 2020. https://www.microstrain.com/
20. Nouri, A., Mediouni, B.L., Bozga, M., Combaz, J., Bensalem, S., Legay, A.: Performance evaluation of stochastic real-time systems with the SBIP framework. Int. J. Crit. Comput. Based Syst. 1–33 (2018)
21. OpenIoT. Accessed on Jan 17 2020.https://github.com/OpenIotOrg/openiot
22. Petković, T., Puljiz, D., Marković, I., Hein, B.: Human intention estimation based on hidden Markov model motion validation for safe flexible robotized warehouses. Robot. Comput. Integr. Manuf. **57**, 182–196 (2019)
23. Raskaliyev, A., Patel, S., Sobh, T.: A dynamic model for GPS based attitude determination and testing using a serial robotic manipulator. J. Adv. Res. **8**(4), 333–341 (2017)
24. ROS.org: ROS - rviz (2012). http://wiki.ros.org/rviz
25. ROS.org: ROS - stage (2012). http://wiki.ros.org/stage
26. Sensorcloud: Accessed on Jan 17 2020. http://www.sensorcloud.com
27. Simic, V., Stojanovic, B., Ivanovic, M.: Optimizing the performance of optimization in the cloud environment-an intelligent auto-scaling approach. Futur. Gener. Comput. Syst. **101**, 909–920 (2019)
28. thethings.io: Accessed on Jan 17 2020. https://thethings.io/
29. Xively.: Accessed on Jan 17 2020. https://xively.com/
30. Younes, H.L.S., Simmons, R.G.: Probabilistic verification of discrete event systems using acceptance sampling. In: Brinksma, E., Larsen, K.G. (eds.) Computer Aided Verification. LNCS, pp. 223–235. Springer, Heidelberg (2002). https://doi.org/10.1007/3-540-45657-0_17
31. Zhou, Y., Hu, H., Liu, Y., Lin, S.W., Ding, Z.: A distributed approach to robust control of multi-robot systems. Automatica **98**, 1–13 (2018)

Virtual Machine Placement for Edge and Cloud Computing

Behdad Partovi[1], Alireza Bagheri[2], Maryam Haddad Kazarji[1(✉)], Claus Pahl[3], and Hamid R. Barzegar[3]

[1] Faculty of Computer Science and Engineering,
Shahid Beheshti University, Tehran, Iran
b.partovi@gmail.com, mhaddad.gozarji@gmail.com
[2] Faculty of Computer Engineering, Amirkabir University of Technology,
Hafez, Tehran, Iran
ar_bagheri@aut.ac.ir
[3] Department of Computer Science, Free University of Bozen-Bolzano, Bolzano, Italy
{hamid.barzegar,claus.pahl}@unibz.it

Abstract. So far, the genetic algorithm has been presented for the energy-aware scheduling of virtual machines to minimize the total busy time of servers. However, this algorithm does not consider the criteria for service-level policies on real-time applications. The convergence speed of the genetic algorithm is quite low in solving many of the large hybrid optimization problems. In other similar studies, heuristic algorithms were used to solve the interval scheduling problem. Such algorithms are not able to find nearly optimal solutions to hard problems. Since the optimization of scheduling is part of the hard problems, it is wise to use meta-heuristic algorithms to find nearly optimal solutions. Accordingly, an energy-aware meta-heuristic scheduling algorithm is presented in this paper for real-time virtual machines. The main goal of this algorithm is to minimize the total busy time of the physical machines in an interval without violating the deadline for virtual machines. The results were collected from the genetic algorithm, the smart water drop algorithm, the optimization of the ant colony, and the first possible downward algorithm for comparison and evaluation. The optimization of the ant colony and the smart algorithm of water drops showed better results than did the other two algorithms.

Keywords: Cloud computing · Edge computing · Real-time virtual machines · Meta heuristic algorithms · Interval scheduling

1 Introduction

The use of energy-efficient resource allocation creates green edge and cloud computing data centers to meet the demands of applications for computational services and save energy. The infrastructures of cloud systems are made up of virtualized data centers with thousands of highly efficient computational servers. A method of reducing energy loss in data centers is the server consolidation

© Springer Nature Switzerland AG 2021
C. Zirpins et al. (Eds.): ESOCC 2020 Workshops, CCIS 1360, pp. 53–64, 2021.
https://doi.org/10.1007/978-3-030-71906-7_5

technique in which the Virtual Machines (VM)s of a data center are placed on a fewer number of physical machines [1]; therefore, the exploitation of server increases. In resource allocation problems, a constant portion of one resource is allocated to a number of competing activities when objective functions are optimized [2]. In [3], interval scheduling was investigated with the purpose of minimizing the busy time of machines. In fact, the busy time means the power-on time of machines. In [4] this problem is enquired by meta-heuristic method, the deadline constraint is not included, as well as this algorithm due to the speed of slow convergence and the long run time, is not appropriate for dynamic programming applications. User requests for services are mapped onto VMs characterized by the necessary intervals and resource capacity. They should be scheduled without violating the deadline and by considering the constraints on the resources of physical machines. This type of schedule should be energy-aware. In other words, the busy time of physical servers should be minimized in a certain period of time so that more idle servers can be turned off. Since this problem is naturally considered a hard problem, energy-aware meta heuristic algorithms are necessary for solving it. Therefore, the ant colony optimization and intelligent water drops meta-heuristic algorithms were used in this study.

The aim of this study is to find a method for optimizing energy consumption for the allocation and scheduling of resources in cloud computing but it can consider in edge computing respectively. It is worth mentioning other alternative approaches such as edge computing drastically can reduce energy consumption due to their nature. For this reason, VMs are considered to be allocable resources in data centers. The allocation of VMs is considered very necessary in such a way that the energy usage of the data center can be controlled over time. The main contribution of this study in comparison to similar studies is to investigate the methods for the energy-aware scheduling of VMs by considering the constraints on resources and deadlines.

The rest of this paper has been organized in the following sections: Section 2 presented a review of the related works. The system model explained in Sect. 3. Section 4 is given the numerical results and system evaluation. Finally, the conclusion is presented in Sect. 5.

2   Related Works

In this section, relevant studies are compared to point out their advantages and disadvantages. In [5–7], the Dynamic Frequency-Voltage Scaling (DVFS) method was used to reduce energy consumption. In this method, the run time may become longer, and efficiency may decrease. Moreover, this method is too hardware-dependent. As a result, turning off additional servers for exploitation improvement is the only method decreasing the operational costs of data centers significantly [8]. In [9], proposed a heuristic method for packaging with a multidimensional box to consolidate the workloads of tasks, although the proposed method depends on the type of workload and application. It is appropriate for an entire edge and cloud environment. The concept of real-time requests for resources (virtual machines) was not taken into account in [9]. In [10–12] the requests for resources were not considered in the intervals. Furthermore, the migration technique was employed for the allocation of VMs. This technique imposes a considerable overhead on the efficiency of allocation. In [13], formulated the energy-aware placement of applications as a continuous optimization in heterogeneous virtualized systems. In every temporal framework, virtual machine placement is optimized to minimize energy consumption and maximize efficiency. The proposed algorithms do not support the Service Level Agreement (SLA) such as the deadline, therefore, the efficiency of applications may decrease with changes in the workload. In [14], no starting points of time were considered for requests for the allocation of VMs. Furthermore, the hill-climbing algorithm was used to solve optimization problems. The convergence speed of this algorithm is quite low in high-dimensional problems. It is also more likely to get trapped in the local optimum in comparison with meta-heuristic methods such as t ant colony optimization which is considered in this study as well.

In [15], the concept of the deadline was not discussed, and the starting points of VMs were considered constant. The greedy heuristic algorithms were used to solve the energy-aware scheduling of VMs with the purpose of reducing the total busy time of servers which might not find the optimal solution. In [3, 16–18], approximate heuristic methods were presented to solve the problem of minimizing the total busy time in the real-time scheduling of tasks by considering the constraints on resources. In [3] a 3-approximation heuristic method named Modified First Fit Decreasing Earliest (MFFDE) has been introduced to schedule VMs in edge and cloud data centers to minimize energy consumption. In [19], the ant colony optimization was used to optimize virtual machine placement with the purpose of consolidating VMs and minimizing the number of physical servers. In this method, the dimension of time was not taken into account. When this dimension is considered, the optimization does not always bear the desired result only with the purpose of minimizing the number of physical servers and solving the problem regarded as a packaging problem with boxes.

In [20], the proposed algorithm was named Self-Adapting Particle Swarm Optimization (SAPSO). It is an algorithm used for the dynamic allocation of VMs based on Particle Swarm Optimization (PSO). It tries to allocate the arriving VMs to physical machines in alternative temporal windows. This algorithm is mainly intended to maximize the appropriate allocation of VMs and reduce energy consumption. PSO adapts to new conditions of the environment dynamically in every temporal window for the sake of optimization. It also uses the migration of VMs to optimize allocation. In the model presented in [21], VMs do not include the starting points of time or deadlines. In [20], the proposed method may reject some requests for the allocation of VMs and VM may not be allocated. In [4], a VM allocation model resembling the proposed VM model was described. It is meant for the energy-aware scheduling problem of VMs w.r.t the total busy time of physical servers. This problem was solved by using the genetic algorithm. The difference between this model and the model presented in this study is that the starting point of time of VMs is a constant value. However, the starting point of each VM can range in a span of integers with respect to the deadline in the algorithms proposed in this study.

3   System Model

In this study, for the first contribution, guaranteeing the deadline was regarded as a condition for the service level policies, and the next contribution was the minimization of the total busy time of servers for the reduction of energy consumption (the total busy time an abstract thing and it can be used in everywhere, in all data centers (cloud, edge)). The innovation of the article is that for the first time we used meta-heuristic algorithms to achieve our goal, decrease the total number of turned-on physical servers over time. Previously, there was only one article that did this just with a genetic algorithm, which was a kind of schedule. We considered the quality of service (QoS) criterion because we have a deadline factor. Given the proposed algorithm, it is done without violating the deadline, it causes the required service to be met in the deadline intended by the end-user, so the quality of experience (QoE) for end-user is also maintained. The proposed algorithms are described in this section.

3.1   Colony Optimization

There are different versions of ant colony optimization. In this paper, the two main versions of this algorithm were used for implementation: Ant System (AS) and Ant Colony System (ACS). The ant colony optimization algorithms use a graph to provide a solution. They put pheromone on the nodes and edges of the graph which is considered to be multilevel. Each level indicates one VM of the VMs list which is set to be allocated. A Load matrix is defined to save the workload status of physical machines. This matrix shows which machine is occupied at that time. The optimization objective function is defined as the total number of servers, the capacities of which have partially been occupied in scheduling. This function is equivalent to the total busy time of physical machines. $Load(t_i, pm_i) =$ the total capacities of VMs allocated to pm_i at t_i.

3.2   Heuristic Information

The heuristic method used to solve this problem has increased the parallelism degree of jobs (VMs) in the proposed ant colony algorithm. It has also decreased the space wasted over time and increased the productivity of physical machines. The gray area of running VMs and the hachured area indicate the empty space and resource/time wastage, respectively Fig. 1A. Two different allocations of the new VM were highlighted bold. Figure 1B shows that the resource/time wastage is lower; therefore, the heuristic method takes a better value.

3.3   Intelligent Water Drops Algorithm

Here this algorithm is implemented to solve the optimization problem of scheduling VMs with the purpose of minimizing the total busy time of servers. Like the ant colony optimization, a multilevel graph is used to solve the problem. The

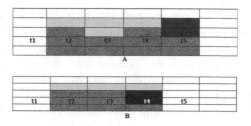

Fig. 1. The heuristic method in the Ant Colony optimization and the Intelligent Water Drops algorithm.

classic Intelligent Water Drop (IWD) algorithm puts the soil on the edges of the graph. In fact, the accumulation of soil or pheromone on edges or nodes indicates that they are weighted. If each node as a specific weight in a weighted graph when the weights of edges are zero, then it can turn into a weighted graph in which the weights are placed on edges. Therefore, the weight of the destination node of each edge can be regarded as the weight of that edge. In the implementation of the proposed IWD algorithm, an amount of soil has been considered to be on the graph nodes, also can be used to measure the soil on the edges. Now the steps of the proposed IWD algorithm: First, all of the static and dynamic parameters are initialized. The static parameters are those which remain constant in the implementation of the IWD algorithm; however, the dynamic parameters are those which are reinitialized in each iteration. Second, the solution graph is a multilevel structure, in which each level represents one VM, and each node shows a pair like (starting point, physical machine) on each level. The VM is allowed to be scheduled on that physical machine at that time. In other words, these pairs include different points of time when a VM can start operating in a way that the VM interval is not violated. To select a pair for the creation of the tour on the path, each water drop selects the nodes which do not violate the resource constraint. Therefore, only valid solutions are created in the graph. After each IWD has completed a tour, the offered solution is evaluated. According to the solution provided by the ant colony optimization, an auxiliary load matrix was used to evaluate the solution in the proposed IWD algorithm. This matrix shows the capacity of every physical machine at any given time. If the physical machine is not working in each time slice, a zero is inserted in the element of the matrix. The total number of non-zero elements show the number of busy physical machines in the scheduling interval. This quantity is equivalent to the total number of time slices in which physical machines are operating. In the classic IWD algorithm, the best solution is selected after providing all solutions in each iteration.

3.4 Utilization of Proposed Algorithm in Dynamic Scheduling

In the proposed dynamic algorithm, VMs enter the system at different time intervals, then they are scheduled. For instance, the VMs arriving in recent time slices are scheduled in each interval (10 min). In other words, scheduling repeatedly occurs (18 times) during the entire period (3 h for instance). In the proposed dynamic algorithm, the ACO or IWD algorithms are used to schedule the arriving VMs every 10 min in compliance with the full capacity of physical machines according to previous scheduling processes. Furthermore, the history of previous scheduling processes is kept in a matrix to determine how limited the resource capacity was and how full the physical machines were over time. It is also important to determine the current busy time, therefore, scheduling can be done in the current interval in a way that the lesser total busy time increases as much as possible.

3.5   Implementing the Basic Genetic Algorithm in Comparison with the Proposed Methods

In the implementation of the genetic algorithm, the problem was regarded as a permutation problem. In other words, the chromosome structure includes the genes indicating a sorted pair (t, pm) or a VM. The different placements of genes of VMs and (t, pm) create the different modes of scheduling. For instance, if there are four times like t_1, t_2, t_3, and t_4 with two physical machines like $p1$ and $p2$ when we want to schedule three VMs like vm_1, vm_2 and vm_3 then once solution can be like Fig. 2 which shows the allocation genes. Different solutions are generated by combining these two types of genes Fig. 2A and B and creating different placements. For instance, Fig. 2C shows one possible chromosome of the solution:

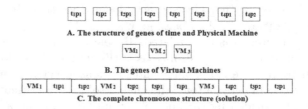

A. The structure of genes of time and Physical Machine

B. The genes of Virtual Machines

C. The complete chromosome structure (solution)

Fig. 2. The chromosome structure (solution) and genes in the Genetic Algorithm.

4   Numerical Results and System Evaluation

This section provides the numerical result and proof of concept for the afore-mentioned algorithms. In fact, here is a comparative evaluation that looks at the time, percentage productivity of resources, cost functions and etc. Our contribution is in the form of AS, ACS, IWD algorithms, which we compared with MFFDE and GA algorithms. As we can see in the diagrams, we have improved the scheduling and minimization of the total busy time.

4.1   Initializing and Generating the Input Parameters of Algorithms

An application was written to generate virtual machines at random. The numbers of ants and water drops were 20 in 100 iterations to run the ant colony optimization and IWD algorithm. The number of population was 40 in 2000 iterations of the genetic algorithm. MFFDE was used to generate the initial solution to the genetic algorithm. There were also 40–45 slices of time, each of which lasted for 5 min. In the tests, each algorithm ran 10 times on average. One of the tests is described in this section.

4.2   Sample Test

There were 100 Virtual Machines (VMs), and Physical Machine (PM) was type 2 in accordance with [22] with 40 compute units. The proposed algorithms were used to solve the problem. Then the charts of PM quantity per time and total resource productivity per PM were drawn. It should be noted that in all figures the total number of necessary PMs were 475 for scheduling by using the AS algorithm. This number is equal to the number of time slices in which physical machines were busy working when scheduling was done.

Comparing the proposed AS algorithm with MFFDE and GA: According to Figs. 3 and 4, the Ant System algorithm has a smaller cost function and operates better than the other two algorithms. Moreover, the maximum number of physical machines for scheduling is smaller in this algorithm compared with the other two. It improved the scheduling by 25.7% and 13.3% compared with the heuristic and genetic algorithms, respectively.

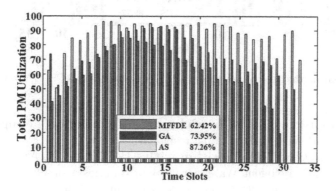

Fig. 3. Comparing the percentage productivity of resources in AS, GA, and MFFDE.

Comparing the Proposed ACS with MFFDE and GA: According to Figs. 5, 6 the Ant Colony System algorithm has a smaller cost function and operates better than the other two algorithms. Moreover, the maximum number of physical machines for scheduling is smaller in this algorithm compared with

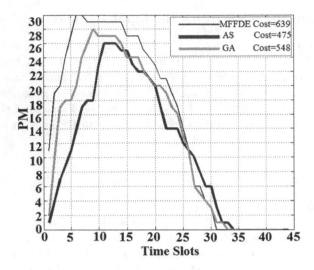

Fig. 4. Comparing the cost6unctions of AS, GA, and MFFDE.

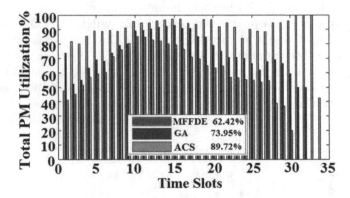

Fig. 5. Comparing the percentage productivity of resources in ACS, GA, and MFFDE.

the other two. It improved the scheduling by 26.9% and 14.8% compared with the heuristic and genetic algorithms, respectively.

Comparing the IWD algorithm with MFFDE and GA: According to Figs. 7 and 8, the Intelligent Water Drop algorithm has a smaller cost function and operates better than the other two algorithms. Moreover, the maximum number of physical machines for scheduling is smaller in this algorithm compared with the other two. It improved the scheduling by 26.3%and 14.1% compared with the heuristic and genetic algorithms, respectively.

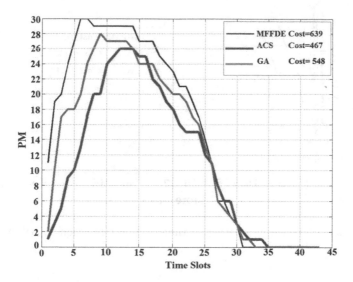

Fig. 6. Comparing the cost functions of ACS, GA, and MFFDE.

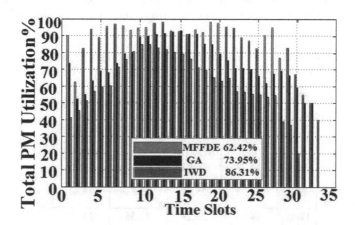

Fig. 7. Comparing the percentage productivity of resources in IWD, GA, and MFFDE.

Table 1. The results of the sample test

Algorithm	Cost Function	Mean Productivity of All Resources (%)	The Maximum Number of Necessary PMs
ACS	467	89.72	26
AS	475	87.26	26
IWD	471	86.31	26
GA	548	73.95	28
MFFDE	639	62.42	30

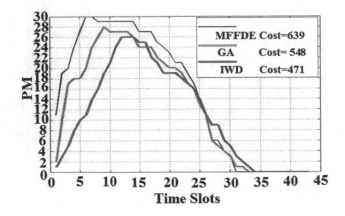

Fig. 8. Comparing the charts of PM per time and cost functions in IWD, GA, and MFFDE.

4.3 Summarizing the Sample Test Results

For a better comparison, the following table shows the outputs of the tested algorithms: According to Table 1, the proposed algorithms minimized the total

Table 2. The improvement percentages of the proposed algorithms compared with the basic algorithms.

	Improvement in Cost Function (%)		Improvement in the Productivity of Resources (%)	
	GA	MFFDE	GA	MFFDE
ACS	14.78	26.92	15.77	27.3
AS	13.32	25.67	13.31	24.84
IWD	14.05	26.29	12.36	23.89

busy time of servers (cost function) and improved the productivity of entire servers in the scheduling intervals. Table 2 shows the improvement percentages of the proposed algorithms in comparison with the basic algorithms.

4.4 System Evaluation

MFFDE tries to schedule on each PM in the first slices of time when the problem constraints allow scheduling. If it cannot do the scheduling on the current PM by meeting the constraints, it adds a new PM and schedules the VM in the first allowed slice of time. Therefore, the number of necessary PMs increases quickly at the beginning of scheduling. Accordingly, the proposed algorithm tries to compress the intervals as much as possible and increase the parallelism degree by delaying the beginning of intervals. As a result, the total busy time of servers decreases, and resource productivity increases. Thus, the density of time intervals increases in the middle of scheduling.

5   Conclusion

In this study, the ant colony optimization and intelligent water drop algorithms were implemented to obtain better results in comparison with the genetic algorithm. Furthermore, the only acceptable ways were the ones in which no intervals of VMs were violated. The deadlines were regarded as a constraint on the problem. In comparison with the basic algorithms, the cost function of scheduling improved. Some methods were proposed to optimize the scheduling of VMs at edge and cloud data centers. The main advantages of these methods were improvements in the minimization of the busy time of servers by 15% and 27% compared with the basic genetic algorithm and the basic heuristic algorithm, respectively, on average. Moreover, resource productivity was improved on average by 16% and 26% in comparison with the basic genetic algorithm and the basic heuristic algorithm, respectively. The proposed algorithms also can be used in the dynamic mode because they run at an appropriate convergence speed and generate nearly optimal solutions. For prospective works, use the proposed algorithm for heterogeneous environments with different resource capacities, collection, and analysis of energy consumption in real data centers, Include server boot time, shutdown time and other real-time overhead are suggested.

References

1. Varasteh, A., Goudarzi, M., Server consolidation techniques in virtualized data centers: a survey. IEEE Syst. J. (2015) (in press)
2. Quang-Hung, N., Son, N.T., Thoai, N.: Energy-saving virtual machine scheduling in cloud computing with fixed interval constraints. In: Hameurlain, A., Küng, J., Wagner, R., Dang, T.K., Thoai, N. (eds.) Transactions on Large-Scale Data- and Knowledge-Centered Systems XXXI. LNCS, vol. 10140, pp. 124–145. Springer, Heidelberg (2017). https://doi.org/10.1007/978-3-662-54173-9_6
3. Tian , W., Yeo, C.S.: Minimizing total busy time in offline parallel scheduling with application to energy efficiency in cloud computing. Concurr. Comput. Pract. Exper. **27**, 2470–2488 (2015)
4. Quang-Hung, N., Nien, P.D., Nam, N.H., Huynh Tuong, N., Thoai, N.: A genetic algorithm for power-aware virtual machine allocation in private cloud. In: Mustofa, K., Neuhold, E.J., Tjoa, A.M., Weippl, E., You, I. (eds.) ICT-EurAsia 2013. LNCS, vol. 7804, pp. 183–191. Springer, Heidelberg (2013). https://doi.org/10.1007/978-3-642-36818-9_19
5. Safari, M., Khorsand, R.: PL-DVFS: combining Power-aware List-based scheduling algorithm with DVFS technique for real-time tasks in Cloud Computing. J. Supercomput. **74**(3), 5578–5600 (2018)

6. Nam, S.A., Bahn, H.: Real-time task scheduling methods to incorporate low-power techniques of processors and memory in IoT environments. J. Inst. Internet Broadcast. Commun. **17**, 1–6 (2017)
7. Mishra, S.K., Puthal, D., Sahoo, B., et al.: Energy-efficient VM placement in cloud data center. Sustain. Comput.: Inform. Syst. **20**, 48–55 (2018)
8. Barzegar, B., Motameni, H., Movaghar, A.: EATSDCD: a green energy-aware scheduling algorithm for parallel task-based application using clustering, duplication and DVFS technique in cloud data centers. J. Intell. Fuzzy Syst. 1–18 (2019) (IOS Press)
9. Carrega, A., Repetto, M.: Energy-aware consolidation scheme for data center cloud applications. In: 2017 29th International Teletraffic Congress (ITC 29), vol. 2, pp. 24–29, IEEE (2017)
10. Zheng, H., Feng, Y., Tan, J.: A hybrid energy-aware resource allocation approach in cloud manufacturing environment. IEEE Access **5**, 12648–12656 (2017)
11. Ranjbari, M., Torkestani, J.A.: A learning automata-based algorithm for energy and SLA efficient consolidation of virtual machines in cloud data centers. J. Parallel Distrib. Comput. **113**, 55–62 (2018)
12. Rahimi, A., Khanl, L.M., Pashazadeh, S.: Energy efficient virtual machine placement algorithm with balanced resource utilization based on priority of resources. Comput. Eng. Appl. J. **4**, 107–118 (2015)
13. Yousefipour, A., Rahmani, A.M.: Energy and cost-aware virtual machine consolidation in cloud computing. Softw.: Pract. Exp. **48**, 1758–1774 (2018)
14. Qiu, Y., Jiang, C., Wang, Y., Ou, D., Li, Y., Wan, J.: Energy aware virtual machine scheduling in data centers. Energi. Multi. Digit. Publ. Inst. **12**, 646 (2019)
15. Askarizade Haghighi, M., Maeen, M., Haghparast, M.: An energy-efficient dynamic resource management approach based on clustering and meta-heuristic algorithms in cloud computing IaaS platforms. Wireless Pers. Commun. **104**(4), 1367–1391 (2018). https://doi.org/10.1007/s11277-018-6089-3
16. Qin, Y., Wang, H., Zhu, F., Zhai, L.: A multi-objective ant colony system algorithm for virtual machine placement in traffic intense data centers. IEEE Access **6**, 58912–58923 (2018)
17. Chau, V., Li, M.: Active and Busy Time Scheduling Problem: A Survey, Complexity and Approximation, pp. 219–229. Springer (2020)
18. Mertzios, G.B., Shalom, M., Voloshin, A., Wong, P.W., Zaks, S.: Optimizing busy time on parallel machines. Theor. Comput. Sci. **562**, 524–541 (2015)
19. Zhao, D.M., Zhou, J.T., Li, K.: An energy-aware algorithm for virtual machine placement in cloud computing. IEEE Access **7**, 55659–55668 (2019)
20. Gill, S.S., Buyya, R., Chana, I., Singh, M., Abraham, A.: BULLET: particle swarm optimization based scheduling technique for provisioned cloud resources. J. Netw. Syst. Manage. **26**(2), 361–400 (2018)
21. Witanto, J.N., Lim, H., Atiquzzaman, M.: Adaptive selection of dynamic VM consolidation algorithm using neural network for cloud resource management. Future Gener. Comput. Syst. **87**, 35–42 (2018)
22. Tian, W.D., Zhao, Y.D.: Optimized cloud resource management and scheduling: theories and practices. Morgan Kaufmann (2014)

Cloud-Edge Microservice Architecture for DNN-based Distributed Multimedia Event Processing

Felipe Arruda Pontes[✉] and Edward Curry

Insight SFI Research Centre for Data Analytics, Data Science Institute,
National University of Ireland, Galway, Ireland
{felipe.arruda.pontes,edward.curry}@insight-centre.org
https://dsi.nuigalway.ie

Abstract. The rise of Big Data, Internet of Multimedia Things (IoMT), and Deep Neural Network (DNN) enabled the growth of DNN-based Computer Vision solutions to Multimedia Event Processing (MEP) applications. When these are applied to a real-world scenario we notice the importance of having a system with a satisfactory speed that can fit in the limited resources of most IoMT devices. However, most solutions for distributed MEP are dependent on a Cloud architecture, which makes these applications migration to the Edge more challenging. As a response to this, we present a microservice architecture for DNN-based distributed MEP over heterogeneous Cloud-Edge environments. We describe our solution that allows for an easier deployment both on the Edge and on the Cloud. We show that choosing the proper tools for an Edge-Friendly solution can lead to 100 times less resource utilisation. Our preliminary investigation shows promising results, with a reduction in energy consumption by 8% with a minor drawback of 15% in throughput in the Edge and a negligible increase in energy consumption on the Cloud.

Keywords: Cloud-Independent · Edge-Friendly · Distributed computing · Multimedia Event Processing · Deep Neural Networks

1 Introduction

Alongside the increase of Big Data and Internet of Multimedia Things (IoMT), we can observe the rise of Multimedia Event Processing (MEP) applications. This is mostly because MEP is useful for handling continuous streams of data that are present in a Big Data scenario, and it provides a framework for the constant multimedia event streams generated from IoMT devices. Another common characteristic of Big Data and IoMT is the fact that they work well with distributed computing architecture, and since both are highly connected to the concepts of Cloud and Edge computing respectively, combining them also presents an interesting scenario where it is common to see this mixed Cloud-Edge environment.

© Springer Nature Switzerland AG 2021
C. Zirpins et al. (Eds.): ESOCC 2020 Workshops, CCIS 1360, pp. 65–72, 2021.
https://doi.org/10.1007/978-3-030-71906-7_6

The general decision of having Deep Neural Network (DNN)-based Computer Vision (CV) solutions as part of MEP applications for Big Data with IoMT accompanies the consolidation of using DNN models for most CV problems. On one side, DNN models are known to require many resources, on the other side, many Edge devices are resource-constrained, with restrictions in energy consumption, CPU/GPU, and memory. Thus, Cloud-Edge Heterogeneity becomes another important characteristic for distributed MEP applications because it is essential to take into consideration the different aspects and limitations of both Cloud and Edge devices.

However, migrating the available distributed MEP solutions to the Edge brings many challenges since they are mostly made with a focus on specific Cloud infrastructures (e.g.: Amazon AWS or Microsoft Azure) [2,10]. As a response to this, we propose a microservices architecture for distributed MEP over heterogeneous Cloud-Edge environments, which is both Edge-Friendly and Cloud-Independent at the same time. Microservices architecture (MSA) is one of the new trends in distributed systems architecture, and have been used by several prominent companies such as Netflix, Amazon, and Uber, in addition, they are accepted as a reliable solution for the overall problems of distributed systems.

In this work, we detail our architecture design and its impact in terms of energy and speed. We describe our tooling decisions and show that choosing the appropriate tools for an Edge-Friendly solution can lead to **100 times less resource utilisation** than a non-optimal tool. Our architecture shows promising preliminary results of **8% of energy reduction** with only a **minor reduction of 15% on the overall speed**.

2   Motivation and Related Works

The basic required components in a MEP application are **sources**, **stream manager**, **stream processor** and **sinks**. An example of the dataflow is depicted in Fig. 1. The use of Computer Vision (CV) techniques to help with Occupational Health and Safety (OHS) in construction sites has been recently explored [6]. The use of a mixed Edge-Cloud is important when we consider that construction sites may be located in isolated regions without access to infrastructure. Some of the problems in this area range from accidents prediction and prevention to safety rule violation alerts. In this case, it is possible to identify the lack of safety helmets or hi-viz vest in dangerous locations by using cameras, Object Detection (OD) models to analyse the video stream from the cameras, and generate an alert to the OHS supervisor, as shown in Fig. 1.

On the use of bandwidth-efficient MEP for drones, Wang et al. [9] uses similar DNN models to ours. However, they focus on the weight of the devices and the models' speed, without taking into account the energy consumption. The EdgeWise system [5] gives stream processing optimisations for mixed Cloud-Edge environments, but it differs from our work since it does not take into consideration Cloud-Edge environment heterogeneity.

Microservice architecture (MSA) is a system architecture style where an application is decomposed into small and autonomous parts that work together

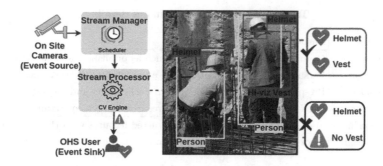

Fig. 1. Multimedia Event Processing on OHS for Construction Sites Safety Rules alerts using OD

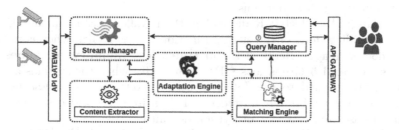

Fig. 2. Microservice architecture for DNN-based Distributed Multimedia Event Processing.

and around business capabilities, with decentralised control of languages and data [4]. Sprocket [1] implements MSA for MEP and takes advantage of well-defined patterns from Amazon AWS. The approach is highly dependent on a single cloud infrastructure, making it harder to apply it to the Edge.

3 MEP Framework Design

Microservices Decomposition: Our approach for defining the boundaries of our MSA is to use a Domain-Driven Design (DDD) decomposition [4] and to improve it over multiple development iterations. This process supported us on avoiding common MSA anti-patterns, such as having the wrong cuts in our architecture. We ended up producing five main sub-domains (see Table 1 and Fig. 2), each containing multiple sub-domains with their respective microservices (19 in total).

Underlying Tooling. Below there is a summary of the selected tools for our MEP framework together with the reason for each choice.

- **Docker**: To get the most of MSA, and to have a Cloud/Edge-Friendly solution, we are using Docker as our containerisation. Docker allows us to have

Table 1. Our main sub-domains details

Sub-domain	Purpose
API gateway	Connection of external entities, such as publishers and subscribers.
Query manager	Parsing, maintaining, optimising, and planning the user queries.
Stream manager	Pre-processing of publisher streams, scheduling and dispatching events.
Content extraction	DNN models for extracting features from the video streams.
Matching engine	Manages the matching of the extracted features with the users queries.
Adaptation engine	Incorporates self-adaptive behaviour into the system

a compartmentalised, independent, scalable, and reproducible development and deployment process. It can be used in both Cloud and Edge devices with a small footprint in resource usage.

– **Streaming**: We selected Redis rather than Kafka because in addition to Redis providing most of the stream functionality as Kafka, when comparing their docker images, Redis uses **100 times less memory, 10 times less disk space and 5 times less CPU** than Kafka when the systems are idle.
– **JSON**: We decided to use JSON to serialise our internal messages. This schemaless format fits our unstructured data from the video streams, it is simple to use, and it is part of Python default libraries.
– **CV**: We selected Python and Tensorflow to work with the DNN models. They are widely used both in the academia and in the industry, and there are versions built especially for common Edge device, with the option of easily setting the amount of GPU allocated for each model. To represent the video streams, we are using Video Event Knowledge Graphs (VEKG) [10].
– **Microservice Monitoring**: We chose Jaeger for the distributed event tracing. It provides a unified front for analysing the path and time of each event on the system. And to monitor the Quality of Service metrics of our MSA we use Prometheus. It also provides a centralised view of each microservice (MS) current metrics. Both tools are used by our Adaptive Engine to ensure that the framework adaptation plans are more precise.

4   Framework Evaluation

4.1   Study Requirements

We selected energy and speed as our study metrics. **Speed** is essential in scenarios where there is a need for a quick response to events identified in the system [9]. **Energy**'s importance comes in three-fold, first in its economical impact, especially for big companies that manage massive cloud infrastructures in their data-centres. Second, for its ecological significance, since recent studies show that 14% of the worldwide energy consumption is for data-centres alone [3]. Being especially true regarding DNN-based models since the carbon footprint of DNN models can produce as much CO_2 as five cars would produce in a lifetime [7]. And third, for the context of resource-constrained Edge devices, where energy is often a limited resource.

Table 2. Device specifications

Device	CPU	Memory RAM	GPU	Disk
Jetson TX2	Dual-core Denver 2 64-bit, quad-core ARM A57 complex	8 GB 128-bit LPDDR4 1866 MHz - 59.7 GB/s	NVIDIA Pascal 256 CUDA cores(FP16)	32 GB eMMC 5.1
Dedicated server	Intel i9-9900K 8 Cores	32 GB Corsair 163301 2× 16 GB DDR4 3200 MHz	MSI GeForce RTX 2080 TI GAMING X TRIO 11 GB	500 GB SSD & 4 TB HD

4.2 Methodology

To measure the impact of Energy and Speed that our framework adds to a DNN-based OD operation on a mixed Cloud-Edge environment, we needed first to execute different state-of-the-art DNN-based OD models with the images from our chosen dataset and calculate their energy consumption and speed in different Edge and Cloud scenarios, and then choose the model that had the best speed in the Edge environment.

Next, we tested our MEP framework architecture in a mixed Cloud-Edge environment. We started a single node of our framework in our Dedicated Server (Cloud environment) without a content extraction microservice. Then, we started a single Object Detection MS in the Jetson (Edge environment) with GPU enabled, using the previously selected DNN model, and had the MS connected to the Cloud node. This way, we get a network of microservices which is composed of a mixed Cloud-Edge environment. Once these services were ready, a publisher was connected to the framework, where each event published represents an image from the dataset. Finally, we compare the framework results against the baseline values of the DDN model execution without our framework.

4.3 Execution Environments

We selected two devices (see Table 2). The first is a Jetson TX as the Edge device. The second, for the Cloud environment, is a Dedicated Server. This setup presents different environments for exploration, encompassing both Edge and Cloud. These environments are: i) **Cloud-Baseline**: Cloud environment at stand-by; ii) **Edge-Baseline**: Edge environment at stand-by; iii) **Edge-SSD-Model**: Edge with GPU enabled with only the DNN model running; iv) **Edge-OD-Service**: Edge with GPU enabled with the DNN model running inside our solution's MS; v) **Cloud-MEP**: Cloud environment running the rest of our architecture.

4.4 Evaluation Method

For our evaluation we followed the same protocol on all experiments, with the method for measuring each one of the targeted metrics as follows:

Speed: We analyse the models' prediction speed for each image and calculate their averages. This is converted to the models' throughput in Frames Per Seconds (FPS), which is a measure of quantity per unit time (Seconds). For our baseline speed, we are using the stand-alone DNN models running without our framework. In this case, the metric is exported to each experiment output. For our framework results, the speed is gathered from the event tracing service and exported to a JSON file once the experiments are done.

Energy Consumption: For energy consumption measurement, we follow on the work of Walker et al. [8]. We are connecting our devices into two smart power plugs monitors that can estimate the energy usage every 10 s, and send it via radio frequency to a smart home gateway device that will save it.

During the experiments' execution, we record the starting and ending timestamps. Later, during the evaluation, we get the energy consumption records that match the experiments start/end timestamps and calculate the average of the energy consumption value for the experiment as a whole. We also analysed both Cloud and Edge devices at stand-by, that is, without running anything on them, to get the baseline energy consumption that these machines consumed by being on. To do that, we gathered the energy consumption of the Jetson and the Dedicated Server for 5 min and calculated the average and standard deviation of them. The results were: **2 W** (standard deviation of 0) and **72.1 W** (standard deviation of 0.3) for the Jetson and the Dedicated Server respectively.

4.5   Object Detection Models and Dataset

We started with three state-of-the-art OD DNN models for our initial comparison: SSD-MobilenetV1, Faster RCNN-InceptionV2, Faster RCNN-Inception-ResnetV2-Atrous. The models are pre-trained on the COCO 2017 image dataset[1] and were gathered from the official Tensorflow model collection. The configurations for the DNN models were: The batch size of 1, GPU memory limit of 70% (except for Faster RCNN-Atrous which was 18%), image input size of 300×300 pixels and detection threshold of 0.5. After analysing the results from the models, we selected the SSD DNN model to test our framework against, since it had the best speed in the Edge device. Curiously, this model showed some nonintuitive behaviour, with its usage on the GPU being more economic in terms of energy and with a lower throughput than when running only on the CPU. This only reiterates how heterogeneous Cloud-Edge environments can affect the performance of an' application.

Since these models were pre-trained on the COCO 2017 Training dataset, we decided to use the COCO 2017 Validation as our OD dataset. This way, we would not need to implement class label mappings. In COCO 2017 Validation dataset, there are 80 classes and 5000 images.

4.6   Framework Impact on Speed and Energy

By analysing the event traces from the OD service running on the Jetson, we could calculate their average time on different processes. In this case, the *"Process Data Event"* process represents the full process of extracting content in the

---

[1] COCO dataset: https://cocodataset.org/.

Table 3. Comparison of Energy and Speed from the different environments studied

Environment	Energy	Throughput	Process	Speed
Edge-baseline	2.0 watts	–	–	–
Edge-SSD-model	6.6 watts	1.3 FPS	Model execution	0.7692 s
Edge-OD-service	6.1 watts	1.1 FPS	Process data event	0.9027 s
			Serialise and write event	0.0166 s
			Tracer injection	0.0001 s
Cloud-baseline	72.1 watts	–	–	–
Cloud-MEP	72.3 watts	–	Rest of MEP	1.3030 s

OD MS, starting from the moment that each imaging event is read and finishing after the event is sent to the next service in the data-flow. This process is broken into, first, *Serialise and Write Event*, where the current event is serialised into JSON format and written to the next service stream in the dataflow; and second, *Tracer Injection*, where the last event trace from the service is added to an event before it leaves the service. This way the next service can retrieve the last event trace id, making the event trace flow in Jaeger clearer to follow.

Table 3 shows that the OD service in this setup had a lower throughput than the bare model, **losing 15% of the throughput** the model originally had. This is expected since we are using a lazy load approach for retrieving the images to reduce the size of the event messages through the system. Our imaging events that are read by the service in the Edge only contains the ID of the image stored in the Cloud Redis server, thus the service needs to retrieve each image from the Cloud before it can load it up into the model, which incurs some latency due to the network communication. We also observe that the use of JSON, Redis and Jaeger did not add much overhead in terms of latency on the resource-constrained Edge device.

We can see that adding our framework shell around the DNN model did not increase the amount of energy usage in the Edge. With an average of 6.1 Watts, it indicates that our solution leads to **8% of reduction in energy consumption** when compared to running the model on its own in the Edge, as can be seen on Table 3. This is probably caused by the network communications while retrieving the image from the Cloud to the Edge device. This leaves the CPU and GPU idle, thus reducing the amount of energy consumed. And for the Cloud environment, this was also negligible when compared to the stand-by baseline.

5   Conclusion

This paper has discussed the importance of a Cloud/Edge-Friendly architecture for DNN-based distributed MEP applications over heterogeneous Cloud-Edge environments; tooling decision can have a direct impact on the usability of resource-constrained Edge devices, greatly benefiting real-world scenarios such as when implementing OHS for construction sites.

The paper proposes an MSA for distributed MEP over heterogeneous Cloud-Edge environments; this system is both Edge-Friendly and Cloud-Independent at the same time. Some preliminary results of the proposed system were presented, starting with an analysis of how different OD models perform in heterogeneous Cloud and Edge scenarios. Initial exploration shows promising results on the impact that the proposed architecture solution impact has in a mixed Cloud-Edge deployment. The solution **reduces the energy consumption by 8%** with only a minor **drawback of 15% in throughput** in the Edge environment, while the energy usage in the Cloud is negligible. At the same time, the overhead for deployment in the different scenarios is very small, requiring only specific changes in the node configuration file.

Further testing of this solution is planned in a broader range of scenarios, such as a complete Edge node that can run independently from any Cloud node, as well as with a varying range of workloads with multiple publishers and subscribers. A self-adaptive scheduler for the DNN-based tasks is being developed which will take into account the different characteristics of the DNN models and the deployment environments. This scheduler will then be applied in a real-world case study for OHS in construction sites.

Acknowledgement. This work was supported by Science Foundation Ireland under grant SFI/12/RC/2289_P2, co-funded by the European Regional Development Fund.

References

1. Ao, L., Izhikevich, L., Voelker, G.M., Porter, G.: Sprocket: a serverless video processing framework. In: ACM Symposium on Cloud Computing. ACM (2018)
2. Aslam, A., Curry, E.: Towards a generalized approach for deep neural network based event processing for the internet of multimedia things. IEEE Access**6**, 25573–25587 (2018)
3. Belkhir, L., Elmeligi, A.: Assessing ICT global emissions footprint: trends to 2040 & recommendations. J. Cleaner Prod. **177**, 448–463 (2018)
4. Fowler, M., Lewis, J.: Microservices a definition of this new architectural term.http://martinfowler.com/articles/microservices.html (2014)
5. Fu, X., Ghaffar, T., Davis, J.C., Lee, D.: Edgewise: a better stream processing engine for the edge. In: 2019 USENIX Annual Technical Conference (2019)
6. Seo, J., Han, S., Lee, S., Kim, H.: Computer vision techniques for construction safety and health monitoring. Adv. Eng. Inform. **29**(2), 239–251 (2015)
7. Strubell, E., Ganesh, A., McCallum, A.: Energy and policy considerations for deep learning in NLP. arXiv preprint arXiv:1906.02243 (2019)
8. Walker, G., et al.: A practical review of energy saving technology for ageing populations. Appl. Ergon. **62**, 247–258 (2017)
9. Wang, J., et al.: Bandwidth-efficient live video analytics for drones via edge computing. In: 2018 ACM Symposium on Edge Computing, pp. 159–173. IEEE (2018)
10. Yadav, P., Curry, E.: VidCEP: complex event processing framework to detect spatiotemporal patterns in video streams. In: 2019 IEEE International Conference on Big Data (Big Data), pp. 2513–2522. IEEE (2019)

16th International Workshop on Engineering Service-Oriented Applications and Cloud Services (WESOACS 2020)

Introduction to the 16th International Workshop on Engineering Service-Oriented Applications and Cloud Services (WESOACS 2020)

Andreas S. Andreou[1], George Feuerlicht[2], Willem-Jan van den Heuvel[3], Winfried Lamersdorf [4], Guadalupe Ortiz[5], and Christian Zirpins[6]

[1] Cyprus University of Technology
andreas.andreou@cut.ac.cy
[2] Unicorn University
george.feuerlicht@unicornuniversity.net
[3] Tilburg University
wjheuvel@uvt.nl
[4] University of Hamburg
lamersdorf@informatik.unihamburg.de
[5] University of Cádiz
guadalupe.ortiz@uca.es
[6] Karlsruhe University of Applied Sciences
christian.zirpins@hs-karlsruhe.de

The International Workshop on Engineering Service-Oriented Applications and Cloud Services (WESOACS), formerly known as WESOA, was established in 2005 in Amsterdam with the aim to promote innovative ideas in research and practice of engineering of service-oriented applications. This year, WESOACS 2020 took place online on 28 September 2020 in conjunction with the 8th European Conference on Service-Oriented and Cloud Computing (ESOCC).

Service-oriented applications and cloud computing play an increasingly important role in enterprise computing today. While there is a good agreement about the main principles for designing and developing application systems based on the principles of distributed software services, there is still intense interest in this research area; in particular, in software service life cycle methodologies, service-oriented enterprise architectures and, more recently, in engineering methods for cloud computing environments. The recent shift towards DevOps and microservices and the extensive use of container-based technologies and architectures necessitates revision of current approaches for developing service-oriented applications. The WESOACS 2020 technical program included three research papers focusing on cloud services and microservices development: *"Modelling service-oriented systems and cloud services with Heraklit"* authored by Peter Fettke and Wolfgang Reisig, *"An Evaluation of Frameworks for Microservices Development"* authored by Isabell Sailer, Robin Lichtenthäler and Guido Wirtz, and *"Mining the Architecture of Microservice-Based Applications from their Kubernetes Deployment"* authored by Giuseppe Muntoni, Jacopo Soldani and Antonio Brogi.

Even though the online format of this year's event made the networking that characterizes WESOACS workshops more challenging, we regard the 16th edition of the workshop as highly successful.

Organization

Workshop Organizers

Andreas S. Andreou   Cyprus University of Technology, Cyprus
George Feuerlicht   Unicorn University, Czech Republic
Willem-Jan van den Heuvel   Tilburg University, Netherlands
Winfried Lamersdorf   University of Hamburg, Germany
Guadalupe Ortiz   University of Cádiz, Spain
Christian Zirpins   Karlsruhe University of Applied Sciences, Germany

Program Committee

Marco Aiello   University of Stuttgart, Germany
David Bermbach   TU Berlin, Germany
Javier Berrocal   Universidad de Extremadura, Spain
Juan Boubeta-Puig   University of Cádiz, Spain
Alena Buchalcevova   Prague University of Economics and Business, Czech Republic
Javier Criado   University of Almería, Spain
Marcelo Medeiros Eler   University of São Paulo, Brazil
Efstratios Georgopoulos   TEI Peloponnese, Greece
Laura González   Universidad de la República, Uruguay
Herodotos Herodotou   Cyprus University of Technology
Massimo Mecella   Sapienza University of Rome, Italy
Pierluigi Plebani   Politecnico di Milano, Italy
Wolfgang Reisig   Humboldt University of Berlin, Germany
Norbert Ritter   University of Hamburg, Germany
Ioannis Stamelos   Aristotle University of Thessaloniki, Greece
Eric Wilde   UC Berkeley School of Information, USA

Acknowledgements

We wish to thank all the authors for their contributions and the program committee members whose expert input made this workshop possible. Special thanks to the ESOCC 2020 workshop chairs Christian Zirpins and Iraklis Paraskakis.

Modelling Service-Oriented Systems and Cloud Services with HERAKLIT

Peter Fettke[1,2]([⊠]) and Wolfgang Reisig[3]

[1] German Research Center for Artificial Intelligence (DFKI), Saarbrücken, Germany
peter.fettke@dfki.de
[2] Saarland University, Saarbrücken, Germany
[3] Humboldt-Universität zu Berlin, Berlin, Germany
reisig@informatik.hu-berlin.de

Abstract. Modern and next generation digital infrastructures are technically based on service oriented structures, cloud services, and other architectures that compose large systems from smaller subsystems. The composition of subsystems is particularly challenging, as the subsystems themselves may be represented in different languages, modelling methods, etc. It is quite challenging to precisely conceive, understand, and represent this kind of technology, in particular for a given level of abstraction. To capture refinement and abstraction principles, various forms of "technology stacks" and other semi-formal or natural language based on presentations have been suggested. Generally, useful concepts to compose such systems in a systematic way are even more rare. HERAKLIT provides means, principles, and unifying techniques to model and to analyze digital infrastructures. HERAKLIT integrates composition and hierarchies of subsystems, concrete and abstract data structures, as well as descriptions of behaviour. A distinguished set of means supports the modeler to express their ideas. The modeller is free to choose the level of abstraction, as well as the kind of composition. HERAKLIT integrates new concepts with tried and tested ones. Such a framework provides the foundation for a comprehensive Systems Mining as the next step after Process Mining.

Keywords: Systems composition · Data modelling · Behaviour modelling · Composition calculus · Algebraic specification · Petri nets · Systems mining

1 Introduction

The development of big service-oriented systems is challenging. Traditionally, models have been a central tool for designing such systems. Currently used modelling methods reach their limits and should be replaced by better concepts.

Presented at the *16th International Workshop on Engineering Service-Oriented Applications and Cloud Services*, Heraklion, Greece, September 28–30, 2020.

The currently prevailing way of developing service-oriented systems is unsatisfactory in many aspects. The development process and its result must be: (a) more manageable for the developer, (b) easy to understand for the user, (c) less error-prone and verifiable, (d) easier to change, faster reachable and cheaper especially for really large systems. These and similar requirements have long been discussed in the relevant literature.

The development of a complex service-oriented system is always preceded by a planning process in which models are used to formulate the structure, function, intended effects etc. of the intended product. In comparison to other engineering disciplines, models are generally not used very often in computer science and business informatics. This is mainly due to the fact that up to now not much benefit can be derived from models. In the practice of system design nowadays mainly diagrams using the Business Process Modeling Notation (BPMN) are propagated for describing the business logic. Such diagrams are limited to the identification of elementary activities and the representation of the control flow. More comprehensive models that take more aspects into account and are more intuitive would be extremely helpful for computer science and business informatics.

We argue for a modelling method whose models are suitable for much more than just the representation of elementary activities and control flows. In particular, a good modelling method should meet the requirements mentioned above. From a more technical point of view, such a method should:

- support the structuring of a large service-oriented systems into modules;
- technically simple, but expressive to compose modules to large service-oriented systems;
- describe the discrete steps in large systems only locally in individual modules;
- represent modules intended for implementation and modules not intended for implementation integrated with the same concepts;
- represent data and consider data dependencies in the control flow;
- abstract from concrete data in order to create instantiations with the same behavior in a schematic way;
- add under-specified data aspects in the later design process or in the event of changes of the system systematically;
- describe activities and events at any level of abstraction and hierarchy levels;
- generate models that are scalable, changeable and expandable;
- support the proof that a model has desired properties;
- extend the proven techniques of Data Mining and Process Mining to general Systems Mining.

In this paper we propose HERAKLIT as a modelling method that meets these requirements. It combines proven mathematically based and intuitively easy to understand concepts that are already used for system specification; we recombine them and complement them with concepts for composition and hierarchical refinement of local components, making this technique suitable for modeling large operational systems.

The objective of this paper is to present an overview on HERAKLIT. Therefore we shortly introduce the central modelling principles in Sect. 2. Section 3 presents a concise case study using HERAKLIT. The paper closes with a discussion of related work (Sect. 4) and some conclusions (Sect. 5).

2 Principles of HERAKLIT

2.1 Big Systems

What are the implications of the statement that a system is "big"? Firstly, some concepts that suit "small" systems do not suit large systems. One of the most obvious of these concepts is the assumption of global states and steps that update global states [17]. Global states and steps adequately describe, for example, the behaviour of s small digital circuit. To describe the behaviour of stakeholders of a business as a sequence of global steps, is, however, conceptually not adequate. In a big system, e.g. a business, cause and effect of a step are locally confined; and this confinement is essential to understand behaviour. As another specific concept, a big system requires conventions to confine validity of names, i.e. to avoid globally valid names, with a few exceptions such as URLs.

In HERAKLIT, single behaviours (runs, executions) of a subsystem can be represented by means of states and steps that are global only within the subsystem. Upon composing two such systems, those local states and steps are not necessarily embedded into global states and steps of the composed system. Instead, single behaviours of the composed system are represented without assuming global states and steps. Local names of a subsystem are confined to the subsystem and its direct neighboring subsystems.

2.2 Composition of Systems

Every "big" real life system is composed from subsystems that are mutually related: they may exchange messages or jointly execute activities. The composition of subsystems is particularly challenging, as the subsystems themselves may be represented in different languages, modelling methods, etc [6]. Modelling techniques for such systems must provide means to compose models of subsystems. Many modelling techniques provide such means; they all come with specific, frequently parameterized composition operators, concentrating on special ways to exchange data, e.g. synchronously or asynchronously. A "big" system, composed from many systems $S_1, \ldots, S_n$, is favorably written

$$S = S_1 \bullet \cdots \bullet S_n, \tag{1}$$

with "$\bullet$" being any version of a composition operator. This bracket free notation requires that the composition operator is associative, i.e. that for any three models R, S, T hold: $(R \bullet S) \bullet T = R \bullet (S \bullet T)$. Typical examples for the notation (1) include supply chains, sequences of production machines in a factory, etc. Associativity of composition is rarely discussed explicitly, but frequently assumed without saying [16].

HERAKLIT offers a simple, universally employable and associative composition operator. In HERAKLIT, the diversity of specific, parameterized composition operators is expressed by help of *adapters*: Specific aspects and properties of the composition $R \bullet S$ of two models R and S are formulated in an adapter A, such that $R \bullet A \bullet S$ expresses the wanted properties. The advantages of this concept are obvious: One technical composition operator fits all content-wise requirements, adapters can themselves be composed, etc.

2.3 Abstraction and Refinement

A number of general principles has been proposed in literature, to adequately cover the abstraction and refinement of systems. In particular, it is most useful to start out with an abstract specification and to refine it systematically, such that properties of the refined system imply the relevant properties of the abstract system. Vice versa, a given system may be abstracted, yielding a more compact version.

Abstraction and refinement should harmonize with the composition. To refine a part T of a system S, one would partition S into T and the environment of T, and then refine T. The remaining subsystems in the environment of T should not be affected by this procedure. Systems on different refinement levels should be composable; an overall concept of hierarchy levels for subsystems should not be required. HERAKLIT suggests concepts for refinement and abstraction that respect these requirements.

2.4 Modelling of Data and Things Equally

In a big system, data, physical items, algorithms, activities of persons, steps of organizations, etc., are entangled. They must be modelled by similar means that differentiate between them only in pragmatical aspects: data can be generated, deleted, transformed into different representations, manipulated by computers, copied, updated, composed, etc. Physical items behave differently: A physical item always occupies a distinguished place in space. In models, one frequently does not want to distinguish "equal" items explicitly; their number matters.

2.5 Behaviour

The behaviour of a large system is composed of single actions. An action updates some local state components. It is up to the modeler to embed local state components into more global views, if wanted. For a really large system, a single execution (run) should not be represented as a sequence of actions (though one may argue that all behaviour occurs along a global time scale). Independence of actions should explicitly be represented and not be spoiled by representing them in an arbitrary order.

HERAKLIT suggests to base the description of behaviour on Petri nets with data carrying tokens [15]. This choice is motivated by multiple aspects:

– Petri nets can easily be specialized to include interfaces: Just select some places, transitions, and even arcs to serve as interface elements.
– The composition of Petri nets with interfaces is again a Petri net with interfaces.
– Petri nets suggest the notion of concurrent runs that partially order actions of a run, thus, avoiding them to be mapped onto a global time scale.

2.6 Describing Systems on a Schematic Level

Data, real life items, as well as entire systems must be describable on an abstract, schematic level. In particular, it must be possible to describe just the existence of data, items, functions, etc., without any concrete description of how they look like, how many of them there are, etc. On this schematic level, it should be possible to describe activities in systems, e.g. the principles of executing a client's order of an enterprise. A concrete enterprise is then an instantiation of the schema.

HERAKLIT provides techniques to model such schemata, and to characterize concrete enterprises as instantiations of such a schema. Here, we adapt notions such as structures, signatures and instantiations of signatures, that are well-known from first order logic and algebraic specifications. (Technically, a signature is just a set of sorted symbols for sets, constants, and functions. An instantiation interprets these symbols consistently). We extend signatures by requirements to exclude "unwanted" instantiations, in the spirit of specification languages such as the Z language.

Signatures and their instantiations can naturally be transferred to define Petri net schemata – we call them HERAKLIT schemata. Such a schema can be instantiated in different ways; each instantiation results in a concrete Petri net. This concept is useful to model, for example, not just a distinguished business, but a class of businesses that all follow the same business rules. Hence, HERAKLIT strongly supports the idea of reference modelling, a core topic of business informatics [13].

2.7 Verification

The notion of correctness has many implications for big systems. Some ideal properties of a big system can be composed of corresponding properties of the component systems. Not all relevant properties can formally be captured, yet they deserve a proper framework to reason about them. Particularly interesting are methods to prove properties at run-time.

HERAKLIT integrates a number of formal and semi-formal verification techniques to support structured arguments about the correct behaviour of modules.

3 Modules and Their Composition

3.1 Modules

In Sect. 1 we discussed a number of principles that are inevitable for modelling big systems: no globally effective structures, associative composition of models of any two systems, composition must be compatible with abstraction, modelling of data and real items, modelling of behaviour, parameterized models. Now we must model systems in such a way that all these principles are met.

We start out with the obvious observation that a real system in general consists of interdependent subsystems. This paves the way for the central notion of HERAKLIT-modules: A HERAKLIT module is a model, graphically depicted as a rectangle, with two decisive components:

- Its inner: this may be any kind of graph or text. Three variants are frequent: (a) the inner consists only of the name of the module, (b) it consists of (connected) submodules, (c) it describes dynamic behaviour.
- Its surface: this consists of gates, each gate is labelled, i.e. inscribed by a symbol. The gates of the surface are arranged on the surface of the module's rectangle. Alternatively, each gate is represented as a line, linking the module's rectangle with the gate's label.

The following Fig. 2 shows typical HERAKLIT modules.

3.2 Composition of Modules

Composing two modules A and B follows a simple idea: two equally labelled gates of A and B are "glued" and turned into an inner element of the module $A \bullet B$. However, in this simple version, the composition is fundamentally flawed: Upon composing three or more modules, the order of composition matters: for three modules A, B, and C, the two modules $(A \bullet B) \bullet C$ and $A \bullet (B \bullet C)$ differ from one another. In technical terms: this version of composition is not associative. But associativity is a central requirement, as discussed in Sect. 2.2.

To solve this problem, we return to modules shaped $S = S_1 \bullet \cdots \bullet S_n$. As discussed in Sect. 2.2: each module S_i generally has a left and a right neighbor (S_0 has no left, S_n has no right neighbor). S is composed by composing S_{i-1} with S_i (for $i = 2, \ldots, n$). In the real world, systems frequently exhibit this kind of structure, physically or conceptually.

Therefore, HERAKLIT partitions the surface of a module L into its left and right interface, written $^*L$ and L^*, resp. To compose two modules L and M, equally labelled gates of L^* and $^*M$ are glued and turn into inner elements of $L \bullet M$. The remaining elements of L^* go to $(L \bullet M)^*$ (together with M^*), and the remaining elements of $^*M$ go to $^*(L \bullet M)$ (together with $^*L$). Most important: A general theorem guarantees that this kind of composition is associative [16].

4   Case Study: A Service System

4.1   The Different Modules of the System

Today, many organizations offer a complex service portfolio for their customers or clients [3,4]. Typical examples are banking or financial services, insurance services, legal services, and the medical or health services offered by a hospital or a medical center.

basic sorts	function symbol
C *clients*	f: S ⟶ P(E) *experts for services*
E *experts*	
R *rooms*	
A *admins*	**variables**
S *services*	c: C
	e: E
	r: R
constant symbols	a: A
EX : P(E) *experts at work*	s: S
RO : P(R) *available rooms*	
AD : P(A) *admins at work*	

Fig. 1. Signature of the service system

Here, we model the organization of such a service system, serving clients, customers, or patients that want confidential consultation about particular services or a particular treatment, provided by experts.

Figure 1 shows the signature of the system: there are five sorts of elements in a service system, indicated by C, E, R, A, and S. Their intuitive meaning is indicated in italic. In a concrete service system, there are sets of experts, available consulting rooms, and admins, symbolically represented by EX, RO and AD. Their type is $P(E)$, $P(R)$, and $P(A)$, resp., with $P(\cdot)$ standing for "powerset". Furthermore, we need a function symbol f and five variables, one for each basic sort. An *instantiation* assigns each basic sort an arbitrarily chosen concrete set, each constant symbol a set of elements of the indicated sort, and f a function that assigns each service the set of experts that offer consultations for this service.

Figure 2a shows a module that represents the behaviour of clients: For every instantiation of the variables c and s by a client and a service, resp., transition a is enabled. Transition a represents the policy that any client may enter the service system with any kind of wish for consultation for a service s. Hence, place A may eventually hold any number of tokens, with each token consisting of a client and a service. Transition b indicates the service systems's help desk, accepting each client's wishes and asking them to wait at place B. There, a client will eventually receive a message either at place C or at place D. A message at place C indicates that no expert is available; so the client leaves the service system along transition c. A message at place D indicates that the client should proceed to the consulting room named or numbered r. The client will do so along transition d and arrow E. He will later on return along arrow F and leave the service system by transition e.

The module in Fig. 2b represents the behaviour of the service system's experts. There is a set of experts, depicted as EX, fixed when the schema is instantiated, and initially represented as unengaged at place G. One might expect this to be expressed by the symbol EX at place G. However, this would indicate one token at place G. This is not what we want: we want each single expert to be represented as a token. This is achieved by means of the function elm: Applied to a token that represents a set M, $elm(M)$ returns each element

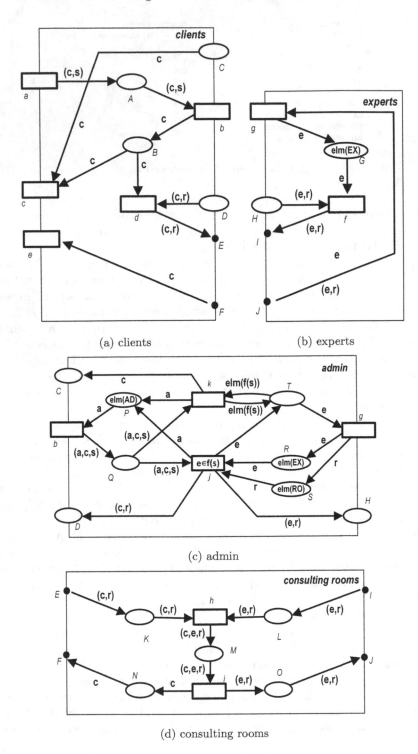

(a) clients

(b) experts

(c) admin

(d) consulting rooms

Fig. 2. The four modules of the system

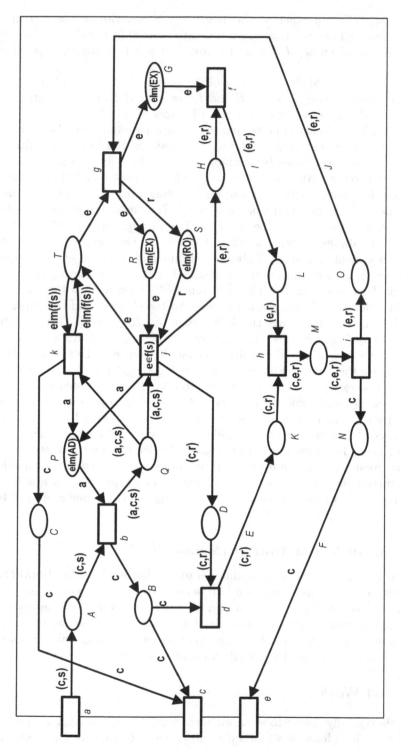

Fig. 3. Overall model of a service system

of M as a token. For an expert e, the message (e, r) arriving at place H indicates that e must go to consulting room r, due to transition f and arc I. He will eventually return along arc J, release room r, and will be again unengaged at place G.

The module in Fig. 2d shows the consulting rooms: A client c and an expert e arriving at room r along the arcs E and I, resp., start their consultation by transition h, end it by i, and leave the room by arcs F and J.

The behaviour of clients, experts, and the consulting rooms must be properly synchronized. The admin module of Fig. 2c organizes this. Place P initially contains each admin as a token (we employ again the function elm as explained above for the experts). An admin a engages with a client c and their request for an expert for service s, along transition b. A token (a, c, s) on place Q then continues either along transition k or transition j. Transition j requires an expert e on place R, such that e offers the service s. The inscription of j indicates this requirement. R always contains a "digital twin" for each expert that is not engaged with a client. The place S always contains a digital twin of each empty consulting room. Hence, transition j is enabled with proper instantiations of all five variables a, c, s, e, and r. The occurrence of j then renders the admin a available in P for new clients, sends messages to the client c, and the expert e to proceed to room r, and moves the digital twin of e to place T. This way, the digital twin of each expert e is either a token in R or in T. With e in T, the expert e eventually indicates by transition g that they finished their consultation and they release the room r. Finally, transition k manages the case where for a token (a, c, s) no expert for service s is available in R. As discussed above, the digital twin of each such expert is a token in T. Hence, all tokens in the set $f(s)$ of experts for s are in T. This is "tested" by means of the loop between k and T. Occurrence of k then renders the admin a available in P for new clients and sends a corresponding message to the client c. Notice the subtle treatment of experts and rooms as a scarce resource: If no corresponding expert is available, a client is turned away, as it may take too long until an expert for s is available. But if no room is available, the client is just waiting as long as one room will be available.

4.2 Overall Model and Abstract Composition

Figure 3 finally "glues" the four modules into one big module. In HERAKLIT, this can just be written as: *clients* • *admin* • *consulting rooms* • *experts*.

Similarly, it is possible to construct an abstract composition of the system. Figure 4 depicts such a composition of the four abstract modules by using the abstraction operator [·], which deletes the inner structure of a module. Formally written as: [*clients*] • [*admin*] • [*consulting rooms*] • [*experts*].

5   Related Work

Modelling is typically understood as an interdisciplinary field that is used in many different disciplines as a method or instrument to capture knowledge or

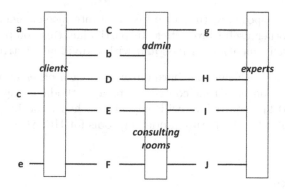

Fig. 4. Abstract composition of the overall model

to assist other (research) actions [2,6]. As we discuss above, HERAKLIT mainly does not invent new modeling concepts but integrates proven and well-known modelling approaches. Compared to other integrated approaches which currently dominate the modelling practice, e.g. BPMN, HERAKLIT provides integrated means to descrive model structure, data, and behaviour. In the central concept of a module, HERAKLIT combines three proven, intuitively easy to understand, and mathematically sound concepts that have been used for the specification of systems in the past:

1. Abstract data types and algebraic specifications for the formulation of concrete and abstract data: since the 1970s such specifications have been used, built into specification languages, and often used for (domain-specific) modelling. The book [18] presents systematically the theoretical foundations and some applications of algebraic specifications. Abstract state machines [8] also belong to this context.
2. Petri nets for formulating dynamic behaviour: HERAKLIT uses the central ideas of Petri nets. A step of a system, especially a large system, has locally limited causes and effects. This allows processes to be described without having to use global states and globally effective steps. This concept from the early 1960s [12] was generalized at the beginning of the 1980s with predicate logic and *colored marks* [7,10]. The connection with algebraic specifications is established by [14]. HERAKLIT adds two decisive aspects to this view: uninterpreted constant symbols for sets in places that use the *elm* function to hold instantiations with many possible initial marks, and the *elm* function as an inscription for an arrow to describe flexible mark flow.
3. The composition calculus for structuring large systems: this calculus with its widely applicable associative composition operator is the most recent contribution to the foundations of HERAKLIT. The obvious idea, often discussed in the literature, of modeling composition as a fusion of the interface elements of modules is supplemented by the distinction of left and right interface elements, and composition $A \bullet B$ as a fusion of right interface elements of A with left interface elements of B. According to [16,17], this composition is

associative (as opposed to the naive fusion of interface elements); it also has a number of other useful properties. In particular, this composition is compatible with refinement/coarseness and with individual (distributed) runs.

These three theoretical principles harmonize with each other and generate further *best practice* concepts that contribute to a methodical approach to modeling with HERAKLIT, and which will only be touched upon in this paper. On the down-side, industrially mature modelling tools for HERAKLIT are still under development.

6   Conclusions

The presented case study clearly demonstrates how HERAKLIT provides an integrated view on structure, data, and locally defined behaviour. Hence, HERAKLIT covers all central aspects of every computer-integrated system. Such a description can be used for different purposes, e.g. business process management, service engineering, software analysis, design, verification, and development. The used techniques are well-known but combined in a novel and innovative way.

By providing such an integrated method for system specification, HERAKLIT paves the way for many important innovations which are currently so much in need [2,9]. In particular, we like to introduce the idea of *Systems Mining*. While Data Mining and Process Mining [1] exploit the knowledge implicitly represented in data tuples and event sequences, respectively, Systems Mining is able to analyze the structure, data, and behaviour of a system. For such analysis, HERAKLIT provides the necessary techniques to specify all essential characteristics of a system. The observed structure of the system can be represented as modules, the observed data is captured by both concrete and abstract data structures, and the observed behaviour is specified as (distributed) runs. Based on such a powerful framework, Systems Mining provide a much richer picture of and deeper insights into big systems.

The presented case study of a service system illustrates powerful possibilities. Based on these HERAKLIT models, Systems Mining can answer a wide spectrum of interesting questions: (1) Do typical communications patterns between the modules of the system exist? (2) Which services are often requested by customers? (3) Do customers follow particular patterns for requesting services? (4) Which particular service requests and assignments of experts and rooms typically cause long waiting times for a customer? (5) Are there particular behaviour patterns and service requests which typically cause customers to leave the service system without getting a service or treatment?

Such questions and many more can easily be specified with HERAKLIT. Additionally, HERAKLIT provides a richer foundation for predictive and prescriptive process management as well as deeper insights for explaining process behaviour [5,11]. Hence, HERAKLIT lays the foundation for the next step after Process Mining.

References

1. van der Aalst, W.: Process mining. Commun. ACM **55**(8), 76–83 (2012)
2. Beverungen, D., et al.: Seven paradoxes of business process management in a hyperconnected world. Business & Information Systems Engineering Online-First (2020)
3. Böhmann, T., Leimeister, J., Möslein, K.: Service systems engineering. Bus. Inform. Syst. Eng. **6**, 73–79 (2014)
4. Chesbroug, H., Spohrer, J.: A research manifesto for service science. Commun. ACM **49**(7), 35–39 (2006)
5. Evermann, J., Rehse, J., Fettke, P.: Predicting process behaviour using deep learning. Decis. Support Syst. **100**, 129–140 (2017)
6. Frank, U., et al.: The research field "modeling business information systems" - current challenges and elements of a future research agenda. Bus. Inform. Syst. Eng. **6**(1), 39–43 (2014)
7. Genrich, Hartmann J., Lautenbach, Kurt: The analysis of distributed systems by means of predicate/transition-nets. In: Kahn, Gilles (ed.) Semantics of Concurrent Computation. LNCS, vol. 70, pp. 123–146. Springer, Heidelberg (1979). https://doi.org/10.1007/BFb0022467
8. Gurevich, Y.: Evolving algebras: the lipari guide. In: Borger, E. (ed.) Specification and Validation Methods. pp. 9–36. Oxford University (2012)
9. Houy, Constantin., Fettke, Peter., Loos, Peter., van der Aalst, Wil M.P., Krogstie, John: BPM-in-the-large – towards a higher level of abstraction in business process management. In: Janssen, Marijn, Lamersdorf, Winfried, Pries-Heje, Jan, Rosemann, Michael (eds.) EGES/GISP -2010. IAICT, vol. 334, pp. 233–244. Springer, Heidelberg (2010). https://doi.org/10.1007/978-3-642-15346-4_19
10. Jensen, K.: Coloured Petri Nets: Basic Concepts, Analysis Methods, and Practical Use. Springer, New York (1982). https://doi.org/10.1007/978-3-662-03241-1
11. Mehdiyev, N., Fettke, P.: Prescriptive process analytics with deep learning and explainable artificial intelligence. In: Rowe, F., et al. (eds.) 28th European Conference on Information Systems - Liberty, Equality, and Fraternity in a Digitizing World, ECIS 2020, pp. 15–17. Morocco, June, Marrakech (2020)
12. Petri, C.A.: Kommunikation mit Automaten. Ph.D. thesis, Institut für instrumentelle Mathematik der Universität Bonn (1962)
13. Rehse, J., Fettke, P.: A procedure model for situational reference model mining. Enterprise Model. Inform. Syst. Archit. Int. J. Conceptual Model. 14, 3:1–3:42 (2018)
14. Reisig, W.: Petri nets and algebraic specifications. Theor. Comput. Sci. **80**, 1–34 (1991)
15. Reisig, W.: Understanding Petri Nets. Springer, New York (2013). https://doi.org/10.1007/978-3-642-33278-4
16. Reisig, W.: Associative composition of components with double-sided interfaces. Acta Informatica **56**(3), 229–253 (2018). https://doi.org/10.1007/s00236-018-0328-7
17. Reisig, W.: Composition of component models - a key to construct big systems (2020)
18. Sanella, D., Tarlecki, A.: Foundations of Algebraic Specification and Formal Software Development. Springer, New York (2012). https://doi.org/10.1007/978-3-642-17336-3

An Evaluation of Frameworks
for Microservices Development

Isabell Sailer, Robin Lichtenthäler[✉], and Guido Wirtz

Distributed Systems Group, University of Bamberg, Bamberg, Germany
isabell.sailer@stud.uni-bamberg.de,
{robin.lichtenthaeler,guido.wirtz}@uni-bamberg.de

Abstract. Accompanying the popularity of the microservices architectural style, frameworks have been released which claim to specifically support the development of microservices-based applications. We investigate how well such frameworks support microservices characteristics both theoretically by a documentation analysis and practically by exemplary implementations. Our findings are that the frameworks cover most of the characteristics, but differ significantly in the way how. Therefore such frameworks can facilitate the development of microservices-based applications, but combining different frameworks can be a challenge.

Keywords: Microservices · Microservices development · Framework comparison

1 Introduction

The microservices architectural style has become a popular trend in software engineering for web- and cloud-based applications [7,10]. According to a recent survey among Java developers, 63% of their respondents were *"either working in, or actively transitioning to, microservices"* [14]. However, developing applications with a microservices architectural style is difficult. The main reason is that microservices-based applications are distributed over the network and functionality is split over several services [7]. While the complexity decreases for a single microservice, because of its limited functional scope, developing and operating numerous interconnected microservices is a challenge. There is no standardized definition of the microservices architectural style [11], instead it is described by a set of characteristics and practices which should be followed, leaving room for interpretations how exactly these characteristics should be realized. Nevertheless, several frameworks have emerged which claim to support the development of microservices-based systems and therefore for software engineers the question arises whether using such frameworks is beneficial. However, this is difficult to assess due to the broad range of aspects to consider on the one hand and the unclear definition of microservices on the other. This work presents a catalog of characteristics derived from the literature to compare existing frameworks with regard to their supported functionality. Selected frameworks are also assessed

© Springer Nature Switzerland AG 2021
C. Zirpins et al. (Eds.): ESOCC 2020 Workshops, CCIS 1360, pp. 90–102, 2021.
https://doi.org/10.1007/978-3-030-71906-7_8

practically by implementing an exemplary microservices-based application. We aim at answering the following research questions:

RQ1: Which microservices-specific characteristics are supported in which way by existing frameworks for microservices development?

RQ2: How easily and efficiently can microservices-specific characteristics be implemented with existing frameworks for microservices development?

In the following, Sect. 2 presents microservices-specific characteristics. In Sect. 3 we describe our approach for the framework comparison. The comparison is presented in Sect. 4, followed by the practical assessment in Sect. 5. In Sect. 6 we discuss our main findings and derive implications for practice and further research. We review related work in Sect. 7 and finish with a final conclusion in Sect. 8.

2 Microserivces Characteristics

Even though there is no standardized definition for the microservices architectural style, certain common characteristics can be identified. We considered a set of works which are commonly referred to when introducing microservices to derive common characteristics: The influential blog post by Fowler and Lewis [9], a survey paper by Dragoni et al. [7], an influential book by Newman [19] and a definition from The Open Group [1]. We unified equivalent but differently named characteristics and defined subcategories to account for different levels of granularity. For this work we only considered technical characteristics, although organizational aspects are equally important. To enable a comparison targeted at specific features of the frameworks, we then enriched the characteristics with subcategories identified from additional literature. In the following, the resulting eight characteristics with their additional subcategories are described.

1. Service Independence. A microservice should be developable and deployable independently from other microservices [1]. To form a larger system, microservices communicate with each other exclusively via interfaces [7], without an update or replacement of a single microservice affecting the entire system [1]. The number of running service instances and their network locations are dynamic. **Service discovery** mechanisms enable determining the up-to-date location of services at runtime independent of specific pre-defined locations [22,24]. Furthermore, **distributed configuration** should be used, which means that the configuration is stored independently from the microservices in a central, external memory [19,23]. Microservices load the configuration at startup and reload it at runtime. This is important to keep microservices independent from differing environment-specific configurations and to avoid redeployments because of changing configurations. General **access control** mechanisms, such as authentication and authorization to secure interfaces and regulate the access to resources, should also be implemented [25] and be customizable per service.

2. Size. Compared to other service-oriented approaches, the size of a microservice should be rather small [7]. However, the size is difficult to specify and impossible to accurately measure, making technical support from a framework difficult. A common approach is to state that a microservice should be concerned only with a single business activity and bounded contexts (originating from Domain-Driven Design (DDD)) [1] can be used to define such business activities. Apart from bounded contexts as a concept to define service scopes, another concept called Command Query Responsibility Segregation (**CQRS**) can be used which aims at separating query functionalities from command functionalities into separate components [6, 19]. It is applied in the context of event-based systems and can also guide the decomposition of functionalities into services.

3. Well-Defined Interface. Because Microservices are independent processes and communicate by remote calls via interfaces, these interfaces must be well-defined and published, i.e. accessible to others. For an interface to be well-defined, it must be suited for the functionalities it offers, predictable, which means that it provides consistent semantics, and adhere to standards and best practices. Documenting an interface with a standardized **interface specification**, also referred to as API description [18], supports developing a well-designed interface, enables the sharing of interface documentations and helps to achieve consistency across entire microservices-based applications [1, 9].

4. Smart Endpoints and Dumb Pipes. For the communication between services, simple mechanism are preferred, such as Representational State Transfer (**REST**) over HTTP [9, 12, 26] to keep complexity in the services and out of the communication channels [1, 9]. Another common approach to also enable asynchronous communication is lightweight **messaging** via a message bus [12]. To provide routing logic and shared functionalities like authentication or rate-limiting, which have traditionally been provided by the infrastructure, specialized services, so-called **API Gateways**, are commonly used [11, 22]. API Gateways also decouple microservices from clients and enable the aggregation of multiple service calls. Cases of complex **service workflows** involving multiple services need special attention, because the loose coupling of services should be preserved while still guaranteeing a certain level of (eventual) consistency. Specialized mechanisms such as the Saga Pattern [20] have been proposed for this.

5. Decentralized Data Management. To ensure loose coupling and independence, the data management is decentralized among microservices as in the case of the database-per-service pattern [22]. This decentralization also enables **polyglot persistence** which means that different services can use different database technologies depending on which technology is suited best [9, 26]. However, data consistency is constrained, because transactions across services should be avoided. Data requiring strict consistency should be contained within one service, otherwise eventual consistency across services should be embraced [1, 9].

6. Design for Failure. Because microservices are distributed over the network, communication failures and node crashes have to be expected. The impact of failures on the whole system, however, should be minimized [1, 9] by employing certain mechanisms. **Timeouts** must be chosen appropriately and **bulkheads** can be used to reduce the impact of failures. The **circuit breaker** pattern can be applied [11, 19] to avoid cascading failures and enable services to recover. To ensure availability, microservices should be replicated across different servers.

To efficiently distribute the network traffic among the service instances, **load balancing** is essential. By autonomously and dynamically adjusting the number of service replicas, it can be ensured that enough replicas are available, even in the case of node failures [1], and if replicas are no longer needed resources can be freed [23]. To detect errors and failures at an early stage, microservices-based applications attach great importance to real-time **monitoring** [9]. To enable a consistent monitoring even for requests which span multiple services, **distributed tracing** should be used [5]. Requests can then be tracked across the individual microservices in order to find the cause in the event of a failure [20]. Furthermore, a thorough monitoring should support different types of **metrics** for each service, such as host-level metrics and application-level metrics [19].

7. Automation. Operating and evolving a complex microservices architecture while guaranteeing stability requires high levels of automation. To ensure correctness even with frequent updates, automated unit-, integration- and performance **testing** during deployment is necessary [9,19]. To run multiple isolated services in a resource-efficient way, **containerization** is typically used. Containers also improve automated scalability, because of their fast start-up times [2,26]. Automated testing and containerization are the basis for **Continuous Deployment** which enables fast evolution of services in a safe way by employing specialized continuous deployment tools [4,26].

8. Evolutionary Design. Microservices-based systems should be designed to encourage evolution. This can for example be achieved by implementing parts that change simultaneously in the same microservice. Ideally, consumers of a microservice should not be affected by its evolution. One approach to achieve this is to use **versioning** [9] which means having different versions of service endpoints coexist to allow consumers to adapt over time [19]. However, versioning should only be used as a last resort. It is preferable for each microservice to be as tolerant as possible so that versioning is not necessary at all [9].

3 Methodology

To select frameworks for our comparison we focused on those claiming to be specifically designed for developing microservices-based applications, although general purpose web frameworks are also frequently used in practice. We considered **Go**, **Java**, **Node.JS** and **Python** as currently popular languages for developing microservices [3] and because polyglot programming is core to the microservices architectural style [26]. In addition, we included the language **Jolie**, which is specifically designed for the development of microservices. An overview of the frameworks with the version we considered is presented in Table 1.

For the theoretical evaluation of which features are supported by the frameworks, we reviewed their documentations as well as the source code repositories. We rated characteristics as *supported*, *not supported* or *no information* and noted how exactly, e.g. by which technology or tools, a characteristic is supported. If few information could be found, but not enough to clearly mark the aspect as supported, it was rated as *no information*.

Table 1. Selected microservices frameworks

Language	Name	Released	Version	Link
Go	Kit	2016	0.9.0	https://gokit.io/
	Micro	2017	2.2.0	https://micro.mu/
Java	Axon	2010	4.2	https://axoniq.io/
	Eventuate	2017	0.2.0	https://eventuate.io/
	Helidon	2018	1.4.1	https://helidon.io/
	Lagom	2016	1.6.0	https://www.lagomframework.com/
	Micronaut	2018	1.2.8	https://micronaut.io/
	MicroProfile	2018	3.2	https://microprofile.io/
	Spring Cloud	2014	2.2.1	https://spring.io/cloud
Jolie	-	2006	1.8.2	https://www.jolie-lang.org/
Node.JS	Moleculer	2017	0.14.5	https://moleculer.services/
Python	Falcon	2013	2.0.0	https://falconframework.org/
	Nameko	2013	3.0.0-rc8	https://www.nameko.io/

Subsequently, we selected one framework of each programming language for the practical assessment, based on how well the frameworks scored in the theoretical evaluation. We then developed the same application with each selected framework and examined whether, and if so how efficiently, the functionalities could be implemented with the respective frameworks. In addition we added aspects specific to the *development perspective* to the assessment.

4   Frameworks Feature Comparison

The result of our theoretical evaluation is the comparison of features offered by the frameworks for the characteristics of the microservices architectural style. Table 2 shows a summary of the evaluation while the detailed comparison can be found online.[1] If characteristics are supported, this is marked with ✓, if not with ✗. When no information could be found, this is marked with ⁓.

Overall, the frameworks offer many features to support the characteristics of a microservices-based architecture. For **Java**, we not only found the most frameworks but also the more comprehensive documentations on how to use the offered features. Spring Cloud and Micronaut have the most supported characteristics which is probably the result of Spring Cloud being one of the most mature frameworks with a longer history as a popular general web framework. Micronaut is comparably newer, but has adopted successful concepts from Spring Cloud. A somewhat special case is Eventuate because it does not offer a broad range of features, but has a special focus on service workflows with support for the implementation of the Saga pattern [20]. In a similar way, Axon and Lagom have a focus on event-driven concepts and therefore other characteristics are less

---

[1] https://github.com/IsabellSailer/ms-framework-comparison.

Table 2. Feature comparison of microservices development frameworks

Characteristic	Go		Java							Jolie	Node.JS	Python	
	Kit	Micro	Axon	Eventuate	Helidon	Lagom	Micronaut	MicroProfile	SpringCloud		Moleculer	Falcon	Nameko
1. Service Independence													
1.1 Distributed Configuration	–	✓	–	–	✓	–	✓	✓	✓	–	✓	–	✓
1.2 Service Discovery	✓	✓	✓	–	–	✓	✓	–	✓	✗	✓	✗	✗
1.3 Access Control	–	–	–	–	✓	✓	✓	✓	✓	✗	✓	✓	–
2. Size													
2.1 CQRS	–	–	✓	✓	–	✓	–	–	–	–	✓	–	–
3. Well-Defined Interface													
3.1 Interface Specification	–	–	✓	–	✓	✓	✓	✓	✓	✓	✗	✓	✓
4. Smart Endpoints and Dumb Pipes													
4.1 API Gateway	–	✓	✓	–	✓	✓	✓	–	✓	✓	✓	✓	–
4.2 REST	✓	✓	✗	✗	✓	✓	✓	✓	✓	✓	✓	✓	✓
4.3 Messaging	✓	✓	✓	✓	✗	✓	✓	✓	✓	✓	✓	✗	✓
4.4 Service workflows	✗	✗	✓	✓	✗	✗	✗	✗	✗	✗	✗	✗	✗
5. Decentralized Data Management													
5.1 Polyglot Persistence	✗	✗	✓	✗	✓	✓	✓	✓	✓	✓	✓	✓	✓
6. Design for Failure													
6.1 Circuit Breaker	✓	✓	✗	–	✓	✓	✓	✓	✓	–	✓	✗	–
6.2 Load Balancing	✓	✓	✓	–	–	✗	✓	–	✓	✓	✓	✗	✗
6.3 Bulkheads	✗	✗	✗	–	✓	✓	✓	✓	✓	–	✓	✗	✗
6.4 Timeouts	✓	✓	✓	✓	✓	✓	✓	✓	✓	✓	✓	–	–
6.5 Monitoring	✓	✓	✓	–	–	✓	✓	✓	✓	✓	✓	✗	–
6.6 Metrics	✓	✓	✓	✓	✓	✓	✓	✓	✓	–	✓	✓	✓
6.7 Distributed Tracing	✓	✓	✓	–	✓	✓	✓	✓	✓	–	✓	✗	✓
7. Automation													
7.1 Containerization	✓	✓	–	✓	–	✓	✓	✓	✓	✓	✓	–	–
7.2 Testing	✗	✗	✓	✗	✗	✓	✓	✓	✓	✗	✓	✓	✓
7.3 Continuous Deployment	✓	✓	–	–	–	✓	✓	–	✓	✓	✓	–	–
8. Evolutionary Design													
8.1 Versioning	–	–	✓	–	–	–	✓	–	–	–	✗	–	–
supported	11	13	14	6	11	17	19	14	18	10	18	7	8
no information	6	4	4	12	7	2	1	6	2	7	0	6	9
not supported	4	4	3	3	3	2	1	1	1	4	3	8	4

relevant. For example, Axon explicitly has no circuit breaker feature, because this is only useful for synchronous service invocations, not for asynchronous event-based messaging. MicroProfile, with its origin in the JavaEE ecosystem, differs from the others, as its focus is on specifications for how certain features should be provided leaving room for vendors to provide actual implementations. For many characteristics, the frameworks rely on other software which has proven its worth. For example, the frameworks include adapters for object-relational mappers to access databases, for messaging systems like RabbitMQ,[2] for monitoring solutions like Prometheus,[3] for service discovery with services like Consul,[4] or for distributed tracing with tools like Zipkin[5] or Jaeger.

The two **Python** frameworks offer less comprehensive features, especially regarding design for failure. Instead, they have a narrow focus on certain aspects. Nameko focuses on asynchronous interactions based on the Advanced Message Queuing Protocol (AMQP), explicitly stating that it is not a general web framework. The documentation of Falcon describes it as a lightweight framework focusing on HTTP to build REST APIs. Kit and Micro, as frameworks for **Go**, offer a comparably large set of features, although some characteristics are insufficiently supported, such as extensive support for polyglot persistence or interface specifications. Micro stands out, because it includes a service runtime at its core which runs along the individual services and internally provides features such as distributed configuration, service discovery and messaging. Moleculer, which is based on **Node.JS**, follows a similar approach and offers a so-called ServiceBroker which provides features such as service discovery, load balancing and monitoring. Overall Moleculer also offers a comprehensive set of features with an extensive documentation. **Jolie**, as the only specific language for microservices development, has a clear academic background and lacks some of the features which are provided by the other frameworks. Its focus is on how to structure the communications between services by making service interfaces a core part of the language. Nevertheless, it is a mature language and has already been used in productive deployments. A feature that is common across many of the frameworks is the support for the OpenAPI[6] specification, if an interface specification is supported.

5   Implementation-Based Comparison

For the practical assessment we investigated how well the different characteristics could be implemented. In addition, we also assessed the general development perspective. To represent each language, we selected Micronaut, Micro, Nameko, Moleculer and Jolie. The use case of our exemplary application is a Beauty Salon with three different services. The high-level architecture is shown in Fig. 1 and highlights the main characteristics based on the numbering from Table 2. Briefly, the intended use case is that a customer could get information about the available treatments from the treatment service (TrS) and then book an appointment via the appointments service (ApS). Upon a request to book an appointment, the

---

[2] https://www.rabbitmq.com/.
[3] https://prometheus.io.
[4] https://www.consul.io/.
[5] https://zipkin.io.
[6] https://www.openapis.org/.

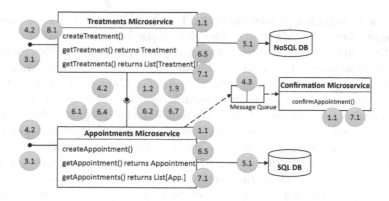

Fig. 1. Architecture of the beautysalon application

ApS queries the TrS via a REST API to validate the request. Then it stores the appointment in its database and sends a message to the confirmation service (CoS) via a message queue. The CoS can then send out a confirmation to the customer. It has to be noted, that the purpose of this application is to show exemplary implementations of microservices characteristics. It is not an example of how to split functionalities into services, because the scope is reduced to a minimum. In the following we describe the implementations, which can be found online (see footnote 1). Due to the limited scope of the sample application, we omitted the characteristics: CQRS, API gateway, Bulkheads, Testing and Continuous deployment.

While for all implementations the configuration is separated from the services, only with Micronaut, true **Distributed configuration** with a configuration service (Consul) could be used. **Service discovery** for the interaction between the ApS and the TrS is implemented with Consul (see footnote 4) for Micronaut, an internal mechanism for Micro and Moleculer and not implemented with Nameko and Jolie. **Access control** is implemented for the API of the treatments service. Direct support is only offered by Micronaut and Moleculer while for the other frameworks it would have been necessary to implement access control manually. Creating and publishing an OpenAPI (see footnote 6) specification is only possible with Jolie and Micronaut. Micro and Moleculer don't offer support for any **interface specification** format and while for Nameko a plugin is available, it was not integrable due to errors. Implementing a **REST** API works equally well for all frameworks, only for Jolie it is not possible to differentiate between HTTP verbs for the same URI or include path parameters. Also implementing **messaging**-based communication works equally well for all frameworks, although the mechanisms differ significantly. Micronaut offers adapters for independent messaging services. Jolie, Micro, Nameko, and Moleculer have internal messaging solutions which work well as long as all services are implemented with the same framework.

To realize **polyglot persistence**, the TrS uses a NoSQL database (Redis in the case of Micronaut, Micro and Nameko; MongoDB in the case of Jolie and Moleculer) and the ApS uses a SQL database (PostgreSQL). The MongoDB connector for Jolie is only in a beta version and has some drawbacks. Micro offers no plugin for database access, therefore general Go libraries are used. Although Nameko offers a plugin to integrate SQLAlchemy,[7] the setup requires significant additional effort using alembic.[8] With Micronaut and Moleculer the desired models could be created in the services and then the framework takes care of creating and handling the required database schemas. The **circuit breaker** pattern is only implemented with Micronaut and Moleculer. For Moleculer however, it can only be used within the Moleculer runtime, not with other external services. For Micro the circuit breaker pattern cannot be used with the module for REST-based communication. **Load balancing** is enabled for Micronaut via the Consul service discovery mechanism. Micro and Moleculer offer load balancing via the internal service discovery. **Timeouts** are set together with retry mechanisms per service or per service call in Micronaut and Moleculer. **Monitoring** and **metrics** are supported by Micronaut via configuring a health and a metrics endpoint respectively. For Moleculer, a combined endpoint can be activated, but without separate monitoring via a health endpoint. Micro offers a wrapper to export basic metrics to Prometheus[3]. Nameko supports exporting metrics to StatsD[9] with a tracer endpoint. However, combining them leads to problems. Micronaut and Moleculer support the OpenTracing API and distributed tracing is therefore implemented with Zipkin[5]. All implementations are available in the form of Docker .**containers**. Moleculer includes prepared Dockerfiles and for the others it is possible to write Dockerfiles based on the documentations with Jolie also offering a Jolie base image. Versioning as an explicit concept is only supported and implemented with Micronaut.

Finally, we considered additional characteristics adopted from Rieger et al. [21] covering the general development perspective. Regarding the **development environment**, frameworks should support integrated development environments (IDE) to facilitate the usage of the framework. For all frameworks the existing language support in IDEs could be used and also Jolie offers extensions enabling the usage of IDEs. In addition, Micronaut and Moleculer offer command line tools to generate pre-configured project templates which enhances the development perspective. The **preparation time** is influenced by the time and effort to install and setup a framework, the quality of the documentation and accompanying tutorials, and the amount and quality of examples. Setup time was equally small for all frameworks, only for Jolie artifacts were initially missing in the installer. For Micronaut, Moleculer and Jolie extensive documentation and helpful guides are available. For Micro and Nameko the provided documentation is sufficient, but could provide more details and examples. Regarding **extensibility**, meaning the possibility to include and use additional third-party

---

[7] https://www.sqlalchemy.org/.
[8] https://alembic.sqlalchemy.org.
[9] https://github.com/statsd.

libraries or other components, all frameworks perform well, because they rely on existing tools for their respective languages. Micro uses Go modules, Micronaut uses `Gradle` or `Maven`, Moleculer uses `npm`, and Nameko uses `pip`. For Jolie it is possible to include Java or JavaScript libraries, but without proper dependency management,

All in all, regarding the implementations we found Micronaut and Moleculer to be most comprehensive, followed by Micro, Jolie and Nameko.

6   Discussion

To explain the differences in the number of supported characteristics, the context of each framework needs to be considered. For example, Eventuate focuses on service workflows or Nameko focuses on asynchronous communication. Both therefore neglect other characteristics, which could be covered by combining them with others. Hence, the suitability of frameworks cannot be assessed in general, but depends on the development context. Nevertheless, frameworks like Micronaut, Spring Cloud or Moleculer are comprehensive in nearly all aspects This is in accordance to the results of Baresi and Garriga [3] who found Java to be the most used language for microservices-based projects on Github.

Regarding **RQ1** we can state that the characteristics are supported to a large extent, but for the ways how, there are significant differences. For example, Micro, Nameko and Moleculer have specialized service runtimes which provide communication and capabilities such as the circuit breaker pattern. However, that means services based on other frameworks are difficult to integrate. For other aspects in turn the support is similar. For example, if an interface specification is supported, it is the popular OpenAPI specification. For Distributed Tracing, there is the OpenTracing API which most of the frameworks support. That means, if an independent and broadly used specification for a characteristic is available, the integration of services built with different frameworks is a lot easier.

Considering **RQ2**, we can similarly state that the characteristics can be implemented efficiently when the same framework is used for all services, but an implementation using the different frameworks in combination, although not covered in this work, would be more challenging.

The emerging questions are then what aspects are the most important to be supported by a framework and which aspects can be realized in another way. From our point of view, frameworks should provide flexibility regarding the integration with other services and other technologies. For example messaging should be flexible by supporting different messaging systems like RabbitMQ or Kafka. The strength of a framework then is if it can combine characteristics, meaning for example that monitoring can be configured easily for messaging or the interaction mechanism used independent of specific technologies.

For some characteristics a shift towards other technologies can be observed. For example, Service Discovery or Distributed Configuration are also features of container orchestration systems such as Kubernetes [15]. Access Control or the

Circuit Breaker pattern are now available from so-called services meshes [17]. If a framework shows flexibility to integrate with other components for such characteristics, it can be adapted more easily and provide long-term value.

7 Related Work

Most of the previous work on Microservices covers architectural foundations [11] or studies on migrations from monolithic architectures to a microservices architecture [2]. Specific microservices development frameworks have been less in focus so far. For Jolie and the development of microservices with Jolie, there is various work, mainly by the developers of Jolie themselves [13]. The only work on a comparison of different microservices frameworks is a thesis [8] by Edling and Östergren. However, their comparison considered only Java and was based on a specific use case rather than general microservices characteristics.

Using an exemplary application for research has been done also by von Kistowski et al. [16]. However, their research focus is on performance benchmarking and therefore significantly different from ours. Nevertheless, their work includes a review of existing exemplary applications which can be compared to our approach, although none exemplary microservices-based application has been presented so far which shows the same application built with different technologies.

To the best of our knowledge an analysis of microservices development frameworks based on characteristics derived from the literature is not yet available.

8 Conclusion

Our comparison of frameworks for developing microservices-based applications shows that overall many of the characteristics important for the microservices architectural style are covered by the frameworks. Because of the broad range of aspects, however, no framework can cover everything. Therefore we found that (1) some frameworks have a strong focus only on certain characteristics, (2) all frameworks rely on and integrate with existing solutions for a substantial part of the characteristics and (3) if a framework shows flexibility, it is overall better suited for the technological heterogeneity inherent to the microservices architectural style. Using a microservices framework can facilitate the development process, but requires a developer to be already familiar with this architectural style to use the features in their intended way. Furthermore, within each framework microservices can be built effectively, but combining frameworks, especially across languages, would be challenging due to the different ways how microservices-specific characteristics are supported.

There are some limitations to our work: We do not cover general web frameworks which are used for microservices in practice, such as Django or Flask. For our theoretical investigation we relied on the accurateness of the documentations and it is a snapshot based on the framework versions at the time of our study. As frameworks evolve, the number of supported characteristics change.

If a software engineer has to choose a microservices framework, this work can serve as a decision support to some extent, but there are additional aspects to consider such as the previous experience with a language. In addition, frameworks offer only technical solutions to the microservices architectural style. To successfully apply the microservices architectural style, however, also organizational aspects have to be taken into consideration, which cannot be covered by the frameworks. Finally, the business context and how to scope and split functionalities between services is an aspect which can hardly be covered by technical solutions like frameworks, although it is a deciding factor for the success of a microservices development project.

References

1. Balakrushnan, S., et al.: Microservices architecture. Technical report W169, The Open Group (2016)
2. Balalaie, A., Heydarnoori, A., Jamshidi, P.: Microservices architecture enables DevOps. IEEE Softw. **33**(3), 42–52 (2016)
3. Baresi, L., Garriga, M.: Microservices: the evolution and extinction of web services? In: Bucchiarone, A., et al. (eds.) Microservices, pp. 3–28. Springer, Cham (2019). https://doi.org/10.1007/978-3-030-31646-4_1
4. Chen, L.: Microservices: architecting for continuous delivery and DevOps. In: ICSA, pp. 39–397. IEEE (2018)
5. Cinque, M., Corte, R.D., Pecchia, A.: Microservices monitoring with event logs and black box execution tracing. IEEE Trans. Serv. Comput. p. 1 (2019)
6. Debski, A., Szczepanik, B., Malawski, M., Spahr, S., Muthig, D.: A scalable, reactive architecture for cloud applications. IEEE Softw. **35**(2), 62–71 (2018)
7. Dragoni, N., et al.: Microservices: yesterday, today, and tomorrow. In: Mazzara, M., Meyer, B. (eds.) Present and Ulterior Software Engineering, pp. 195–216. Springer, Cham (2017). https://doi.org/10.1007/978-3-319-67425-4_12
8. Edling, E., Östergren, E.: An analysis of microservice frameworks (2017)
9. Fowler, M., Lewis, J.: Microservices (2014). https://martinfowler.com/articles/microservices.html. Accessed 03 July 2020
10. Francesco, P.D., Lago, P., Malavolta, I.: Migrating towards microservice architectures: an industrial survey. In: ICSA, pp. 29–2909. IEEE (2018)
11. Francesco, P.D., Lago, P., Malavolta, I.: Architecting with microservices: a systematic mapping study. J. Syst. Softw. **150**, 77–97 (2019)
12. Garriga, M.: Towards a taxonomy of microservices architectures. In: Cerone, A., Roveri, M. (eds.) SEFM 2017. LNCS, vol. 10729, pp. 203–218. Springer, Cham (2018). https://doi.org/10.1007/978-3-319-74781-1_15
13. Guidi, C., Lanese, I., Mazzara, M., Montesi, F.: Microservices: a language-based approach. Present and Ulterior Software Engineering, pp. 217–225. Springer, Cham (2017). https://doi.org/10.1007/978-3-319-67425-4_13
14. JRebel: 2020 java developer report. Technical report, Perforce Software, Inc. (2020)
15. Khan, A.: Key characteristics of a container orchestration platform to enable a modern application. IEEE Cloud Comput. **4**(5), 42–48 (2017)
16. von Kistowski, J., Eismann, S., Schmitt, N., Bauer, A., Grohmann, J., Kounev, S.: TeaStore: a micro-service reference application. In: (MASCOTS), pp. 223–236. IEEE (2018)

17. Li, W., Lemieux, Y., Gao, J., Zhao, Z., Han, Y.: Service mesh: challenges, state of the art, and future research opportunities. In: (SOSE), pp. 122–1225. IEEE (2019)
18. Lübke, D., Zimmermann, O., Pautasso, C., Zdun, U., Stocker, M.: Interface evolution patterns. In: EuroPLop 2019, pp. 1–24. ACM Press (2019)
19. Newman, S.: Building Microservices. O'Reilly Media Inc., Sebastopol (2015)
20. Richardson, C.: Microservices Patterns. Manning Publications, Shelter Island (2019)
21. Rieger, C., Majchrzak, T.A.: Towards the definitive evaluation framework for cross-platform app development. Syst. Softw. **153**, 175–199 (2019)
22. Taibi, D., Lenarduzzi, V., Pahl, C.: Architectural patterns for microservices: a systematic mapping study. In: CLOSER, pp. 221–232. SciTePress (2018)
23. Toffetti, G., Brunner, S., Blöchlinger, M., Dudouet, F., Edmonds, A.: An architecture for self-managing microservices. In: AIMC 2015, pp. 19–24. ACM Press (2015)
24. Wolff, E.: Microservices: Grundlagen flexibler Softwarearchitekturen. dpunkt. (2018)
25. Zdun, U., Wittern, E., Leitner, P.: Emerging trends, challenges, and experiences in DevOps and microservice APIs. IEEE Softw. **37**(1), 87–91 (2020)
26. Zimmermann, O.: Microservices tenets. CSRD **32**(3–4), 301–310 (2016)

Mining the Architecture
of Microservice-Based Applications
from their Kubernetes Deployment

Giuseppe Muntoni, Jacopo Soldani$^{(\boxtimes)}$, and Antonio Brogi

University of Pisa, Pisa, Italy
jacopo.soldani@unipi.it

Abstract. Microservice-based applications can include hundreds of interacting software components. This makes their design, implementation, and operation complex, costly, and error-prone. While the availability of a description of the software architecture of microservice-based applications can help to analyse and maintain them, manually generating an architectural description of microservice-based applications is costly because of the number of services and of service interactions. In this paper, we propose a solution for automatically mining the architecture of a microservice-based application starting from its deployment in Kubernetes, and for generating the corresponding architecture description with the OASIS standard TOSCA. Our solution extracts information both statically, from the manifest files specifying the application deployment in Kubernetes, and dynamically, by deploying and monitoring the application on Kubernetes. We also present a first proof-of-concept implementation of our solution.

Keywords: Microservices · Microservices architectures · Software architecture mining

1 Introduction

Microservices are gaining momentum in enterprise IT, with major IT companies (e.g., Amazon, Facebook, Google, Netflix, and Spotify) adopting them to deliver their businesses [22]. Microservice-based architectures are service-oriented architectures satisfying some additional key principles, e.g., shaping services around business concepts, ensuring their independent deployability and horizontal scalability, and isolating failures [23]. As exploiting microservices to architect enterprise applications is becoming commonplace, checking whether an application adheres to the main design principles of microservices, and—if not—understanding how to refactor it, are two key issues [19].

μTOSCA and μFRESHENER [12] enable modelling, analysing, and refactoring the architecture of microservice-based applications to enhance their adherence to the key design principles of microservices. μTOSCA enables representing the architecture of microservice-based applications with the OASIS standard TOSCA [9]. A microservice-based application is represented by a topology graph, whose nodes model the services, integration components (e.g., API gateways,

© Springer Nature Switzerland AG 2021
C. Zirpins et al. (Eds.): ESOCC 2020 Workshops, CCIS 1360, pp. 103–115, 2021.
https://doi.org/10.1007/978-3-030-71906-7_9

message queues, or load balancers), and databases forming the application, and whose arcs indicate the runtime interactions occurring among them. Given the μTOSCA specification of a microservice-based application, μFRESHENER enables automatically checking whether an application contains architectural smells that may violate some key design principle of microservices, as well as reasoning on how to refactor an application to resolve the occurrence of smells.

In order to use μFRESHENER, application administrators were required to manually specify the architecture of their microservice-based applications in μTOSCA, i.e., to describe all the components forming the application and all the interactions occurring among them. Even if μFRESHENER supports application administrators in graphically editing such μTOSCA specifications, microservice-based applications can include hundreds of interacting components [22]. This obviously was making the specification of the architecture of microservice-based applications complex, time-consuming, and error-prone [12].

To further support application administrators, in this paper we propose a solution for automatically deriving the architecture of a "black-box" microservice-based application. Our solution indeed works without needing to access the sources of the components in an application, but it rather enables deriving the architecture of a microservice-based application only from the declarative specification of its deployment in Kubernetes. This is done by performing three subsequent steps, i.e., (i) by statically mining information from the manifest files specifying the application deployment in Kubernetes, (ii) by dinamically mining information by monitoring the interactions among application components in a running application deployment, and (iii) by refining the information mined statically and dinamically to identify components implementing well-known integration patterns.

The static mining step enables eliciting the services and databases forming a microservice-based application, while the dynamic mining step complements the mining of the application architecture by monitoring the interactions that occur among such services and databases at runtime. The information monitored during the dynamic mining step is then also used by the final refinement step, which refines the mined architecture by distinguishing services from integration components implementing well-known message-based integration patterns, e.g., message queues or load balancers [16]. The refined architecture can then be automatically marshalled to μTOSCA, to obtain a specification that can be fed to μFRESHENER to check whether the application adheres to the key design principles of microservices and to refactor it, if this is not the case.

We also present a proof-of-concept implementation of our solution, realising the three aforementioned steps (i.e., static mining, dynamic mining, and refinement) to automatically derive the μTOSCA specification of the architecture of a microservice-based application, starting from its deployment in Kubernetes. The implementation is designed to support additional plugins that can enable both deriving the architecture of microservice-based applications from the application deployment with other technologies (e.g., Chef or Docker) and exporting its representation in other specification languages (e.g., UML).

The rest of this paper is organised as follows. Section 2 provides some background on μTOSCA. Section 3 illustrates our microservice-based architecture mining solution, while Sect. 4 presents our proof-of-concept implementation. Sections 5 and 6 discuss related work and draw some concluding remarks, respectively.

2   Background: μTOSCA

TOSCA [9] is a standard for representing multi-component applications as typed topology graphs, where nodes represent software components, and oriented arcs represent the interactions occurring among such components. μTOSCA [12] provides the building blocks for exploiting TOSCA to model the architecture of microservice-based applications (Fig. 1).

Fig. 1. The node types, relationship types and group types defining μTOSCA.

Topology nodes can be services, communication patterns, or data stores. A Service is a component running some business logic, e.g., a service managing users' orders in an e-commerce application. A CommunicationPattern is an integration component implementing a messaging pattern for decoupling the communication among two or more components. μTOSCA includes two communication patterns from [16]: MessageRouter (e.g., load balancers, API gateways) and MessageBroker (e.g., message queues). Finally, a DataStore is a component storing the data pertaining to a certain domain, e.g., a database of orders in an e-commerce application.

Topology nodes can be interconnected via InteractsWith relationships, to model that a source node invokes functionalities offered by a target node. Such relationships can be enriched by setting the boolean properties circuit_breaker, timeout and dynamic_discovery. The first two properties indicate whether the source node is interacting with the target node via a circuit breaker or by setting timeouts, to avoid that the source fails/gets stuck waiting for an answer from the target when the latter is unresponsive. Property dynamic_discovery specifies whether the endpoint of the target of the interaction is dynamically discovered, e.g., through client-side service discovery [21].

Finally, topology nodes can be placed in an Edge group, to define the subset of application components directly accessed from outside of the application.

3   Mining Microservice-Based Architectures

We hereafter illustrate our solution to automatically determine the μTOSCA topology graph modelling the architecture of a microservice-based application, given its Kubernetes deployment. As shown in Fig. 2, our solution incrementally builds such topology graph by first mining information from the static description of the application deployment (Sect. 3.1). It then dinamically mines

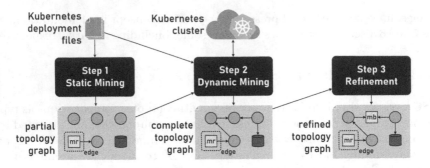

Fig. 2. Our three-steps approach for mining the architecture of a microservice-based application from its Kuberenetes deployment.

component-to-component interactions to be included in the topology graph by sniffing the network packets exchanged among the components of a running instance of the application (Sect. 3.2). Finally, the topology graph is refined by analysing the sniffed network packets to automatically identify integration patterns exploited to structure the application (Sect. 3.3).

3.1   Step 1: Static Mining

The manifest files specifying the deployment of an application in Kubernetes are first used to elicit the topology nodes modelling the software components forming an application. As each pod defines the deployment unit for the container hosting one application component[1], a topology node is added to the topology graph for each pod in the application deployment. If the pod runs a container from the official Docker image of some database component, the topology node is assigned the type DataStore. Otherwise, the component is assumed to implement some business logic and its corresponding topology node is typed Service.

The set of topology nodes is completed by including the message routers that can be added when specifying the deployment of an application in Kubernetes, i.e., Kubernetes services and ingress resources. A Kubernetes service is a message routing component that allows forwarding and balancing the requests sent to the multiple replicas of a pod [10]. Hence, for each Kubernetes service defined in an application deployment, a MessageRouter node is added to the topology graph, together with InteractsWith relationships outgoing from the newly added topology node and targeting the topology nodes corresponding to the pods handled by the Kubernetes Service. In addition, if a Kubernetes service is specified

---

[1] Following the guidelines in Kubernetes documentation [10], our solution assumes each pod in a Kubernetes deployment to form a single cohesive unit of service, i.e., that a single container is deployed to host a service, integration component, or data store. We hence abstract from "sidecar" containers accompanying such container in a pod (e.g., for monitoring and logging purposes), since they are not to be included architectural representation of a microservice-based application.

to be a *NodePort* or *LoadBalancer*, then it is publicly accessible from outside of the Kubernetes cluster where the application is deployed [10]. If this is the case, a MessageRouter node modelling the Kubernetes service is placed in the Edge group of the μTOSCA topology graph (to reflect the fact that such component can be accessed from external clients).

Kubernetes ingress resources are instead message routing components allowing to define API gateways managing the access of external clients to the services and pods running in the Kubernetes cluster where an application is deployed [10]. Ingress resources are associated with ingress controllers, i.e., a pod actually implementing the message routing defined by the corresponding ingress resource. For each ingress controller associated with an ingress resource in the manifest files specifying the Kubernetes deployment of an application, a MessageRouter node is added to the topology graph and included in the Edge group.

3.2   Step 2: Dynamic Mining

The dynamic mining step enriches the topology graph statically obtained from the manifest files specifying the deployment of an application in Kubernetes. In particular, after configuring the application deployment to enable sniffing the network packets containing the messages exchanged in component-to-component interactions, the application deployment is actually enacted and monitored in a Kubernetes cluster. The monitored information (i.e., the sniffed network packets) is then used to elicit the interactions occurring among application components, as well as to identify the possible usage of ingress controllers already existing in the cluster to implement ingress resources, if any.

Configuring the Deployment of an Application. To enable monitoring the interactions occurring among the pods in the Kubernetes deployment of an application, a monitoring container is included within each of such pods. The specification of each pod is extended by including a container running a packet sniffer (e.g., WireShark [8]), which is configured to sniff all network packets sent to/from the container running in the pod. In addition, to uniquely identify the source and destination of each network packet, each pod is assigned with an unique hostname, either being the pod hostname (if specified in the original Kubernetes deployment) or automatically generated.

It is worth noting that Kubernetes also allows application deployments to specify an ingress resource (e.g., providing the message routes for implementing an API gateway for the application), without associating it with an ingress controller actually implementing the specified message routing. In this case, ingress controllers already available in a Kubernetes cluster are by default exploited to implement the message routing defined by ingress resources defined the application and not associated with any controller [10]. To capture this case as well, each ingress controller already available in the cluster is also equipped with a sidecar packet sniffer, to monitor the network packets sent to/from such ingress controller as well (to enable checking whether such controller is used by Kubernetes to implement some ingress resource of the application).

Enacting and Monitoring the Application Deployment. After automatically configuring the Kubernetes deployment as described above, the deployment is enacted to start monitoring the packets exchanged between the containers running the application components. The application is kept running for a given amount of time, which can be customised by the application administrator. In addition, to make application components interact, a load test is executed. The latter can be provided in the Kubernetes deployment of the application (e.g., in a pod running a service that invokes functionalities offered by the application component), or it can be given in the form of a script invoking the application components that are accessible from outside of the Kubernetes cluster where the application is running. The application is then undeployed by also ensuring that all containers or artifacts pertaining to the application deployment are removed from the Kubernetes cluster where it was running (e.g., to avoid that WireShark containers continue to sniff the network packets exchanged by the ingress controllers installed in the cluster).

While the deployed application is running, the injected WireShark containers sniff the network packets exchanged between the containers running in the deployed pods. Such packets are stored to enable determining the interactions occurred among components, as shown hereafter.

Determining Interactions Among Components. A component interacts with another if the former invokes some functionality offered by the latter at runtime. This is modelled in μTOSCA by a InteractsWith relationship, whose source and target nodes correspond to the source and target components of an interaction. To grasp this information from the network packets sniffed by the WireShark instances accompanying application components, the source and target of component-to-component interactions are identified. This is done by analysing the TCP segments of sniffed packets: If a segment specifies SYN equal to 1 and ACK equal to 0, this means that a connection is being opened for allowing the component sending the packet to interact with the component receiving the packet. Starting from this observation, our solution is to include an InteractsWith relationship connecting a component to another if there exist a network packet sent by the former to the latter with SYN and ACK set to 1 and 0, respectively.

Each of the newly introduced InteractsWith relationships is also temporarily associated with all network packets concerning the corresponding interactions. The information contained in such packets will then be exploited in the refinement step, to understand whether a topology node is implementing some well-known integration pattern (Sect. 3.3).

Identifying the Exploitation of Ingress Controllers. As already noticed, Kubernetes exploits the ingress controllers already existing in a cluster to implement ingress resources in an application deployment, if no ingress controller is associated with them in the manifest files specifying the application deployment itself [10]. Our solution analyses the network packets sent by already existing ingress controllers to check whether they were actually exploited to implement the message routing defined by some ingress resource in the Kubernetes deployment of the application. For each such ingress controller, a MessageRouter node is added to the topology graph and included in the Edge group. The network packets sent by such ingress controller are further analysed to identify the interactions starting from the controller and targeting the components of the deployed application. Each identified interaction is represented in the topology graph by including a corresponding InteractsWith relationships, with the same approach as described above.

3.3   Step 3: Refinement

Given the topology graph obtained after the static and dynamic mining steps, and given the network packets associated with the InteractsWith relationships in the graph, the topology graph is refined by identifying the nodes in the graph that implement well-known integration patterns, i.e., message-routing or message-brokering. Each of such nodes is then assigned with the corresponding type in μTOSCA, i.e., MessageRouter and MessageBroker. In addition, the network packets associated with the InteractsWith relationships in the graph are analysed to determine whether the corresponding interaction is exploiting client-side service discovery, i.e., whether the source of the interaction has dynamically discovered the endpoint of the target [21]. If this is the case, the property dynamic_discovery of the corresponding InteractsWith relationship is set to true.

Identifying Message Routers. Microservices mostly rely on HTTP to intercommunicate [13], which means that components implementing message routing can set the HTTP header X-Forwarded-For. The latter is the standard approach for identifying the IP address of the client that sent a message, when such message passed through one or more HTTP proxies or load balancers. Hence, if the messages sent by a component contain the HTTP header X-Forwarded-For, the component is implementing some sort of message routing. This can be easily checked by looking at the network packets associated with the InteractsWith relationships outgoing from a node in the topology graph. If they contain the HTTP header X-Forwarded-For, the node is typed MessageRouter.

Identifying Message Brokers. Message brokers use standard messaging protocols [17], e.g., AMQP (*Advanced Message Queuing Protocol*), MQTT (*Message Queuing Telemetry Transport*), or STOMP (*Simple Text Oriented Message Protocol*). A component is hence identified as implementing the message broker integration pattern if all communications ingoing and outgoing from such component are done throughout one among such messaging protocols. The corresponding check is done by looking at the messages contained in the network packets associated with the InteractsWith relationships ingoing and outgoing from the topology node modelling a component: The messages in such network packets must be structured according to either AMQP, MQTT, or STOMP.

The above check is however not enough: A service only communicating with a message broker would be wrongly identified as being itself a message broker. AMQP, MQTT, and STOMP are however client-server messaging protocols, all distinguishing in the header of their messages whether a message is sent from a client to the server or vice versa. The additional conditions to check is that the network packets received by a component include messages sent to the message broker by its clients, and that the network packets sent by a component include messages sent by the message broker to its clients. If this is the case, then the corresponding node in the topology graph is typed MessageBroker.

Identifying Client-Side Discovery. Client-side service discovery occurs whenever a component dynamically resolves the IP address of another component, with which the former wishes to interact [21]. To recognise whether this happened in the deployed application, our solutions looks at the network packets associated with each InteractsWith relationship in the topology graph. If the IP address of the target of the interaction varies among such network packets, this means that client-side service discovery occurred, with the source component connecting to different instances of the target component. The property dynamic_discovery of the considered InteractsWith relationship is hence set to true.

4   Proof-of-Concept Implementation

To assess the feasibility of our approach, we have developed an open-source proof-of-concept implementation, called μMINER[2], where we exploited the tshark command-line version of WireShark to enact packet sniffing. Figure 3 illustrates the modular architecture of μMINER: The main module offers a command-line interface enabling application administrators to provide the manifest files specifying the application deployment in Kubernetes. Given such files, the main module starts orchestrating the other modules to enact the architecture mining, i.e., (i) it first invokes the miner to enact the static and dynamic mining steps in our approach, (ii) it then invokes the refiner to refine the mined topology as described in the refinement step in our approach, and (iii) it finally invokes the exporter to marshal the mined architecture to μTOSCA.

Steps (i) and (ii) incrementally build and refine the architecture of the analysed microservice-based application by relying on the topology module, which enables instantiating and updating topology graphs. Step (iii) then picks the mined topology graph from the topology module and marshals it to μTOSCA.

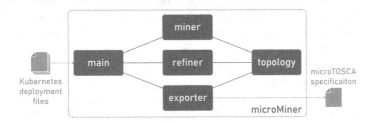

Fig. 3. Architecture of the proof-of-concept implementation of our solution.

---

[2] https://github.com/di-unipi-socc/microMiner (MIT License).

μMINER enables application administrators to mine the architecture of their microservice-based applications by issuing the following command:

```
$ sudo python3.8 -m microMiner generate kubernetes \
                        source target [time] [test] [name]
```

where **source** and **path** are mandatory and enable to specify the path to the folder containing the Kubernetes manifest files and the path where to store the generated μTOSCA specification, respectively. The optional parameters **time**, **test**, and **name** instead allow to indicate how long the application deployment is to be run, the Python module containing the load test to run, and the name to be assigned to the application in the μTOSCA specification, respectively.

It is finally worth noting that μMINER must run with **sudo** privileges on the master node of the Kubernetes cluster where to deploy and monitor the application. This allows μMINER to interact with the Kubernetes engine running on the master node to suitably configure, enact, and manage the deployment of the given applications on the cluster.

5   Related Work

Several recent contributions allow to elicit the architecture of microservice-based applications. For instance, [18] presents a solution for determining the service dependency graph modelling the interactions occurring among the services in a microservice-based application, based on the static analysis of their Java sources. [11] proposes a methodology for modelling the architecture of microservice-based applications by statically analysing their source code, based on a set of rules for mapping source code to modelling constructs. [20] illustrates a solution to reconstruct the architecture of microservice-based applications by statically analysing their source code under the different perspectives of domain experts, developers, and operators. [11], [18], and [20] however differ from our approach since they all follow a "white-box" approach, by requiring the source code of the software components forming an application to be available. Our solution can instead work also in "black-box" scenarios where such sources are not available, as it only requires the Kubernetes deployment of a microservice-based application to automatically determine its architecture. In addition, while our solution is fully automated, both [11] and [20] require application administrators to manually intervene for completing the mining of a microservice-based architecture.

Similar considerations apply to MicroART [14,15], a semi-automatic approach for determining the architecture of a microservice-based application. MicroART can however be considered closer to our solution, as it statically analyses the source code to determine the services forming an application, and it dynamically runs and monitors the services to grasp the interactions occurring among them. MicroART then requires the application administrator to manually refine the obtained architecture by removing the infrastructure components used by the services forming an application (e.g., service discovery components) and the corresponding interactions. Our approach hence differs from MicroART since it fully automates the mining of architectures, and since it can be applied also to microservice-based applications whose source code is not available. In addition, our approach automatically distinguishes services and databases in an application from integration components implementing well-known integration patterns (e.g., message queues or load balancers), which is something not featured by neither MicroART nor by [11], [18], or [20].

It is also worth relating our approach with existing tooling for visualising and monitoring Kubernetes-based application deployments. Kiali [2], KubeView [3], and WeaveScope [7] are three different tools displaying the structure of applications deployed in Kubernetes. Being developed for monitoring the Kubernetes-based deployment of generic applications, they only visualise the deployed Kubernetes objects (e.g., pods and services) and how they are interconnected. Our solution instead enables distinguishing among services, integration components, and data stores forming the architecture of a microservice-based

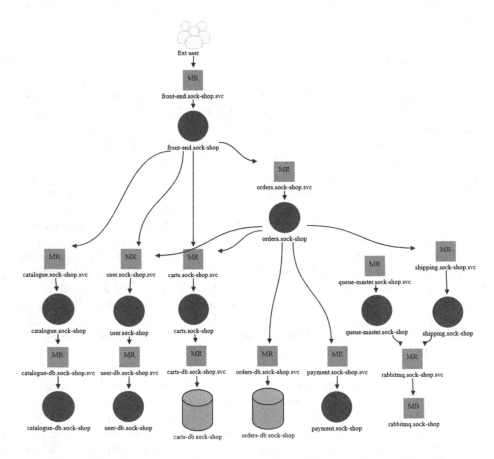

Fig. 4. Visualisation in μFRESHENER of the architecture of *Sock Shop* [6].

application, as well as to recognise whether component-to-component interactions involve some form of client-side service discovery.

Instana [1] makes a step further in this direction, by enabling to visualise services and data stores forming a microservice-based application deployed in Kubernetes, together with service-to-service and service-to-database interactions. Our approach however differs from Instana as we not only enable visualing service and data stores, but also recognising whether some software component is implementing message-based integration patterns, as well as whether client-side service discovery is enacted in some service-to-service interaction. In addition, while Instana is a commercial and subscription-based tool, our approach is publicly available in a free open-source implementation.

6   Conclusions and Future Work

We have presented a solution to automatically determine the architecture of a microservice-based application. Given the manifest files specifying the deployment of an application in Kubernetes, our solution first statically analyses such files to start drafting the partial topology graph modeling the architecture of the application. Our solution then configures, enact, and monitors a deployment of the application to automatically extract the information needed to complete the topology graph, which is then refined by automatically identifying whether some application component is implementing well-known integration patterns.

We have also presented a first proof-of-concept implementation of our solution, which enables automatically obtaining a specification of the mined architecture in μTOSCA. To experiment our solution, we have exploited our proof-of-concept implementation to generate the architecture description of three existing open-source microservice-based applications (i.e., *Online Boutique* [4], Robot shop [5], and *Sock Shop* [6]), successfully obtaining the representation of their architecture in μTOSCA in all the three cases. The obtained μTOSCA were then fed as-is to μFRESHENER, which enabled us to graphically visualise the mined architecture of their microservice-based applications, as shown in Fig. 4.

At the same, the proof-of-concept implementation of our solution works under some assumptions, e.g., requiring to run it in the master node of a Kubernetes cluster or that in-cluster component-to-component communications are not encrypted. We plan to engineer our implementation into a working prototype releasing such assumptions (e.g., by remotely interacting with the master node of a Kubernetes cluster and enabling to configure secrets so that in-cluster communication can be encrypted) and enforcing security to mitigate the risks deriving from executing potentially malicious applications in a Kubernetes cluster.

We also plan to extend our solution to work also with other container-based orchestration systems (e.g., Docker Swarm, OpenShift). The current implementation of our solution already features a pluggable architecture, based on the strategy design pattern, with the Kubernetes-based architecture mining plugged as a strategy supported by the implementation itself. Adding support for other existing container-based orchestration systems hence just requires to implement the corresponding strategy and to plug it into the current implementation.

References

1. Instana. https://www.instana.com
2. Kiali. https://kiali.io
3. KubeView. https://github.com/benc-uk/kubeview
4. Online Boutique: A Cloud-native Microservices Demo Application. https://github.com/GoogleCloudPlatform/microservices-demo
5. Robot Shop: Sample Microservice Application. https://github.com/instana/robot-shop
6. Sock Shop: A Microservices Demo Application. https://microservices-demo.github.io
7. WeaveScope. https://www.weave.works/oss/scope
8. WireShark. https://www.wireshark.org
9. TOSCA Simple Profile in YAML, version 1.2. OASIS Standard (2019)
10. Kubernetes documentation (2020). https://kubernetes.io/docs
11. Alshuqayran, N., Ali, N., Evans, R.: Towards micro service architecture recovery: an empirical study. In: 2018 IEEE International Conference on Software Architecture (ICSA), pp. 47–4709 (2018)
12. Brogi, A., Neri, D., Soldani, J.: Freshening the air in microservices: resolving architectural smells via refactoring. In: Yangui, S., et al. (eds.) ICSOC 2019. LNCS, vol. 12019, pp. 17–29. Springer, Cham (2020). https://doi.org/10.1007/978-3-030-45989-5_2
13. Fowler, M., Lewis, J.: Microservices (2014). http://martinfowler.com/articles/microservices.html. Accessed 7 Aug 2020
14. Granchelli, G., Cardarelli, M., Di Francesco, P., Malavolta, I., Iovino, L., Di Salle, A.: MicroART: a software architecture recovery tool for maintaining microservice-based systems. In: 2017 IEEE International Conference on Software Architecture Workshops (ICSAW), pp. 298–302 (2017)
15. Granchelli, G., Cardarelli, M., Di Francesco, P., Malavolta, I., Iovino, L., Di Salle, A.: Towards recovering the software architecture of microservice-based systems. In: 2017 IEEE International Conference on Software Architecture Workshops (ICSAW), pp. 46–53 (2017)
16. Hohpe, G., Woolf, B.: Enterprise Integration Patterns: Designing, Building, and Deploying Messaging Solutions. Addison-Wesley, Boston (2003)
17. Korab, J.: Understanding Message Brokers. O'Reilly Media Inc., Sebastopol (2017)
18. Ma, S., Fan, C., Chuang, Y., Lee, W., Lee, S., Hsueh, N.: Using service dependency graph to analyze and test microservices. In: 2018 IEEE 42nd Annual Computer Software and Applications Conference (COMPSAC), vol. 02, pp. 81–86 (2018)
19. Neri, D., Soldani, J., Zimmermann, O., Brogi, A.: Design principles, architectural smells and refactorings for microservices: a multivocal review. SICS Softw. Inensiv. Cyber Phys. Syst. 35, 3–15 (2020). https://doi.org/10.1007/s00450-019-00407-8
20. Rademacher, F., Sachweh, S., Zündorf, A.: A modeling method for systematic architecture reconstruction of microservice-based software systems. In: Nurcan, S., Reinhartz-Berger, I., Soffer, P., Zdravkovic, J. (eds.) BPMDS/EMMSAD -2020. LNBIP, vol. 387, pp. 311–326. Springer, Cham (2020). https://doi.org/10.1007/978-3-030-49418-6_21
21. Richardson, C.: Microservices Patterns. Manning Publications, Shelter Island (2018)

22. Soldani, J., Tamburri, D.A., Van Den Heuvel, W.J.: The pains and gains of microservices: a systematic grey literature review. J. Syst. Softw. **146**, 215–232 (2018)
23. Zimmermann, O.: Microservices tenets. Comput. Sci. Res. Develop. **32**(3–4), 301–310 (2016)

ESOCC 2020 PhD Symposium

Preface to the PhD Symposium

The PhD Symposium at ESOCC is an international forum for PhD students to present and discuss their work with senior scientists and other PhD students working on related topics. As for the main conference, the topics welcomed by the PhD Symposium span all aspects of service-oriented and cloud computing, e.g., service and cloud computing models, service and cloud computing engineering, technologies, and business and social aspects of service and cloud computing. In contrast to the main conference, the research reports presented and discussed at the PhD symposium typically present unfinished research work or "just started" PhD research projects.

The program committee of the 2020 edition of the ESOCC PhD Symposium carefully selected three contributions, based on the review reports on the submissions, each of which was reviewed by at least two PC members. In addition to the precise description of the problem to be solved, preliminary results, and first ideas for solving the main problem, the selected contributions also included a work plan. All these issues were discussed at the symposium between selected senior scientists and the PhD students. After the symposium, the PhD students were invited to incorporate all feedback from reviewers and from the live discussion at the PhD symposium into their papers, to make such papers mature for a scientific publication. This post-symposium proceedings include such revised selected papers.

We wish to thank all the PhD students who contributed to the PhD symposium for their submissions and careful revisions of their papers, as well as the PC members and symposium attendees for their detailed and constructive feedback suggesting valuable improvements. We are also grateful to Kyriakos Kritikos (General Chair of ESOCC 2020), to Antonio Brogi and Wolf Zimmermann (Program Chairs of ESOCC 2020), and to Christian Zirpins and Iraklis Paraskakis (Workshop Chairs of ESOCC 2020) for their organizational support, even in these trouble times. Without all these people, such an enjoyable, virtual, and successful 2020 edition of the ESOCC PhD Symposium would not have been possible.

November 2020

Jacopo Soldani
Massimo Villari

Organization

Program Committee Chairs

Jacopo Soldani   University of Pisa, Italy
Massimo Villari   University of Messina, Italy

Program Committee

Uwe Breitenbücher   University of Stuttgart, Germany
Antonio Brogi   University of Pisa, Italy
Schahram Dustdar   TU Wien, Austria
Paul Grefen   Eindhoven University of Technology,
                                Netherlands
Kung-Kiu Lau   University of Manchester, UK
Zoltán Ádám Mann   University of Duisburg-Essen, Germany
Ulf Schreier   Hochschule Furtwangen University, Germany

Trusted Orchestrator Architecture in Mobile Edge Cloud Computing

Van Thanh Le[✉]

Department of Computer Science, Free University of Bozen/Bolzano,
Bolzano, Italy
vanle@unibz.it

Abstract. In recent years, shifting part of the computation and data management from the center of the cloud to its edges has brought huge benefits for end-users. Mobile Edge Computing (MEC) represents a huge step towards high preferment cloud services. MEC can deploy dedicated services dynamically based on the request types and the specific context. In the transportation context, services need not only to be installed in the closest MEC but also be able to follow the vehicles as they move to keep providing the same service. This scenario raises different challenges in terms of service migration and security. This paper presents a MEC based trusted orchestrator architecture to address these issues with the target to enable migrating services transparently and guaranteeing requests with high-security levels.

Keywords: MEC · Blockchain · Service continuity · Orchestration

1 Introduction

Cloud Computing technology plays an essential role in computer system resource management, especially with data storage and computing power. Resources can be accessed from anywhere followed by the distributed user demand, and applications are preferable to be deployed into cloud since its flexibility and high availability. However, these computation resources traditionally are located in a centralized data-center, which leads to high latency in handling user requests. The new concept of Mobile Edge Computing (MEC) [1,11] is presented to build a micro-cloud which can be set up in close proximity to the users. A part of computations and resources is moved from the main cloud to the edge node, which allows low data latency and context-aware services. With MEC, we do not have to send data to the main cloud for analysis, instead, it can be pre-processed before transferring it to the cloud, thus MEC will reduce a massive amount of bandwidth usage to the main cloud and boost the user connection speed.

MEC is mainly deployed on top of low cost resource constrained devices which makes it affordable, nevertheless, these devices may suffer from security

Supervisors: Claus Pahl (cpahl@unibz.it), Nabil El Ioini (nelioini@unibz.it).

C. Zirpins et al. (Eds.): ESOCC 2020 Workshops, CCIS 1360, pp. 121–132, 2021.
https://doi.org/10.1007/978-3-030-71906-7_10

issues [28] since the used hardware platform lack robust security mechanisms. Therefore, we need a robust and secure network to control MEC, which is also our purpose to build a trusted orchestrator architecture for MEC.

The remainder of the paper is structured as follows, the next section presents the problem statement and reference scenario, Sect. 3 shows our methodology, the orchestrator architecture is demonstrated in Sect. 4, and then simulator environment is discussed in Sect. 5, Sect. 6 presents our current work and future plan, then Sect. 7 discusses related studies. The last section describes our conclusion and future work.

2   Problem Statement and Reference Scenario

A reference scenario is defined in this section to show the problems we are addressing. Transportation is one of the cases where MEC could bring benefits. In 4G network (LTE - Long-Term Evolution), vehicles need to connect with eNodeB (Evode Node B) as a gate for user equipment (UE) to the Internet, in our scope, MEC is also set up in eNodeB and work as an RSU (Road Side Unit) to response with specific services (e.g., mapping, gaming).

In our scenario, we choose the example of video streaming that depends mainly on the Vehicle to Infrastructure (V2I) architecture for real time services. In order to watch a video in a car, customers have to pay a subscription fee to the service provider (MEC infrastructure provider and multimedia service provider), after that, a video will be streamed from a hosting service to the customer vehicle. When the car is moving, the streaming service will send requests to do buffering the video resources. In general, the following **Research Challenges** motivates through the video streaming use case:

- Low latency: which reflects user experience when watching a video, when the video streaming service is deployed into the nearest MEC, we can have lower end-to-end latency.
- High availability: to watch any films from anywhere, the service has to follow the car to maintain the connection, in other words, it always has to be deployed into the closest MEC. The behavior for transferring service from a MEC to another MEC is called **service migration** and maintaining service sessions without interruption is called **service continuity**. Therefore keeping service continuity will guarantee high availability.
- High security: since it is related to the customer payment, so we need to have a secure channel for the user payment and to be sure the customer rights to access media resources.

MEC nodes or service applications could belong to different providers, so their communication and collaboration could be a challenge when they do not trust each other but still want to get customer information from others or share the market. Moreover, in case of providers do not make any agreement for service migration, requests have to follow roaming routes to the home network which reduces user experiences and can not get any benefits of MEC. We will define methodologies to overcome these problems in the next section.

3   Methodology

We focus on MEC to MEC communication without the need to access the core network, localizing handover process could speed up the context transfer. The direct connection among MECs facilitates reducing latency because the car does not have to send requests to the main cloud and wait for the acceptance, instead, MEC will control procedures. Context transferring includes moving current sessions and service migration, while session data is sent via point-to-point connection of MECs, which is already executed by mobile operators, migrating services is still a challenge, which mainly comes from service provider collaborations, different policies or infrastructure, and low level of security in MECs.

To address the challenges set in the reference scenario, three main areas are being investigated:

3.1   Mobility Simulator

Device-to-device communication in the transportation model is complicated with multiple participants, in other words, while handover process belongs to LTE infrastructure, service migration is executed in the cloud layer and belongs to MEC providers, these services should be run in parallel in the demand of service continuity. However, testing new strategies in the real LTE devices is cumbersome and time wasting in deployment, thus, a simulator running LTE environment and supporting MEC devices could be a solution that will be discussed in Sect. 5.

3.2   Containerization

Services are packed and built a flexible environment, it is a lightweight alternative for a full machine visualization, it encapsulates applications in a container with its own environment isolated from the host. D. Bernstein in [7] explained the container concept which presented a need for an isolated and multi-tenancy layer, dependencies and resources are separated from the host. Docker[1] is the most common application of container now, in our scope, we apply Docker to deploy a stateful video streaming service.

Considering service migration, H.Abdah et al. in [2] presented three main kinds of service migration as follow, services are packed in Docker containers or VM (Virtual machine):

- Cold migration: the running process will be paused or terminated white the service state is transferring.
- Pre-copy live migration: will move the memory of the service through several iterations before the VM is restarted, the service still runs while migration process is executing.
- Post-copy live migration: similar to pre-copy one, but this type only sends the virtual CPU and device state at the initial step.

---

[1] https://www.docker.com.

CRIU[2] is currently the well-known technique to support migration techniques, however, it now does not support live-migration in Docker container so we need to investigate other techniques in the future work.

3.3 Blockchain and Trust Mechanism

MEC is built on top of constrained devices and container is a lightweight machine, they are all vulnerable and easy to be attacked while full firewall mechanization becomes overload for these technologies, blockchain could be a solution to build a secure channel and security gate. It is a distributed, decentralized database composed of a growing list of records, called blocks. In the blockchain network, a consensus among maintaining nodes strengthens security and prevent tampering. In our scenario, some platforms as Bitcoin[3] or Etherum[4] could support customer payments or Hyperledger could build an environment for vendors to exchange information.

In the environment of MEC, service migration requires multiple actions and participants, among them, authentication is crucial while reconnecting to the next MEC, which also takes a huge amount of time if users have to transfer via various intersection regions. A trust mechanism could contribute here to build a trust network among MECs based on specific attributes, when the next MEC is trust-able, authorization process will not be skipped that speeds up the migration process.

3.4 Prediction Mechanization

Prediction mechanization will forecast the car status to decide which strategies are used for service migration, this will answer the question when and where to migrate. Migrating services lead to service interruption while not migrating, in other words, roaming results in the transmission delay when the user gets far from the current host and requests have to be sent via many layers to come back the host.

A survey [25] showed the three most updated service migration optimization strategies as follow me cloud [21], dynamic service migration [27] and time window based service migration [26]. This work will be the baseline for our prediction model.

4 Trusted Orchestrator Architecture

We propose an architecture to orchestrate containers based on blockchain which enables service continuity on the MEC (Fig. 1). Each MEC node can serve vehicles within its range by downloading and instantiating the needed services.

---

[2] https://criu.org.

[3] https://bitcoin.org.

[4] https://ethereum.org.

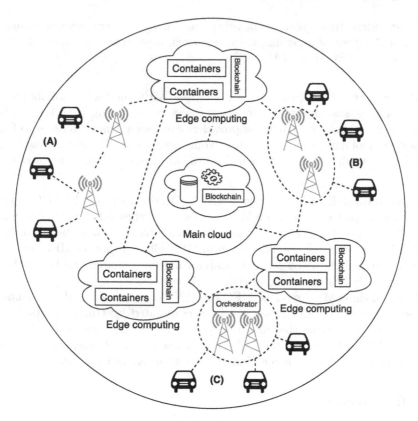

Fig. 1. Trust orchestrator infrastructure

MEC nodes can work independently or collaboration can be established between MEC nodes even belongs to different providers when exchanging information is required. When users move, the vehicle will communicate with MEC for the movement and inform when the migration process is needed, the MEC after that will notify the main cloud for the service transfer. Blockchain joins as a verification gate for service payment and user authentication, in other words, any requests from users as creating, migrating or stopping services should be verified to guarantee the network security.

The orchestrator will decide credential checking and migration activities followed by sub-scenarios below, to simplify the scenario, we suppose that all service providers share the same blockchain platform, once a user pays a subscription fee, he has a right to access all services of all providers. We have identified three flavors of MEC models.

4.1 MEC Models

Single MEC. Each MEC node works independently with the others and they orchestrate by themselves, it is similar to the case of independent service providers. In our scenario of video streaming, the user credentials must be verified at any time of accessing video resources, after that a service is deployed on the nearest MEC (Fig. 1(A)).

MEC Cluster. The cluster allows multiple MEC nodes to collaborate to increase service availability and reduce the service migration (Fig. 1(B)), MEC nodes that could belong to different providers can join a cluster in order to facilitate service deployment and continuity. Nodes will share UE common data, once a MEC node verifies a user, other nodes can skip the step and trust in the UE.

MEC Swarm. MEC nodes are controlled by an orchestrator (Fig. 1(C)) which will manage requests to and from MEC nodes, the orchestrator will decide which node will execute the task and communicate with blockchain on behalf of MEC nodes. The sub scenarios are different from MEC Cluster that all MEC nodes are under the control of an orchestrator, all information is shared and the authentication step only has to be triggered once.

Based on these MEC models, MEC-to-MEC communication also depends on trust score for each MEC which will be accumulated by trust aspects. In our scenario, before starting the migration process, the MEC source has to verify the trust-ability of the next MEC, if the next one is not reliable, other solutions could be proposed based on the kind of trust shortage of the next.

4.2   Trust Aspects

MEC is deployed in IoT devices, so we will demonstrate trust aspects for IoT devices here, these aspects already are discussed in [9,12], since we would concentrate on scenarios of MEC, thus there are three aspects will be considered:

Capacity Based Trust. Capacity based Trust (CBT) refers to the reliability of resources in a MEC, since IoT devices only have a constrained resource and can run limited number of services. Therefore, the resources should be under control to guarantee the device does not run any unreliable or untrusted services, it also checks the sufficient of resources when deploying new service after receiving migration requests.

To be detailed, the capacity trust score is computed based on three resource values, *(i)* before-deployment resource capacity (BDR), *(ii)* after-deployment resource capacity (ADR), and *(iii)* service usage resource (SUR). Each of the resource values considers three parameters, namely *CPU, RAM, DISK usage*.

$$CBT = BDR + SUR/ADR \tag{1}$$

Considering the resource sufficient for service migration, the values of ADR will be used to do a comparison with the service resource requirement.

Security Based Trust. Security in cloud computing has been discussed in many papers [4, 13, 19] and it is a wide concept and covers various aspects as authentication, authorization, integration. In our scope, an IoT device will deploy Docker containers to build services for users which could lead to two security levels, one comes from security in containers and another one is from IoT system.

Docker security is analyzed in [8], the author states that hypervisor-based virtualization techniques (VM) are more secure as they added an extra layer of isolation between the applications and the host. An application running inside a VM is only able to communicate with the VM kernel, not the host kernel while containers can directly communicate with the host kernel that enables hackers to break the host system easily.

The most common OS used for cloud servers is Ubuntu because of its security, versatility, and stability however incident activity involving outdated certificates or the unchanged default passwords could make the system more vulnerable. Thus, for both containers and system security, we will investigate related aspects and score the Security based Trust (SBT) values.

We use Lynis[5] to perform an automated audit of an OS based on a security benchmark and propose the system hardening suggestions, from reports by Lynis, we can score the security of the OS (SOOS). For the security score of Docker container (SOD), security benchmark for Docker[6] could support to verify the security of both Docker environment as volumes, containers and images. In summarize, the MEC security score (SBT) will be the average of SOD and SOOS.

$$SBT = Average(SOOS, SOD) \tag{2}$$

Behavior Based Trust. Behavior based Trust (BBT) refers to the outcomes of MEC nodes since its quality also affects the trust of MEC, if the reports from MEC is unreliable or users suffer from slow responses, the MEC behavior score will be decreased. There are three behavior aspects we would consider:

- Live time: followed [29], the live time of a MEC will be evaluated by direct-connected MECs and forwarded to other MECs to synchronize trust values. MECs have to respond to any communication requests to maintain the network status.
- Success rate of service deployment: if service deployment fails, users will have to wait a lot of time and also to find another solution which reduces the quality of experience (QoE) of the users. The rate is only scored as the number of successful deployment per total number of requests.
- Success rate of service migration: Service continuity requires multiple actions and communication as [16], network instability or missing system files could break the migrated service. In the scope of trust, we only consider the success rate of migration in the received migrated MEC.

---

[5] https://cisofy.com/lynis/.
[6] https://github.com/docker/docker-bench-security.

In summarize, BBT, SBT and CBT will be merged and used to decide the next MEC is reliable or not, in case of untrust, alternative solutions will be made to maintain the user QoE, for example, reduce the quality of services in term of capacity or redirect service requests to the previous MEC in cases of low security score.

$$BBT = Average(TLT, SSD, SSM) \tag{3}$$

5   Simulation Environment

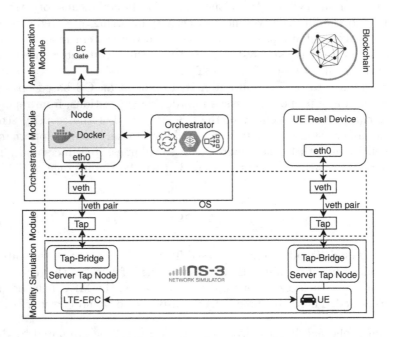

Fig. 2. MEC trusted orchestrator architecture

We have developed a simulation environment relying on existing open source projects. Our architecture contains three main modules as mobility simulation module, orchestrator module, and authentication module (see Fig. 2).

The mobility module is based on NS3 [20] which stands for network simulator, it is a discrete-event network simulator for Internet systems. The core of NS3 is written in C++ to facilitate library reusing and executing standalone application, besides that, the core is wrapped by Python application to set up simulation scenarios. NS3 supports the LTE-EPC module [5] that includes common components for the LTE infrastructure as Packet Gateway (PGW), Serving Gateway (SGW), Mobility Management Entity (MME). NS3 communicates with the real world via tap bridge, tap devices from the simulator will connect with the port eth0 of the corresponding nodes of the orchestrator module.

The authentication module is built from blockchain which creates a secure channel for participants, the module will verify requests, execute transactions or log behaviors from the orchestrator via blockchain gateway, the gateway provides a restful API for the MEC node access.

The Orchestrator module is designed to manage MEC nodes, any requests from UEs will be sent to the nearest node, and then verified by the authentication module before forwarding to the orchestrator, it will decide the working flow of MEC nodes. The UE status is collected and analyzed by the prediction engine that will trigger the migration process. The orchestrator also controls the load balancer to allocate tasks for suitable nodes. Our main architecture is also deployed in this module, a MEC controller will be setup in MEC Node to manage requests, it will act as the orchestrator for Single MEC and MEC Cluster, in MEC Swarm, we need a separated orchestrator to manipulate requests to the MEC controller.

6   Our Current Work and Future Research Plan

Currently, I am in my second year PhD and we are part of an EU project[7] where we are investigating solutions for smart mobility in the scenario of crossing border and context transfer. We have investigated research papers related to blockchain, MEC, IoT, service continuity and trust management, which gave us an overview of the research topic. Trust orchestrator architecture and service continuity are still new concepts that need to be studied in various aspects.

For the future work, we will implement the entire architecture with three modules and follow three scenarios, evaluate end-to-end latency and prediction results for service migration. The work will follow 5G-CARMEN project requirements to get closer to real infrastructure, data from the project partners will be used for the prediction process.

7   Related Work

Our previous work [15] proposed a blockchain based architecture for MEC, is deployed by SimuLTE [24] and OMNetpp [23] however SimuLTE is no longer supported by developers from 2016, so now it is almost outdated. Moreover, OMNetpp environment only works on its simulation time, so real-world communication from the simulator is limited and does not perform the real connection, this study is still a baseline for our architecture and is our first approach to deal with migration overheads.

Follow me cloud (FMC) concept has been first introduced in [21] to solve the problem of using services when changing access points. Taleb et al. show that a service migration decision mainly depends on network operator policies, and

---

[7] http://5gcarmen.eu.

particularly on the P-GW relocation procedure. A. Aissioui et al. [3] proposed the Follow Me edge-Cloud (FMEC) concept and implement a demonstration based on MEC, their experiments showed migration approaches in detail and are close to our mobility simulation. However, their work does not show fully connections among LTE devices, for example, PGW connects SGW via S5 socket, so their experience can not present fully the LTE communication.

Migration strategies for service continuity is also proposed by Abdullaziz et al. via [14], instead of controlling user mobility in MME as current LTE architecture, the task is moved to edge with a vMME module, the module will interact with the target MME in the core network. For the service migration in edge, authors applied CRIU to do pre-copy migration to reduce end-to-end latency after changing APs. Their simulation is built on top of NextEPC[8] and all edge node belongs to an LTE network, but they have not solved the problem with roaming when a node moves to a new network.

Related to blockchain-based architecture for MEC, Pahl et al. in [17] proposed an architecture pattern which is namely trusted orchestration management (TOM) for IoT edge cloud. TOM will verify activities and requests from IoT devices, the idea of TOM comes from the W3C Provenance framework[9] that logs behaviors from IoT to enable the trust. N.El Ioini in [10] implements a TOM system based on permissioned blockchain Hyperledger Fabric[10], the orchestrator verify the identity provenances before grant access to IoT devices. We will also follow the similar ideas to track requests from users, and reports from MEC.

Trust management systems (TMS) for IoT devices are presented in [22,28]. Capacity of IoT is one of the most common concerns which is also its limitation. Zahariadis et al. in [22] calculates the trust value of nodes from the success rate of requests with the weighted factors from nodes. In the model, nodes are in wireless sensor network (WSN), thus, the node connection and communication is also taken into account to increase the battery lifetime. Ben et al. [6] proposed a TMS model for multi-services based on a cognitive learning algorithm which will analyze the service capacity and the changes of IoT device resources from historical data. Pirzada et al. [18] focused on trust communication in IoT, a central trust authority is developed to build a trusted based communication in ad-hoc network. Each node will be a trust agent and assist other nodes by sending data and control packets to others, after that it will summarize the trust value also with each weighted factor. In our architecture, IoT devices are supposed to deploy in eNodeB and work as MECs to receive requests from the main cloud and deploy services, trust factors are inherited from these papers to calculate trust values, historical data and resource capacity also can be used to support the process.

---

[8] https://nextepc.org.
[9] https://www.w3.org/TR/prov-overview/.
[10] https://www.hyperledger.org/use/fabric.

8   Conclusion and Future Work

In this paper, we proposed an architecture to enable service continuity in MEC. Ns3 facilitates a comprehensive LTE network which provides an ideal environment to build on top services, our design can get advantages of both MEC and containerization for service continuity but still maintain security levels by blockchain. Sub-scenarios could cover almost cases that separate each level of sharing UE information for each level of trust among nodes. Trust aspects will reduce the migration downtime, in other words, increase the QoE of users.

For the future work, we will implement each component of the architecture, evaluate end-to-end latency and prediction results for service migration.

References

1. Abbas, N., Zhang, Y., Taherkordi, A., Skeie, T.: Mobile edge computing: a survey. IEEE IOT J. **5**(1), 450–465 (2018)
2. Abdah, H., Paulo Barraca, J., Aguiar, R.L.: QoS-aware service continuity in the virtualized edge. IEEE Access **7**, 51570–51588 (2019)
3. Aissioui, A., Ksentini, A., Gueroui, A.M., Taleb, T.: On enabling 5G automotive systems using follow me edge-cloud concept. IEEE Trans. Veh. Technol. **67**(6), 5302–5316 (2018)
4. Grundy, J., AlMorsy, M., Müller, I.: An analysis of the cloud computing security problem. In: Proceedings of the APSEC 2010 Cloud Workshop (2010)
5. Baldo, N.: The NS-3 LTE module by the LENA project. Center Tecnologic de Telecomunicacions de Catalunya (2011)
6. Saied, Y.B., Olivereau, A., Zeghlache, D., Laurent, M.: Trust management system design for the Internet of Things: a context-aware and multi-service approach. Comput. Secur. **39**(PART B), 351–365 (2013)
7. Bernstein, D.: Containers and cloud: from LXC to docker to kubernetes. IEEE Cloud Comput. **1**(3), 81–84 (2014)
8. Bui, T.: Analysis of docker security (2015). arXiv preprint: arXiv:1501.02967
9. Chahal, R.K., Kumar, N., Batra, S.: Trust management in social Internet of Things: a taxonomy, open issues, and challenges. Comput. Commun. **150**(2019), 13–46 (2020)
10. El Ioini, N., Pahl, C.: Trustworthy orchestration of container based edge computing using permissioned blockchain. In: The Fifth International Conference on Internet of Things: Systems, Management and Security (IoTSMS), Oct 2018
11. ETSI. Mobile Edge Computing - A key technology towards 5G (2015). https://www.etsi.org/images/files/ETSIWhitePapers/etsi_wp11_mec_a_key_technology_towards_5g.pdf. Accessed 2020
12. Guo, J., Chen, I.R., Tsai, J.J.P.: A survey of trust computation models for service management in Internet of Things systems. Comput. Commun. **97**, 1–14 (2017)
13. Iankoulova, I., Daneva, M.: Cloud computing security requirements: a systematic review. In: Proceedings - International Conference on Research Challenges in Information Science, pp. 1–7 (2012)
14. Ibrahiem, O., Talat, S., Chiu, C.-H.: Mobile service continuity for edge train networks. In: 2019 IEEE 30th Annual International Symposium on Personal, Indoor and Mobile Radio Communications (PIMRC), pp. 1–6, September 2019

15. Van Le, T., El Ioini, N., Pahl, C.: Blockchain based service continuity in mobile edge computing. In: 2019 Sixth International Conference on Internet of Things: Systems, Management and Security (IoTSMS), pp. 136–141, October 2019
16. Machen, A., Wang, S., Leung, K.K., Ko, B.J., Salonidis, T.: Live service migration in mobile edge clouds. IEEE Wirel. Commun. **25**(1), 140–147 (2018)
17. Pahl, C., El Ioini, N., Helmer, S., Lee, B.: An architecture pattern for trusted orchestration in IoT edge clouds. In: 2018 3rd International Conference on Fog and Mobile Edge Computing, FMEC 2018, pp. 63–70 (2018)
18. Pirzada, A.A., McDonald, C.: Establishing trust in pure ad-hoc networks. In: Proceedings of the 27th Australasian Conference on Computer Science, vol. 26(c), pp. 47–54 (2004)
19. Ramachandra, G., Iftikhar, M., Aslam Khan, F.: A comprehensive survey on security in cloud computing. Procedia Comput. Sci. **110**(2012), 465–472 (2017)
20. Riley, G.F., Henderson, T.R.: The *ns-3* network simulator. In: Wehrle, K., Gross, J. (eds.) Modeling and Tools for Network Simulation, pp. 15–34. Springer, Berlin (2010). https://doi.org/10.1007/978-3-642-12331-3_2
21. Taleb, T., Ksentini, A.: Follow me cloud: interworking federated clouds and distributed mobile networks. IEEE Network **27**(5), 12–19 (2013)
22. Zahariadis, S.V.T., Leligou, H.C., Trakadas, P.: Trust management in wireless sensor networks. Trans. Emerg. Telecommun. Technol. **25**(3), 294–307 (2014)
23. Varga, A., Hornig, R.: An overview of the OMNeT++ simulation environment. In: Proceedings of the 1st International Conference on Simulation Tools and Techniques For Communications, Networks and Systems & Workshops, p. 60. ICST (2008)
24. Virdis, A., Stea, G., Nardini, G.: SimuLTE - a modular system-level simulator for LTE/LTE-A networks based on OMNeT++. In: 4th International Conference on Simulation and Modeling Methodologies, Technologies and Applications (SIMULTECH), pp. 59–70 (2014)
25. Wang, S., Jinliang, X., Zhang, N., Liu, Y.: A survey on service migration in mobile edge computing. IEEE Access **6**, 23511–23528 (2018)
26. Wang, S., Urgaonkar, R., He, T., Chan, K., Zafer, M., Leung, K.K.: Dynamic service placement for mobile micro-clouds with predicted future costs. IEEE Trans. Parallel Distrib. Syst. **28**(4), 1002–1016 (2017)
27. Wang, S., Urgaonkar, R., Zafer, M., He, T., Chan, K., Leung, K.K.: Dynamic service migration in mobile edge computing based on Markov decision process. IEEE/ACM Trans. Netw. **27**(3), 1272–1288 (2019)
28. Zhang, Z.-K., Cho, M., Wang, C.-W., Hsu, C.-W., Chen, C.-K., Shieh, S.: IoT security: ongoing challenges and research opportunities. In 2014 IEEE 7th International Conference on Service-Oriented Computing and Applications, pp. 230–234, November 2014
29. Zhao, H., Li, X.: VectorTrust: trust vector aggregation scheme for trust management in peer-to-peer networks. J. Supercomput. **64**(3), 805–829 (2013)

Towards Resolving Security Smells in Microservice-Based Applications

Francisco Ponce(✉) ⓘ

Universidad Técnica Federico Santa María, Valparaíso, Chile
francisco.ponceme@usm.cl

Abstract. Microservices architecture has become enormously popular because traditional monolithic architectures no longer meet the needs of scalability and rapid development cycle, and the success of some large companies in building and deploying services is a strong motivation for others to consider making the change. Microservices bring new security challenges that were not present in traditional monolithic applications due to the nature of these systems and the way they are deployed. Some of these challenges are associated with decisions that can negatively impact system quality. These decisions are known as architectural smells and directly affect lifecycle properties. In this research work, we want to focus on detecting architectural smells associate with security in microservices-based applications. So we have generated a taxonomy of microservice security smells and the refactoring's to resolve them, and we plan to define a set of strategies for detecting the security smells of our taxonomy and develop a software tool that will allow practitioners to automatically detect these security smells in their system.

Keywords: Microservices security · Architectural smells · Security smells · Microservice architecture.

1 Introduction

Microservices architecture has become enormously popular because traditional monolithic architectures no longer meet the needs of scalability and rapid development cycle [10], and the success of some large companies in building and deploying services is a strong motivation for others to consider making the change. Typical issues associated with monolithic architecture are technical (e.g., the system becomes highly coupled, hard to maintain, presents side effects) or business-related (e.g., long time to release new features, low productivity of developers). In some cases, migrating towards microservices architecture represents the best option for resolving existing issues and at the same time improving the system maintainability and the frequency of product releases [3].

Microservices bring new security challenges, and opportunities, that were not present in traditional monolithic applications [13]. Some of these challenges

PhD Advisor: Hernán Astudillo[0000-0002-6487-5813].

C. Zirpins et al. (Eds.): ESOCC 2020 Workshops, CCIS 1360, pp. 133–139, 2021.
https://doi.org/10.1007/978-3-030-71906-7_11

are associated with the decisions made in the project, in this context are the architectural decisions and architectural smells.

An architectural smell is a common (although not always intentionally) used architectural decision that negatively impacts system quality. Architectural smells may be caused by applying a design solution in an inappropriate context, mixing design fragments that have undesirable emergent behaviors, or applying design abstractions at the wrong level of granularity. Architectural smells most directly affect lifecycle properties [5].

Although there is already research associate with architectural smells in the context of microservice-based applications [1,2,9,11,12], to the best of our knowledge, there is not currently work done in microservice security smells.

So in this research work, we want to focus on detecting security smells in microservices-based applications and propose the necessary refactoring to correct them (in most cases an architectural refactoring will improve the system quality).

The remainder of the article is structured as follows: Sect. 2 describes the fundamental concepts; Sect. 3 describe the context of the problem that will be addressed in this investigation; Sect. 4 describes the research plan, the associated challenges and the expected results.

2 Background

2.1 Microservices Architecture

The microservices architecture (MSA) style is an approach to developing a single application as a suite of small services, each running in its own process and communicating with lightweight mechanisms (e.g. HTTP API's) [7]. Microservices are built around business capabilities and independently deployable by fully automated deployment machinery. Because of their size, they are easier to maintain and more fault-tolerant since the failure of one service will not break the whole system, which could happen with a monolithic architecture. Therefore, this style allows designing architectures that should be flexible, modular and easy to evolve [7].

In recent years, many large systems evolve from self-contained *monolithic* applications built of interconnected, interdependent components to a collections of small, autonomous, lightweight-connected services. The market's high pace of demand for new application features requires changes both in the applications themselves (loose coupling and high scalability) and in the way they are built (loose team dependencies and fast deployment). Microservices address both concerns since small services can be built and deployed by independent development teams; the concomitant freedom allows teams to focus on improving each service and increase business value. Hence, in practice, DevOps (Development and Operations) and Continuous Delivery are a close fit for microservice architectures [4].

2.2 Architectural Smells

Besides smells on the code level, smells can also be identified on a higher level, e.g. if the defined interface of a subsystem has been circumvented. Since this higher design level is known as the architecture of a system, these smells are known as architecture smells. Both kinds of smell refer to the design of the software, but on different levels [8].

An architectural smell is a common (although not always intentionally) used architectural decision that negatively impacts system quality. Architectural smells may be caused by applying a design solution in an inappropriate context, mixing design fragments that have undesirable emergent behaviors, or applying design abstractions at the wrong level of granularity [5].

Architectural smells most directly affect lifecycle properties, such as understandability, testability, extensibility, and reusability, but they may have harmful side effects on other quality properties like performance and reliability. Architectural smells are remedied by altering the internal structure of the system and the behaviors of internal system elements without changing the external behavior of the system [5].

Architectural smells always involve a trade-off between different properties, and the system architects must determine whether an action to correct the smell will result in a net benefit. Furthermore, refactoring to reduce or eliminate an architectural smell may involve risk and almost always requires an investment of developer effort. Architectural smells do, however, indicate that in most cases an architectural refactoring will improve the system quality [5].

3 Problem Statement

3.1 Microservices Security

Microservices bring new security challenges, and opportunities, that were not present in traditional monolithic applications. These challenges include establishing trust between individual microservices and distributed secret management; concerns that are of much less interest in traditional web services, or in highly modular software that only runs locally [13].

Microservices needs more complex communication because of its fined granularity. Therefore, there is not only a risk that message data could be intercepted but also the threat that competitors might be able to infer business operations from message data [14].

Since Microservices are often deployed into cloud environments, Microservices also suffers from privacy issues in addition to message transfer and cloud consumers also have the concern that their stored information could be compromised or used inappropriately [14].

3.2 Microservices Smells

In [2] we can find 5 architectural smells proposed by the authors that they found after analyzing 58 different sources of information from academia and gray literature, which are: Single Layer Teams, Greedy Service Container, Single DevOps Toolchain, Dismiss Documentation, Grinding Dusty or Coarse Services. In this work, we can find a description of each smell and how they affect the system design. We haven't found an extension for this work.

In [9] the authors carried a multivocal review of white and grey literature in order to identify the most recognized architectural smells for microservices and to discuss the architectural refactorings allowing to resolve them. They identified 7 smells which are: Multiple services in one container, No API Gateway, Endpoint-based service interactions, Wobbly service interactions, ESB misuse, Shared persistence, Single-layer teams. In [1] we can find the extension of this work. Here the authors present a methodology to systematically identify the architectural smells that possibly violate the main design principles of microservices. They also present a prototype implementing the methodology, based on a representation of microservices using TOSCA.

In [11] the authors extended an existing tool (Arcan) developed for the detection of architectural smells to explore microservices architecture through the detection of three microservice smells (identified by them): Cyclic Dependencies, Hard-Coded Endpoints, and Shared Persistence. In this work, we can find some preliminary results obtained with Arcan for the analysis of 5 open-source projects with a microservices nature and reported a total of 8 instances of microservices smells. It is not yet possible to find an extension of this work because it is a recent publication.

In [12] to identify microservice-specific bad smells, the researchers collected evidence of bad practices by interviewing developers experienced with microservice-based systems. They then classified the bad practices into 11 microservice bad smells frequently considered harmful by practitioners. The authors provide a catalog of microservice smells, that contains a brief description of each smell, the problem that it may cause, and the possible solutions to each one.

3.3 Proposal

Although there is already research associate with architectural smells in the context of microservice-based applications [1,2,9,11,12], to the best of our knowledge, there is not currently work done in microservice security smells.

The main focus of this research work is the development of a software tool that allows practitioners to automatically detect the security smells in their system design and offer them the possible solutions that they could consider in order to improve the quality of their current system.

4   Research Plan

This research consists of several stages that are summarized in Fig. 1, and which are described below.

First, as recommended in [6] to capture both the state of the art and the state of practice in the field, we conducted a Multivocal Literature Review (MLR) of

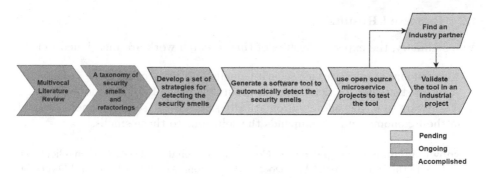

Fig. 1. Proposed research plan

the existing literature, including both white literature and grey literature. We have analyzed blog posts, videos, white papers, book chapters, conference papers, and journals. After applied our inclusion and exclusion criteria, we ended with 57 selected candidates.

We have classified and analyzed the data captured from the 57 selected candidates, and with this information, we have generated a taxonomy that includes security smells and the refactorings needed to resolve them. Currently, our taxonomy is composed of 14 smells, and we have associated at least one refactoring with each one.

Based on the taxonomy generated in the second stage, we plan to develop a set of strategies that will allow us to identify when one of the security smells is present in a determined system. Here we can take as a basis the works carried out in [1,9,11].

Using the result of the third stage, we will develop a software tool that allows practitioners to automatically detect the security smells in their system design.

We plan to test the software tool with open source projects, As was done in [11], and then we will try to find an industry partner to validate our software tool in an industry context.

4.1   Research Challenges

The current research challenges that we are facing are associated with the development of the strategies to detect the security smells. That is because the 14 security smells that we have found belong to 3 different levels. We have smells that are associated with the development process, we have smells associated with the design process, and we have smells that are transversal.

Also one of the main challenges of this work is to correctly define the information that will be processed by the tool developed to be able to automatically detect the security smells. This means that we must determine whether to use a custom system description or to rely on the current information of the system.

4.2   Expected Results

As a summary, the expected results of this research work are mentioned below:

– A taxonomy of microservice security smells and refactoring's.
– A set of strategies for detecting the security smells of our taxonomy.
– A software tool that allows automatically scan for the security smells defined in the taxonomy and recommends the solutions to those smells.

Acknowledgements. Supported by Comisión Nacional de Investigación Científica (CONICYT) through grants PCHA/Doctorado Nacional/2019-21191132 and Dirección de Postgrado y Programas Universidad Técnica Federico Santa María.

References

1. Brogi, A., Neri, D., Soldani, J.: Freshening the air in microservices: resolving architectural smells via refactoring. In: Yangui, S., et al. (eds.) ICSOC 2019. LNCS, vol. 12019, pp. 17–29. Springer, Cham (2020). https://doi.org/10.1007/978-3-030-45989-5_2

2. Carrasco, A., Bladel, B.v., Demeyer, S.: Migrating towards microservices: Migration and architecture smells. In: Proceedings of the 2nd International Workshop on Refactoring, pp. 1–6. IWoR 2018, Association for Computing Machinery, New York, NY, USA (2018). https://doi.org/10.1145/3242163.3242164

3. Di Francesco, P., Lago, P., Malavolta, I.: Migrating towards microservice architectures: an industrial survey. In: 2018 IEEE International Conference on Software Architecture (ICSA), pp. 29–2909, April 2018. https://doi.org/10.1109/ICSA.2018.00012

4. Fowler, S.J.: Production-ready Microservices: Building Standardized Systems Across an Engineering Organization. O'Reilly Media Inc., Sebastopol (2016)

5. Garcia, J., Popescu, D., Edwards, G., Medvidovic, N.: Identifying architectural bad smells. In: 2009 13th European Conference on Software Maintenance and Reengineering, pp. 255–258 (2009). https://doi.org/10.1109/CSMR.2009.59

6. Garousi, V., Felderer, M., Mäntylä, M.V.: The need for multivocal literature reviews in software engineering: complementing systematic literature reviews with grey literature. In: Proceedings of the 20th International Conference on Evaluation and Assessment in Software Engineering. EASE 2016. Association for Computing Machinery, New York, NY, USA (2016). https://doi.org/10.1145/2915970.2916008

7. Lewis, J., Fowler, M.: Microservices: a definition of this new architectural term. https://martinfowler.com/articles/microservices.html. Accessed 27 Dec 2019

8. Lippert, M., Roock, S.: Refactoring in Large Software Projects: Performing Complex Restructurings Successfully. Wiley, New York (2006)

9. Neri, D., Soldani, J., Zimmermann, O., Brogi, A.: Design principles, architectural smells and refactorings for microservices: a multivocal review. SICS Softw.-Intens. Cyber-Phys. Syst. **35**(1–2), 3–15 (2019). https://doi.org/10.1007/s00450-019-00407-8

10. Newman, S.: Building microservices: designing fine-grained systems. O'Reilly Media Inc., Sebastopol (2015)

11. Pigazzini, I., Fontana, F.A., Lenarduzzi, V., Taibi, D.: Towards microservice smells detection. In: Proceedings of the 3rd International Conference on Technical Debt, pp. 92–97. TechDebt 2020, Association for Computing Machinery, New York, NY, USA (2020). https://doi.org/10.1145/3387906.3388625
12. Taibi, D., Lenarduzzi, V.: On the definition of microservice bad smells. IEEE Software **35**(3), 56–62 (2018). https://doi.org/10.1109/MS.2018.2141031
13. Yarygina, T., Bagge, A.H.: Overcoming security challenges in microservice architectures. In: 2018 IEEE Symposium on Service-Oriented System Engineering (SOSE), pp. 11–20 (2018). https://doi.org/10.1109/SOSE.2018.00011
14. Yu, D., Jin, Y., Zhang, Y., Zheng, X.: A survey on security issues in services communication of microservices-enabled fog applications. Concurr. Comput. Pract. Exp. **31**(22), e4436 (2019). https://doi.org/10.1002/cpe.4436

Towards Citizen-Centric Marketplaces for Urban Sensed Data

Heiko Bornholdt(✉)

Department of Informatics, University of Hamburg,
Vogt-Kölln-Straße 30, 22527 Hamburg, Germany
bornholdt@informatik.uni-hamburg.de

Abstract. Due to increasing urbanization, the competition for cities' finite resources is intensifying. To maintain a high quality of life for citizens, more efficient use of these resources can be targeted. One way to achieve this goal is to use sensor networks that collect real-time information about the conditions in a city and improve citizens' understanding of their environment. Nevertheless, many existing sensor networks make their data available only locally, are not interconnected, and target companies and experts instead of average citizens.

Many citizens already operate sensors on several devices but cannot share their sensor data with other citizens in a secure manner. Therefore, we describe building blocks to construct a fully distributed city-wide marketplace for urban sensor data. By this, citizens can be offered a secure possibility to share their data by keeping their data sovereignty.

Keywords: Smart city · Distributed marketplace · Urban sensing · Participatory sensing · Urban participation · Data space

1 Introduction

In 2018, 4.2 billion people lived in urban areas. The UN expects that this number will rise to 6.7 billion people by 2050 [14]. Through such growing urbanization, cities and their citizens will be confronted with ecological, economic, and social challenges as well as an increasing competition for the city's finite resources. Such a competition must be solved to maintain the citizens' quality of life, welfare, health, and productivity. To allow cities to optimize resource usage, a comprehensive understanding of their environment and the city's context is necessary. There is an increasing number of sensor networks deployed in cities to gather this information. These networks are usually closed systems operated centrally by business organizations, governments, or other central authorities, which make their data only locally available - if at all.

However, a city consists of citizens - some of them already measure sensor data for private use. Sensor networks should be designed open to enable citizen

---

H. Bornholdt—Supervised by: Winfried Lamersdorf, University of Hamburg, Department of Informatics, Vogt-Kölln-Straße 30, 22527 Hamburg, Germany, lamersdorf@informatik.uni-hamburg.de.

C. Zirpins et al. (Eds.): ESOCC 2020 Workshops, CCIS 1360, pp. 140–150, 2021.
https://doi.org/10.1007/978-3-030-71906-7_12

participation in collecting sensor data. By interconnecting the individual sensor networks, a city-wide data space of urban information can be generated. This data space can be seen as the city's digital twin, which can serve as a foundation for an urban data marketplace. On such a marketplace, citizens should be able to offer the data generated by their sensors as well as request data, e.g., two neighbors with different outdoor sensors can exchange weather and environmental data in real-time, or a crowd of citizens measures particulate matter to generate a detailed overview of a city's air quality.

The increasing number of data breaches has led to a negative connotation of sharing data. Therefore, the marketplace must be designed to ensure sovereignty and incentives have to be created to motivate citizens to participate and share data.

The research project presented in this article is dedicated to designing a distributed marketplace for the exchange of urban sensor data between citizens under previously negotiated terms and conditions. The envisioned marketplace should enable every citizen to share privately collected sensor data with other citizens while maintaining data sovereignty. Since the marketplace runs on already existing citizens' hardware, no special hardware is required to participate. Thereby, the search for data on the marketplace should be as easy as surfing the WWW. The project's target is presenting a requirements catalog and a reference architecture for an event-based smart city middleware to exchange information in an entirely distributed system between technically diversified citizens. These different marketplace components are divided into individual building blocks, which simplifies reusing our research results. Insights gained from this work should provide information on how and with which limitations such a middleware can be realized.

This paper's remainder is composed as follows: First, in Sect. 2, related work is outlined. Then, in Sect. 3, the challenges of this research project are stated. Section 4 lists and describes the targeted research objectives. Section 5 presents preliminary results, and Sect. 6 presents the remaining research plan.

2   Related Work

This section's related work inspired the research project and revealed open issues in the research field.

Civitas, SmartCityWare, VITAL, CityHub, and *GAMBAS* present approaches to create a smart city middleware allowing cities to connect heterogeneous sensors from different sources [1,7,8,10,15]. Such a middleware can be used to create services and applications. Each approach uses a two-layer architecture: The first layer is responsible for connecting sensors using special adapters, which have to be provided for each sensor to allow a uniform sensor interaction. Based on this, the second layer consists of a centralized/distributed platform running on centrally/independently operated server-grade devices. This platform interacts with the sensors to offer services and applications. Additionally, Filipponi et al. introduce a distributed event-driven architecture for sensor data [5]. By using Complex

Event Processing, they can obtain higher-quality information from simple events emitted by each sensor. Via distributed publish-subscribe, cities can react in real-time to changes in the city's context. The approach is used to monitor public spaces on a large scale. Furthermore, *CrowdSC* is a crowdsourcing framework for smart cities to connect citizens with local governments [2]. By installing an application on the citizen's smartphone, the government can request and collect data (such as damage to public properties caused by vandalism). A multi-step process with a feedback loop is used during data collection to achieve high data quality. Besides, the *Machine eXchange Protocol* presents a concept for operating a city-wide low-power wide-area network [6]. Privately owned gateway nodes are used to connect nearby sensors to the internet. Such gateways are open for other people and can be used for a small fee. Payments provide incentives to set up gateways and are processed via an own blockchain-based cryptocurrency. Based on this network, the presentation of a marketplace for the sensor data is planned for 2021. In contrast, *Streamr* already offers a working centralized marketplace to exchange data streams [13]. Users can browse and subscribe to data sources offered on a website. The individual data sources are provided by other participants free of charge or for an hourly fee. Users can then use flow-based programming via a web-based WYSIWYG editor to process the data streams.

Nevertheless, every work covered in this section represents a single building block required to create the marketplace envisioned for this research project. The mentioned work mostly presents rough visions and does not offer concrete solutions or running examples for outlined problems. Furthermore, citizens' needs are not addressed as citizen-to-citizen interaction without the need of a central platform is often not considered. Besides, the central storage and processing of data planned by some approaches are likely to lead to additional privacy-concerns among citizens. This data collection outside the citizen's sphere will decrease the envisaged marketplace's acceptance rate.

3   Problem Statement

This section describes several problems that need to be addressed when creating a distributed marketplace to exchange urban sensor data between citizens.

First, the marketplace should be open and accessible to a broad range of citizens. Therefore, it has to be ensured that publishing, requesting, and receiving data is easy and does not require above-average technical knowledge, e.g., it should be possible to access the marketplace via a mobile or web-based application installed on citizen's existing devices. Integrating existing sensors should also be supported since many citizens already collect data about their environment via smartphones, fitness trackers, or smart home devices. Furthermore, citizens should be able to participate without having to purchase expensive special-purpose hardware.

Second, data sovereignty is one of the crucial pillars of the envisaged marketplace: Omnipotent central parties should be avoided to meet citizens' privacy concerns. Therefore, an entirely distributed system is preferable, in which all citizens are equal and share responsibilities. The citizen should be seen as the sole owner of the data generated by their sensors and should exclusively be able to decide which data they want to share with whom, for how long, under what conditions of use, and at what price. These usage policies must be guaranteed either technically or through control mechanisms on the marketplace. Since there will be no central supervisory authority, these "rules of the game" must be clear to all participants in advance and respected by them. The price must be either a monetary or non-monetary payment. Compared to centralized storage, distributed data storage on citizens' devices would further increase their data control. Furthermore, the digital footprint of every citizen on the marketplace should be as small as possible. Such design decisions support the citizen's data sovereignty and ensure that users are more willing to provide data.

Third, incentives must be created to improve not only the quantity of shared data but also its quality: Due to the use of sensors of different quality, poor maintenance, or incorrect usage, the data collected from citizens is of varying quality. On the one hand, the sharing of highly requested data or high-quality data should be rewarded to promote a sharing society. On the other hand, it can not be excluded that participants intentionally publish bad or wrong data. Therefore, a mechanism is needed to determine the data quality and to detect and punish malicious users.

Fourth, to enable a fast, efficient, and scalable searching for data on the marketplace, a distributed data structure is needed. Since each sensor and data value could potentially be unique, the search must be complete. In addition, as the various nodes are operated by citizens, heterogeneous computing power, network connectivity, and availability must be taken into account. The structure must be resilient to this.

Finally, all market components should be open source and—if available—use open standards. The city's citizens should manage the future development of the marketplace.

Overall, these problems can be seen as single building blocks within a preferred marketplace design. In this research project, the mentioned building blocks will be further discussed. Crucial parts are planned to be implemented as prototypes to show the feasibility.

4   Research Objectives

The following research challenges have been identified. They must be suitably addressed to overcome the problems mentioned in the previous section.

1. **Design of a Reference Architecture Model:** According to Otto et al., the following four architectures should help to outline the planned marketplace [9]:

    The *business architecture* describes the roles, rights, and duties of each participant. Typical business processes are explained, e.g., posting data, searching for data, negotiating trades, transferring data, and billing.

The *data and service architecture* describes necessary functions for the operation of the marketplace and the resulting services that must run on the individual nodes of the P2P network. Thus, the node's various tasks (e.g., sensor data integration, storage of sensor data, data exchange, visual interface) are described. They should be encapsulated in individual services and be (de)activatable individually, allowing the nodes to take different roles. This architecture does not make decisions on the use of specific technologies.

The concrete implementation of the data and service architecture is described in the *software architecture*. This architecture describes the technical implementation of the functions of the previous architectures. Furthermore, the different components of the marketplace are described (e.g., protocol bindings for the various sensor protocols, event bus for processing received sensor data, blackboard for matching data offers, and requests).

The *security architecture* deals with various aspects of security: participants must be uniquely identifiable, communication channels have to be confidential and provide integrity. The overall system must be designed to be resilient to attacks by harmful users. The previously negotiated terms and conditions of exchanged data must be applied by design.

2. **Data Integration:** In a city, sensors from different manufacturers are deployed. As the sensors are using different protocols, data formats, and interface semantics, their heterogeneity must be abstracted using a description language for higher-level marketplace components. Smooth integration of existing smart homes' sensors must be provided to fill the marketplace with data quickly right from the start. Additionally, it should be possible to integrate other existing smart city data spaces/other repositories in the form of so-called virtual sensors.

3. **Overcoming Network Heterogeneity and Barriers:** The envisaged marketplace should be structured in an entirely distributed manner. For this purpose, a city-wide P2P network should connect citizens as well as all sensors. Furthermore, citizens' should be able to run their nodes on smartphones or other devices in the citizens' PAN or LAN. As these networks are restricted (e.g., firewalls, NATs, unreliable connections), a bidirectional connection between different peers is not always possible. A transport overlay can overcome such barriers with different techniques (e.g., rendezvous-servers, relays, or hole punching). It provides secure and reliable communication channels for higher-level marketplace components.

4. **Distributed Data Structure:** After integrating sensors and solving communication restrictions by providing a transport overlay (challenges 2 and 3), an additional data overlay is required that acts as a distributed storage system. This overlay is used to structure the data in the P2P network and enables effective searches. The data structure should also support complex search queries to allow sensor data to be found by different criteria (e.g., location, timespan, type of data, or usage policies). Existing approaches (e.g., distributed hash tables) are not sufficient because privacy-concerned citizens cannot control their data's locality. Once the desired data has been found

using the data overlay, the previously mentioned transport overlay can handle the actual data transfer.

5. **Incentives for Active Participation:** Like security, incentives are an aspect that must be considered by the overall system design. For the success of the marketplace, a broad variety of high-quality data and a high degree of citizen participation is necessary. Therefore, incentives must be created to encourage citizens to provide data. On the one hand, the technical, monetary, and privacy-concerned barriers for posting data should be kept as low as possible. On the other hand, citizens should be rewarded for providing data (e.g., provide monetary or non-monetary, reputation-based, score-based, advantages). Malicious or non-contributing participants (known as *Free Riding* [3]) should be incentivized to provide their data on the marketplace (e.g., by restricting access to the marketplace). Not only the quantity of shared data is important, but also the quality. Therefore, the provided data quality should be assessed by comparing them with nearby located sensors. The reward should be based on the demand and quality of the shared data.

6. **Data Governance:** Citizens offer their sensor data on the marketplace under pre-defined usage rules (e.g., for private use only, for users above a certain reputation value). As these "rules of the game" are only defined by the creator, the data owner must be "pinned" to each data set. The marketplace is intended to support or guarantee compliance with these rules of use.

5 Preliminary Results

In this section, we present preliminary results as well as our current work in progress. First, we summarize the vision about a distributed citizen-centric marketplace called *Incorum* that we have already published [4]. Afterward, we present our work in progress for the research objectives (see Sect. 4).

In 2019, we already described and published some requirements and system architecture of a citizen-centric marketplace in an envisioned marketplace approach called *Incorum* [4]. The marketplace is based on a completely distributed P2P application consisting of so-called *Incorum Nodes*. These nodes are represented by software that can be installed on internet-enabled devices (such as citizens' smartphones or Raspberry Pi-alike single-board computers located in citizen's smart home). Every citizen participating in the marketplace is represented by a unique cryptographic identity and can operate any number of nodes. These nodes' main task is to collect and (temporarily) store all sensor data of the citizen. Furthermore, the node can offer these sensor data under restrictions previously defined by the citizen and request sensor data of other citizen's Incorum Nodes. Thereby, the node should allow intuitive operation by offering a graphical (web-based) user interface.

Ideally, citizens will just need to install the Incorum Node software as a mobile application on their smartphones or purchase single-board computers with pre-installed Incorum Node software. Once the Incorum Node software is started, it automatically searches for the citizen's sensors. If the node runs on a smartphone, the software will search for locally installed or accessible sensors via Bluetooth and Wi-Fi. If it is running on a single-board computer in citizens home instead, it can be used as a Wi-Fi access point, proxy, VPN server, MQTT broker, ZigBee coordinator, etc., to detect additional sensors. All detected sensors are displayed as so-called Internal Data Source (IDSs) and represent a source of a continuous flow of data sets consisting of the type of sensor, location of the sensor, time of measurement, and additional metadata. The citizen is now free to (temporarily) store this data, use it exclusively for his own needs, or share it with other citizens in the form of so-called External Data Source (EDSs). However, IDSs do not necessarily have to be mapped 1:1 to EDSs (Fig. 1).

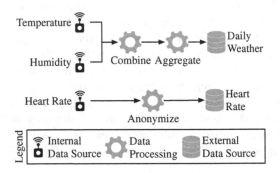

Fig. 1. The raw data received from citizen's sensors (so-called Interenal Data Source) are processed on a workflow basis before being shared with other citizens as so-called External Data Source.

Citizens can define workflows for data processing and control which data emitted by an IDS is published via an EDS. In this way, citizens can apply several data processing tasks on the data (e.g., anonymize, aggregate, delay, or combine data) before it is getting published. In addition, citizens can specify with whom they want to share the data, at what price, and under what conditions of use.

In parallel, the Incorum Node connects to other citizen's nodes and exchanges the available EDSs. Now, the user may request specific data about the city via their Incorum Node. To receive this data, they have to specify which data is needed for what purpose, whether it is a one-time request, temporary, or a permanent request, and what maximum price they are willing to pay. Then, the Incorum Node searches the marketplace for the desired data and uses a reverse auction to find the data's cheapest provider. The purchase will then be recorded in a distributed ledger. Only the seller, buyer, and some validator nodes have access to the recorded data. As soon as both sides have accepted the trade, the data transfer between their Incorum Nodes begins. Thereby the buyer subscribes to the EDS of the seller. As soon as the sensor pushes or pulls new data to the Incorum Nodes of the seller, the data is emitted by the corresponding IDS, processed by the previously mentioned workflow, and emitted by the corresponding

EDS. The data is transferred from the EDS to the buyer and the buyer's node can then process the data. The buyer can now also define the further processing of the data using his workflows (e.g., to combine the purchased data with his sensor data). Figure 2 (taken from [4]) exemplarily shows how data retrieval happens between two citizens and Incorum Nodes.

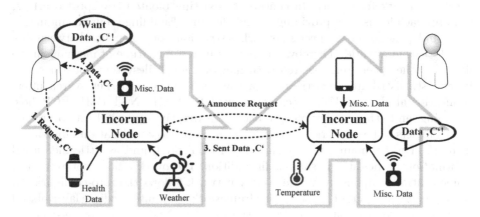

Fig. 2. Process of requesting and transferring sensor data between two citizens, each deployed an Incorum Node at their smart home.

Next, we want to present the work in progress for research objectives 2, 3, and 4. We present concrete additions to the previously described Incorum approach:

In this paragraph, we will take a closer look at data integration. As described in the previous chapter, the sensors and the communication is heterogeneous. For the integration of sensor data, the *W3C Web of Things Thing Description* is used to provide a uniform description of the sensors, interaction interfaces, and used data formats [17]. This description divides the interfaces of a sensor into Properties, Events, and Actions. The Properties are attribute-based parameters, that can be read and, if supported, written to in a pull or push manner (e.g., sense current temperature, control overheating alarm status). Subscriptions to Events can be set up to receive information about certain notifications in a push-based mode (e.g., smoke detected). Actions are used for physical (and therefore time-consuming) processes (e.g., switch sensor on or off). The description is based on JSON documents for each sensor and the different data formats are described via ontologies. Moreover, we have used the *W3C Web of Things Architecture*. That architecture describes how a unified program interface for sensor interaction derived from each Thing Description has to be designed to create a Web of Things [16]. We have evaluated these two W3C Recommendations' feasibility with a prototype receiving information from sensors via HTTP, WebSocket, MQTT, and CoAP. We have successfully established integration with various smart home, LPWAN, and virtual sensors with this prototype. The prototype can be found on GitHub[1]. This prototype will be integrated into the above mentioned Incorum Node and will handle the interaction between the node and different local sensors owned by the citizen.

In addition to data integration, the networks' heterogeneities and barriers must also be overcome so that the Incorum Nodes can connect with each other. For this, we have developed a lightweight, extensible general-purpose transport overlay network framework. In contrast to existing bloated transport overlays, our approach focuses on providing a single feature: Enabling secure communication - independent of the peer's network restrictions/deployment - between any two devices in a world. Thereby, our overlay uses a multitude of mechanisms to discover other peers (e.g., shared local memory, local filesystem, local network broadcast, distributed registries) by acting as a global ethernet switch interconnecting all devices. Using techniques like UPnP-IGD, NAT-PMP, PCP, hole punching, and other rendezvous protocols, our overlay framework can overcome most barriers. The network was developed with privacy and data minimization in mind. The communication is end-to-end encrypted, and as little individual information as possible is shared. In addition, the overlay does not rely on a single central component. As the overlay network follows the zero-configuration principle, it works out of the box. This framework as an intermediate layer placed between the application (in our case, the Incorum Node) and internet-enabled network interfaces, thus serving as a transport middleware. In addition, the overlay is extensible to provide additional network capabilities to the application (e.g., membership management or a distributed data structure). The presentation of the overlay's architecture and the framework is planned for a paper later this year, but the current work-in-progress prototype can be viewed on GitHub[2]. This prototype will be integrated into the above mentioned Incorum Node and will handle the interaction between the nodes.

We are currently evaluating the SkipNet approach [15] to create a distributed data structure containing all sensor data available on the envisioned Incorum marketplace. Unlike other overlays like Chord [12], CAN [11], Pastry [11], and Tapestry [18], SkipNet allows us to control the stored data's location. Since the amount of data shared with other citizens is minimized, such a control is desirable to protect citizens' privacy. Also, the routing of searches can be limited locally to strengthen the searching citizen's privacy. We plan to build the SkipNet approach on our previously mentioned overlay network to create a city-wide data space with all urban sensor data.

6   Research Plan

In this section, we will describe our next steps. For better understanding, we have put these steps in a sequence. We have chosen an iterative development approach, so this order does not necessarily reflect our development order.

---

[1] https://github.com/sane-city/wot-servient/.

[2] https://github.com/drasyl-overlay/drasyl.

Step 1 Further concretization of the reference architecture: The reference architecture will be concretized to understand better the problems that need to be solved. The insights gained through the other steps will help in this process.

Step 2 Work on missing building blocks: Until now, the focus has been on creating the reference architecture, integrating sensor data, and eliminating the network barriers by creating a transport overlay network (objectives 1, 2, and 3). Next, we will focus on creating a distributed data structure, an incentive model to increase participation in the marketplace, and mechanisms to support data governance (objectives 4, 5, and 6).

Step 3 Integration of the building blocks into one marketplace system: To ensure that the individual building blocks work individually and with each other, they will be integrated into an overall system. The system shall be partially implemented to get a running prototype.

Step 4 Evaluation of the envisioned middleware approach: Finally, the architecture and the prototype will be evaluated according to the previously defined requirements. The results will be discussed.

Acknowledgment. This work was partially supported by the DFG (German Research Foundation) under the Priority Programme SPP1593: Design for Future – Managed Software Evolution.

References

1. Apolinarski, W., Iqbal, U., Parreira, J.X.: The GAMBAS middleware and SDK for smart city applications. In: 2014 IEEE International Conference on Pervasive Computing and Communication Workshops, PERCOM WORKSHOPS 2014, pp. 117–122. IEEE (2014). https://doi.org/10.1109/PerComW.2014.6815176
2. Benouaret, K., Valliyur-Ramalingam, R., Charoy, F.: CrowdSC: building smart cities with large-scale citizen participation. IEEE Internet Comput. **17**(6), 57–63 (2013). https://doi.org/10.1109/MIC.2013.88
3. Bhakuni, A., Sharma, P., Kaushal, R.: Free-rider detection and punishment in Bit-Torrent based P2P networks. In: Souvenir of the 2014 IEEE International Advance Computing Conference, IACC 2014, February 2014, pp. 155–159 (2014). https://doi.org/10.1109/IAdCC.2014.6779311
4. Bornholdt, H., Bade, D., Posdorfer, W.: Incorum: a citizen-centric sensor data marketplace for urban participation. In: Bhatia, S.K., Tiwari, S., Ruidan, S., Trivedi, M.C., Mishra, K.K. (eds.) Advances in Computer, Communication and Computational Sciences. AISC, vol. 1158, pp. 659–669. Springer, Singapore (2021). https://doi.org/10.1007/978-981-15-4409-5_59
5. Filipponi, L., Vitaletti, A., Landi, G., Memeo, V., Laura, G., Pucci, P.: Smart city: an event driven architecture for monitoring public spaces with heterogeneous sensors. In: Proceedings of the 4th International Conference on Sensor Technologies and Applications, SENSORCOMM 2010, July 2010, pp. 281–286 (2010). https://doi.org/10.1109/SENSORCOMM.2010.50
6. MXC Foundation: machine exchange protocol: premium network infrastructure, infinite data stream commisioned (2018)

7. Lea, R., Blackstock, M.: City hub: a cloud-based IoT platform for smart cities. In: Proceedings of the International Conference on Cloud Computing Technology and Science, CloudCom 2015, February 2015, pp. 799–804 (2015). https://doi.org/10.1109/CloudCom.2014.65

8. Mohamed, N., Al-Jaroodi, J., Jawhar, I., Lazarova-Molnar, S., Mahmoud, S.: SmartCityWare: a service-oriented middleware for cloud and fog enabled smart city services. IEEE Access **5**, 17576–17588 (2017). https://doi.org/10.1109/ACCESS.2017.2731382

9. Otto, B., et al.: Industrial data space white paper. Fraunhofer-Gesellschaft, Munich (2016)

10. Petrolo, R., Loscrì, V., Mitton, N.: Towards a smart city based on cloud of things. In: WiMobCity 2014 - Proceedings of the 2014 ACM International Workshop on Wireless and Mobile Technologies for Smart Cities, Co-Located with MobiHoc 2014, pp. 61–65 (2014). https://doi.org/10.1145/2633661.2633667

11. Ratnasamy, S., Francis, P., Handley, M., Karp, R., Schenker, S.: A scalable content-addressable network (CAN). Comput. Commun. Rev. **31**(4), 161–172 (2001). https://doi.org/10.1145/964723.383072

12. Stoica, I., Morris, R., Karger, D., Kaashoek, M.F., Balakrishnan, H.: Chord: a scalable peer-to-peer lookup service for internet applications. Comput. Commun. Rev. **31**(4), 149–160 (2001). https://doi.org/10.1145/964723.383071

13. Streamr: unstoppable data for unstoppable apps: datacoin by streamr (2017)

14. United Nations: world urbanization prospects: the 2018 revision, key facts. Technical report (2018)

15. Villanueva, F.J., Santofimia, M.J., Villa, D., Barba, J., Lopez, J.C.: Civitas: the smart city middleware, from sensors to big data. In: Proceedings of the 7th International Conference on Innovative Mobile and Internet Services in Ubiquitous Computing, IMIS 2013, No. 3, pp. 445–450. IEEE (2013). https://doi.org/10.1109/IMIS.2013.80

16. World Wide Web Consortium: Web of Things (WoT) architecture. https://www.w3.org/TR/wot-architecture/. Accessed 31 July 2020

17. World Wide Web Consortium: Web of Things (WoT) thing description. https://www.w3.org/TR/wot-thing-description/. Accessed 31 July 2020

18. Zhao, B.Y., Huang, L., Stribling, J., Rhea, S.C., Joseph, A.D., Kubiatowicz, J.D.: Tapestry: a resilient global-scale overlay for service deployment. IEEE J. Sel. Areas Commun. **22**(1), 41–53 (2004). https://doi.org/10.1109/JSAC.2003.818784

ESOCC 2020 EU Projects Track

EU Projects Track

ESOCC traditionally includes a special track, named the *European Projects* track, entirely devoted to presenting recent results and research perspectives of EU-funded projects on Service-Oriented and Cloud Computing. This track offers an opportunity both for the project consortia to disseminate the results of their activities and for the track participants to get an updated view of the ongoing research at the European level.

In this edition of ESOCC, six main EU projects took advantage of this opportunity to show and report the results of their work touching upon different research challenges arising in Cloud, Fog and Edge environments. In more detail, the RADON project shows the advantages of adopting machine learning techniques to evolve the Infrastructure-as-Code in Cloud environments. Machine Learning techniques are also involved in the ANITA project to propose solutions for revealing and fighting criminal activities on the web. 5G-CARMEN focuses on the need to ensure service continuity in mobile settings while using 5G as communication infrastructure. SODALITE proposes a quality assurance framework for applications deployed on heterogeneous environments combining HPC and Cloud. A recently started project, FogProtect, discusses the importance of ensuring end-to-end protection when considering the data flow along the continuum between edge and cloud. Finally, ENFORCE introduces a framework to monitor virtualized services for interactive TV applications, where huge volumes of data are transferred.

We thank all the authors that submitted and presented their work in the EU project track. Their work significantly contributed to make this track a relevant venue to those who are interested in disseminating their results as well as keeping informed about how the European Projects in the Cloud and Service domain are running. We are also grateful to all the members of the Program Committee, who have given us great support in reviewing and organizing the track.

December 2020

Giuliano Casale
Pierluigi Plebani

Organization

Program Committee Chairs

Giuliano Casale   Imperial College London, UK
Pierluigi Plebani   Politecnico di Milano, Italy

Program Committee

Cristina Chesta   Concept Reply, Italy
Elisabetta Di Nitto   Politecnico di Milano, Italy
Nicolas Ferry   Université Côte d'Azur, France
José Merseguer   Universidad de Zaragoza, Spain
Dana Petcu   West University of Timisoara, Romania
Dimitris Plexousakis   ICS-FORTH, Greece
Vlado Stankovski   University of Ljubljana, Slovenia
Damian A. Tamburri   Eindhoven University of Technology,
     The Netherlands
Stefan Wesner   Ulm University, Germany

Additional Reviewers

Kostas Magoutis   ICS-FORTH, Greece
Indika Weerasingha Dewage   Tilburg University, The Netherlands
Giuseppe Cascavilla   Eindhoven University of Technology,
     The Netherlands

DevOps and Quality Management in Serverless Computing: The RADON Approach

Stefano Dalla Palma[1]([✉]), Martin Garriga[1], Dario Di Nucci[1],
Damian Andrew Tamburri[2], and Willem-Jan Van Den Heuvel[1]

[1] Jheronimus Academy of Data Science, Tilburg University,
Tilburg, The Netherlands
{s.dallapalma,m.garriga,d.dinucci,W.J.A.M.vdnHeuvel}@uvt.nl
[2] Jheronimus Academy of Data Science, Technical University of Eindhoven,
Eindhoven, The Netherlands
d.a.tamburri@tue.nl

Abstract. The onset of microservices and serverless computer solutions has forced an ever-increasing demand for tools and techniques to establish and maintain the quality of infrastructure code, the blueprint that drives the operationalization of large-scale software systems. In the EU H2020 project RADON, we propose a machine-learning approach to elaborate and evolve Infrastructure-as-Code as part of a full-fledged industrial-strength DevOps pipeline. This paper illustrates RADON and shows our research roadmap.

Keywords: Infrastructure code · Serverless computing · Microservices computing · Software Quality · DevOps · Machine-Learning for Software Quality · DataOps

1 Introduction

Not so long ago, companies and individuals used to provision and manage their software on their in-house server and computing infrastructure. This behavior implied several costs, such as the costs involved in buying and maintain machines or hiring IT personnel. Therefore, those companies started outsourcing some responsibilities (for example, the management and maintenance of the infrastructure). The cloud has come, which, combined with virtualization and containerization, laid the ground for Infrastructure-as-a-Service, Platform-as-a-Service, and Software-as-a-Service. These technologies allow for more outsourcing and, as a result, a more focus on the business logic while delegating the management of the infrastructure to those having great expertise in the field. Therefore, the lead time has shortened, and the creation of software and its deployment has become relatively easier, cheaper, and quicker. Serverless Function-as-a-Service (FaaS) is a step forward in this evolution.

© Springer Nature Switzerland AG 2021
C. Zirpins et al. (Eds.): ESOCC 2020 Workshops, CCIS 1360, pp. 155–160, 2021.
https://doi.org/10.1007/978-3-030-71906-7_13

Function-as-a-service is a serverless way to execute modular pieces of code on the edge. FaaS lets developers write and update a piece of code on the fly, which can then be executed in response to an event, such as a user clicking on an element in a web application. It allows for code scalability and is a cost-efficient way to implement microservices. Serverless FaaS came with several advantages, among them:

- the business logic is deployed to the host in the cloud as code units in forms of functions, which are fully managed by the provider (e.g., Amazon AWS, Azure Lambda, Google Cloud Functions);
- the lead time, that is, the latency between the initiation and completion of the development process, has shortened;
- less server-side work is needed: the provider is responsible for managing the host machine. Thus, developers can focus on building the business logic.

In general, there are reduced costs and risks. However, serverless FaaS is not a silver bullet, and new challenges arise.

From a survey conducted with serverless adopters, recurrent problems in adopting serverless have emerged [2]. First, serverless is still relatively in its infancy, and hence only a bunch of best practices for its adoption and operations are available. Second, there are few design principles and patterns for composing and triggering serverless functions. Third, few definitions of bad practices exist in the digital-native technical domain, which should be amended.

Furthermore, the rising of serverless solutions, combined with microservices, has forced an ever-increase demand for tools and techniques to establish and maintain them across the entire DevOps lifecycle [1]. With those challenges in mind, the RADON approach for serverless computing comes to play.

2   Objectives

RADON stands for "rational decomposition and orchestration for serverless computing", and is a project funded by the Horizon-2020 European program. It aims to unlock the benefits of serverless computing and Function-as-a-Service (FaaS), and broaden their adoption within the European software industry by developing a model-driven DevOps framework and methodology to create and manage applications based on fine-grained and independently deployable microservices exploiting the serverless paradigm through FaaS and container technologies.

In particular, this work introduces the key tools on the RADON methodology, the user workflow, and their integration and cooperation in the context of DevOps. The methodology strives to tackle complexity, harmonize the abstraction, enforce action-trigger rules, avoid Faas lock-in, and optimize decomposition and reuse through model-based FaaS-enabled development and orchestration.

3 Early Results

We have currently defined the RADON Architecture, including (i) several workflows to organize and display the possible interactions between the tools of the RADON framework and the identified actors and (ii) a tool-chain to define microservices-based serverless applications with focusing on design-, development-, and run-time.

In particular, RADON envisions a model-based approach to manage and orchestrate modern, distributed, cloud-native application systems that will typically apply a microservice architecture and exploit the FaaS model. The overall RADON framework features rotate around the RADON modeling environment. The other tools are responsible for the correctness and quality of the generated artifacts, such as the Verification, Continuous Testing, and Defect Prediction tools. The framework uses the Topology and Orchestration Specification for Cloud Applications (i.e., OASIS TOSCA) [3] as a baseline to define the RADON models. TOSCA describes the topology generated via the Graphical Modeling tool and the orchestration of cloud applications in a declarative manner. The orchestration process takes place through the Orchestration tool, making it possible to integrate changes and deploy and monitor the application. An overview of the architecture is depicted in Fig. 1.

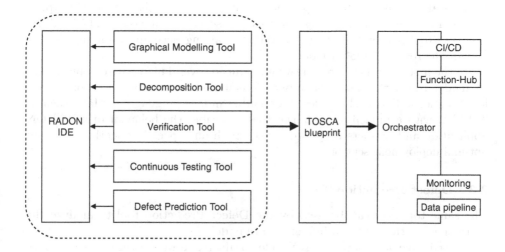

Fig. 1. A broad overview of the RADON framework architecture

3.1 Graphical Modeling Tool

Rather than modeling the environment by manually define TOSCA blueprints, the *graphical modeling tool* (GMT) enables the creation, development, and modeling of TOSCA applications through a web-based software solution. Its main goal is combing TOSCA service templates that represent the applications deployed using the RADON Orchestrator. RADON users can then package their applications as a CSAR (i.e., Cloud Service Archive) before it is deployed into production by using the RADON Orchestrator.

In the first year of the project, the main achievements provided the foundation to graphically maintain RADON applications using the TOSCA Simple Profile standard in version 1.3. Relying on Eclipse Winery as a baseline and by extending it with the respective YAML-based modeling features, allowed a comprehensive modeling tool to graphically (i) create and adapt reusable modeling entities, such as TOSCA Node Types and Policy Types; (ii) compose RADON application structures in the form of TOSCA Service Templates; (iii) enrich existing RADON applications with test-related and performance-specific attributes using TOSCA Policies; and(iv) export a portable archive containing all information to execute the deployment by using the RADON Orchestrator.

3.2   Decomposition Tool

The topology generated by the GMT, or anyone imported into the tool, can be passed as input to the *decomposition tool* to find the optimal decomposition solution for an application based on the microservices architectural style and the serverless FaaS paradigm, taking into account those constraints.

The tool provides suggestions to map abstract components to concrete technologies and adjust the topology itself. For example, to split a monolithic application into microservices or microservices into serverless functions. The feedback from the tool is sent back to the GMT, containing decomposition suggestions and/or the revised TOSCA model.

In the first year of the project, we introduced several modularized approaches to model the performance of applications based on microservices or serverless functions. This tool enables to extend standard languages for IaC, such as TOSCA, with a modeling formalism that describes the behavior of a RADON application and predicts its performance. Such an aspect is essential to obtain optimal deployment schemes.

3.3   Defect Prediction Tool

The same topology can be used by the Defect Prediction tool to analyze the correctness of the delivered infrastructure code.

Indeed, like any other source code artifacts, infrastructure files (such as TOSCA topology definitions or Ansible configuration files) may contain defects that can preclude their correct functioning. The quality of these files should evolve and be maintained through the entire system's life-cycle. The *defect prediction tool* supports the correctness of the infrastructure code developed using the RADON framework and allows DevOps engineers to focus on critical files that may be failure-prone while skipping the others. Thus, allocating resources more efficiently, for example, for testing or code audit.

In the first year of the project, we designed and implemented its architecture to automatically gather meaningful data to improve model performance.

More specifically, we developed a set of tools and framework to (i) automatically crawl and mine projects from Github and Gitlab; (ii) extract code and process metrics from Ansible playbooks and TOSCA blueprints; (iii) support DevOps engineers in training defect-prediction models and identifying snapshots of files containing defects. The tool exposes RESTful APIs that can be used locally or deployed online to interact with the defect prediction tool. The APIs and the MongoDB database will be publicly accessible to retrieve the models trained during our in-vitro experimentations and those added by the community in the future. However, organizations that do not want to expose their data/models can deploy the APIs starting from an empty DB on-premises and grant access to specific users. A command-line client was also developed to use the defect prediction tool in a CI/CD pipeline. It provides functionalities to (i) train a model from scratch using different configurations in terms of data balancing, normalization, feature selection, and classifiers; (ii) download a model from the online APIs; (iii) predict unseen instances based on the model trained with (i) or collected with (ii).

3.4 Verification Tool

The *verification tool* enables a user to verify that a RADON model conforms to a set of constraints (e.g., privacy, security, design pattern violations) before deployment. While modeling the application via the GMT, the Software Designer can set desired properties and constraints (e.g., security/privacy requirements) using a Constraint Definition Language (CDL). The Software Designer can provide examples of the desired behavior through the RADON IDE or manually. Upon the generated models, the software designer or the DevOps engineer can use this tool to perform static checking upon their validity. When a violation is encountered (e.g., circular calls, or privacy violations), the engineer can open the corresponding artifact(s) in the RADON IDE for debugging.

During the first year of the project, the CDL and the command-line version of the verification tool have been developed. It currently supports the verification and the correction of a RADON model and can detect inconsistencies with the constraints expressed in the CDL.

3.5 Continuous Testing Tool

The *testing tool* comprises several modules for microservices/FaaS testing and a data pipeline that will support the continuous testing workflow of RADON. It will provide a set of functionalities to support three main usage scenarios: (i) test case definition, (ii) test execution, and (iii) test maintenance. Such scenarios will help RADON users correctly test their application by creating, executing, inspecting, and removing test cases. In the first year of the project, we specified the requirements of the tool, designed its architecture, envisioned its integration with the other tools of the framework, implemented a prototype, and showcased a proof-of-concept based on two sample applications.

4   Conclusions and Research Roadmap

The RADON project aims to define a decision-making toolkit to optimize micro-services in terms of size, dependencies, and costs by leveraging a reference set of architectural patterns and service templates [1]. To support this goal, the RADON methodology will integrate a workflow that enables decision making on architecture optimization through the *decomposition tool*. To avoid defective infrastructures, it will detect defects through the *defect prediction tool*. To test the application, the framework will check the application invariants against the changes through the *testing tool*. Furthermore, the methodology will define the operations and workflows to use the tools and how they should be integrated and should cooperate. Finally, RADON aims at organizing and accelerating the micro-services evolution in a team-based fashion. Security and privacy policies will be automatically enforced in the run-time environment of the framework to ensure protection for sensitive data and services.

References

1. Guerriero, M., Garriga, M., Tamburri, D.A., Palomba, F.: Adoption, support, and challenges of infrastructure-as-code: insights from industry. In: 2019 IEEE International Conference on Software Maintenance and Evolution (ICSME), pp. 580–589. IEEE (2019)
2. Lenarduzzi, V., Daly, J., Martini, A., Panichella, S., Tamburri, D.: Towards a technical debt conceptualization for serverless computing. IEEE Softw. **38**, 40–47 (2020)
3. Matt Rutkowski, C.N., Lauwers, C., Curescu, C.: TOSCA simple profile in YAML version 1.3 (2019). http://docs.oasis-open.org/tosca/TOSCA-Simple-Profile-YAML/v1.3/TOSCA-Simple-Profile-YAML-v1.3.html

5G-CARMEN: Service Continuity in 5G-Enabled Edge Clouds

Hamid R. Barzegar$^{(\boxtimes)}$, Nabil El Ioini, Van Thanh Le, and Claus Pahl

Faculty of Computer Science, Free University of Bozen-Bolzano, Bolzano, Italy
`Hbarzegar@unibz.it`

Abstract. Mobile Edge Computing (MEC) places part of the cloud resources to the edge of the network to increase performance and provide context-aware services. In combination with the expected high performance 5G, many of the limitations for today's infrastructure could be solved. In the context of the EU 5G-CARMEN project, one of the main challenges is service continuity across organisational and territorial boundaries in a road, motorway and railway settings. The project addresses this challenge by designing and implementing MEC-based services that act as bridges between the different domains, while taking advantage of the high performance and reliability of 5G. Four uses cases have been defined to capture to potential uses of this new paradigm in the mobility domain. In this paper, we present the on going development of service continuity mechanisms within the 5G-CARMEN project.

Keywords: 5G-CARMEN · 5G mobile communication · Edge computing · Cloud computing · Service continuity · CCAM · EU-project · MEC

1 Introduction

Cooperative, connected and automated mobility (CCAM) platform is one of the EU-supported infrastructure initiatives, that investigates advanced cloud and communications solutions. Since the introduction of wireless communication and consequently introduction of mobile internet connection, demands created by connected mobility have increased drastically. Over time, many solutions have been discussed and developed to improve quality-of-experience (QoE) as well as quality-of-service (QoS). Currently, the fifth generation (5G) of mobile communication and the advancement of edge computing represent a huge step toward bringing cloud capabilities closer to the actual applications at the edge of the network [7].

The European Union (EU) supports projects in this context such as 5G-CARMEN, which aims to develop a new platform (CCAM) that supports safer, greener and more intelligent transport system across European countries. The goal of this project is to maintain service continuity in a cross-border scenario. However, to have a seamless connection while users cross the boarders is a big

© Springer Nature Switzerland AG 2021
C. Zirpins et al. (Eds.): ESOCC 2020 Workshops, CCIS 1360, pp. 161–165, 2021.
https://doi.org/10.1007/978-3-030-71906-7_14

challenge that goes beyond simple technique such as network re-selection between different Mobile Network Operators (MNOs), requiring MEC-coordinated support.

The **5G-CARMEN**[1] ("5G for Connected and Automated Road Mobility in the European unioN" project goal is to build a 5G infrastructure corridor from Bologna to Munich to implement different scenarios that improve cross-border mobility use cases. One of the major challenges in the proposed use cases is service continuity across organisational and territorial boundaries in a motorway setting i.e., when vehicles or mobile users cross boarders there is a tangible latency while network re-selection tacks place. This latency has a significant impact on the overall performance of the services in the 5G and MEC space. Therefore, the main objective of 5G-CARMEN is to increase services reliability and reduce latency across European boarders to improve the QoE.

For this project several techniques have been considered. In [1], a MANagement and Orchestration (MANO) system for physical and virtualized resources is proposed. Exploiting Key Performance Indicators (KPIs) in recent 5G networks and next-generation MANO architectures in multi-domain settings has been studied in [2]. The utilization of mobile (also called multi-access) edge clouds (MEC) close to the road side to improve the reliability and low-latency-aware requires a management platform for virtual network function (VNF) placement and service migration [3]. In [4,5], an evaluation of Vehicle to Vehicle (V2V) infrastructure and 5G is carried out, considering a network not being able to cover the entire roadway. The authors in [6] propose a monitoring architecture which enables tracking of the location and current status of distributed and virtualized service functions, for both physical and virtual resources.

The rest of this paper is organised as follows. Main use cases of 5G-CARMEN are discussed in Sect. 2, then followed by the proposed 5G-CARMEN architecture in Sect. 3. In order to illustrate the project, selected contributions around service continuity are explained in Sect. 4. Section 5 concludes the paper.

2   5G-CARMEN Use Cases

In order to investigate SC from different perspectives, four main use cases have been considered in 5G-CARMEN as follows:

- Cooperative Maneuvering: to have a safe, secure and efficient navigation between drivers, the highly important aspect is cooperation among them through in situations like intersections, lane changing, overtaking, entering/exiting motorways.
- Situation Awareness: both human drivers as well as automated vehicles are limited in their ability to ensure safe and efficient travels only based on their perception of the road traffic situation. Here, the utilization of local sensors for human drivers and automated vehicles are important. Two main key scenario for situations awareness are i) back-situation awareness of an emergency vehicle arrival and ii) vehicle sensors and state sharing.

---

[1] https://5gcarmen.eu/.

- Video Streaming: the on-demand streaming of videos is one of the passenger expectation for autonomous vehicles which increases the QoE no matter where they are. Two important factors are the prediction of the expected network QoS and the avoidance of interruptions in the service whenever possible. It is important to guarantee high-quality services, even in cross-country and inter-operator scenarios.
- Green Driving: European road operators and authorities have extended their management capabilities to air quality and air pollution in addition to safety and traffic efficiency. Nevertheless, 5G-CARMEN investigates solutions towards the promotion of greener driving.

3 Proposed System Architecture

SC is a complex undertaking, sensitive to different factors and spans across multiple dimensions. The heterogeneity of the supporting cloud and communications infrastructures and the variability in the different handover scenarios call for a reliable architecture. The introduction of 5G definitely plays an important role. However, challenges in the service and resource management still need to be addressed in order to provide reliable end-to-end solutions. The first challenges concerns the services placement awareness, where services practically follow the moving vehicles by having them deployed at the closest MEC nodes. The second challenge concerns cross organizational boundaries awareness, that is the ability to provide services independently from the underlying provider or technology used. The goal is to build an abstraction layer that isolates the provided services from all the involved parties. Figure 1 represents the system architecture for service migration in mobile edge computing between two countries while users are faced with network re-selection.

4 Service Continuity Solutions

This section explains some contribution in the project of the authors in order to illustrate specific concerns. Our contributions are i) develop and setup a new simulator environment, ii) propose an AI prediction algorithm, iii) investigating data protection for SC where we propose blockchains to provide accountability, and iv) develop and setup a lab environment based on the Raspberry Pi[2] IV to test the proposed algorithms in a lightweight MEC setting.

4.1 Simulation Environment Setup

To simulate a cross-provider MEC scenario, we implemented a prototype, which integrates a number of simulation frameworks that combines components such as, OMNet++, INET-Framework, SimuLte, Veins and Sumo on top of Ubuntu

---

[2] https://www.raspberrypi.org/.

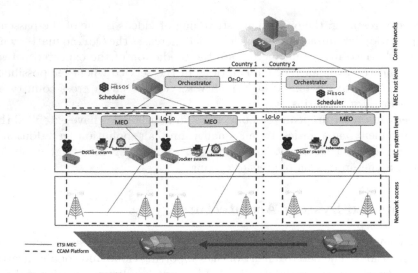

Fig. 1. System architecture of service migration in mobile edge computing between two countries.

16.04 LTS. The combination with Vein, Sumo, SimuLte enable us to demonstrate TCP message flow and smart mobility behaviors, especially the service handover event when changing scenarios. Also, feasibility of NS3 simulation is under investigation.

4.2   AI Algorithm for Prediction Algorithm

There are two algorithm proposed for this part. The first is **gNB** based, which acts based on the signal strength of UE and gNB. In this algorithm, two thresholds have been defined. When UE crosses the first threshold, then the migration application or services will be triggered. The second one is **GPS** based that in this case from the beginning of the journey the network is aware of cross bordering. Therefore, the network is able to estimate when a car is going to cross the boarder and the MEC has sufficient time to establish the requirements on the other side of the border.

4.3   Blockchain-Based Service Continuity

The CCAM platform requires a huge amount of data to be exchanged between different parties (e.g., vehicles, road operators, mobile and MEC providers). This results in users losing physical control over their data. To maintain data confidentiality, encryption has been the predominant mechanism used over the years. However, many of the strong encryption schemes require heavy computation, which might be an obstacle for some CCAM components such as IoT sensors and low computational power MECs. Exploiting data protection for SC which here possibility of blockchain has been taken into account.

4.4 Emulation Environment Setup

In order to test the proposed algorithms, we set up a cluster of Raspberry Pi as a lightweight edge cloud test-bed. The Raspberry Pi is a type of small single-board computers. We are expanding our work on container-based lightweight edge clusters here.

5 Conclusions

The main goal is to enable large scale SC cross organizational boundaries is to maximize service availability and reliability with the highest level of transparency to the user. The recent advancements in cloud and edge computing in combination with 5G could bring here a radical change by providing the proper infrastructure for delivering the needed mechanisms for service continuity. In this paper, we have presented the current status of 5G-CARMEN and our proposed solution for SC, laying down the main open challenges that need to be addressed in the coming next years.

Acknowledgement. This work has been performed in the framework of the EU Horizon 2020 project 5G-CARMEN co-funded by the EU under grant agreement No. 825012.

References

1. Yousaf, F.Z., Sciancalepore, V., Liebsch, M., Costa-Perez, X.: MANOaaS: a multi-tenant NFV MANO for 5G network slices. IEEE Commun. Mag. **57**(5), 103–9 (2019)
2. Sciancalepore, V., et al.: A future-proof architecture for management and orchestration of multi-domain NextGen networks. IEEE Access **7**, 79216–32 (2019)
3. Slamnik-Kriještorac, N., de Resende, H.C.C., Donato, C., Latré, S., Riggio, R., Marquez-Barja, J.: Leveraging mobile edge computing to improve vehicular communications (2019)
4. Elia, G., et al.: Connected transports, V2X and 5G: standard, services and the TIM-telecom Italia experiences. In: AEIT International Conference of Electrical and Electronic Technologies for Automotive, pp. 1–6 (2019). IEEE
5. Garcia-Roger, D., et al.: 5G functional architecture and signaling enhancements to support path management for eV2X. IEEE Access **7**, 20484–20498 (2019)
6. Femminella, M., Reali, G.: Gossip-based monitoring of virtualized resources in 5G networks. In: IEEE INFOCOM 2019-IEEE Conference on Computer Communications Workshops (INFOCOM WKSHPS), pp. 378–384. IEEE (2019)
7. Barzegar, H.R., El Ioini, N., Pahl, C.: Service continuity for CCAM platform in 5G-CARMEN. In: 2020 International Wireless Communications and Mobile Computing (IWCMC), pp. 1764–1769. IEEE, 15 June 2020

Services Computing for Cyber-Threat Intelligence: The ANITA Approach

Daniel De Pascale[1]([⊠]), Giuseppe Cascavilla[2], Damian A. Tamburri[2], and Willem-Jan van den Heuvel[1]

[1] JADS, University of Tilburg, Tilburg, The Netherlands
`d.de.pascale@tue.nl`
[2] JADS, Eindhoven University of Technology, Eindhoven, The Netherlands

Abstract. Major cybersecurity and threat intelligence analysts agree that online criminal activity is increasing exponentially. Technologies, newspapers, the internet, and social media made the dark web an accessible place to almost everyone. The ease of accessing the dark side of the web makes the problem more critical than ever. For this reason, the European Union financed the ANITA project, consisting of different tools for monitoring and fighting illegal criminal activities on the Dark Web. In the ANITA project, we propose different Big Data analytic tools for the analysis of all data extracted from illegal marketplaces. In this survey paper we present our developed tools for detecting trends and analyzing the incoming information with respect to illegal trafficking. The tool extracts information about specific trends, analytics and produces actionable insight on buying and transaction habits and user behaviors. The tool extracts statistics in order to support and guide investigators and law enforcement agencies for the detection of criminal activities.

1 Introduction

Over the recent years, online illegal trafficking activities have hugely elaborated and expanded so that to operate at global level with worldwide supply chains, production facilities and administrative offices, while their legal, economic and sustainability state is optimised [1]. For tackling these emerging challenges, a significant part of LEAs' (Law Enforcement Agencies) efforts has been invested on training activities to equip officers and practitioners with the necessary knowledge and skills related to this emerging and continuously/rapidly evolving scenery [2].

Accordingly, the European Union financed the EU H2020 ANITA project, consisting of different services for monitoring and fighting online criminal activities. ANITA's primary goal is twofold: a) to boost the LEA's investigation process and to significantly increase their operational capabilities, by introducing a set of innovative tools for efficiently addressing online illegal trafficking challenges (namely online data source analysis, blockchain analysis, Big Data analytics, knowledge modelling, incorporation of human cognitive function in the

© Springer Nature Switzerland AG 2021
C. Zirpins et al. (Eds.): ESOCC 2020 Workshops, CCIS 1360, pp. 166–172, 2021.
https://doi.org/10.1007/978-3-030-71906-7_15

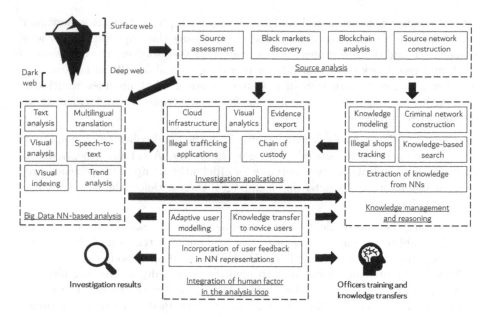

Fig. 1. Graphical representation of the ANITA action.

analysis pipelines, user-oriented intelligence applications), and b) to significantly facilitate the novice officers training process and to optimize the learning curve (by collecting, integrating and re-using knowledge from multiple expert officers and through the development of a recommendation functionality to transfer the acquired 'know-how' to the new officers). This paper discusses the different approaches part of the ANITA action.

2   Concept and Approach Overview

ANITA, as explained in the graphical representation in Fig. 1, is divided into five different steps:

1. *Source Analysis toolbox;*
2. *Big Data NN-based analysis;*
3. *Knowledge management and reasoning box;*
4. *Investigation application box;*
5. *Integration of human factor in the analysis loop.*

Source Analysis Box: The first necessary steps in the analysis chain comprise the detection, assessment and analysis of potentially interesting sources that can be found on Surface/Deep/Dark Web. In particular, a new generation of data collection tools is developed, specific to LEAs needs. Specifically, dedicated services are responsible for: a) Anonymous identification of new relevant content with a balance between speed and precision; b) High performance download and storing in a secure repository; and c) Assessing the importance (i.e. level of relevance and dangerousness) of the examined Web sources, the discovery of black markets, block chain analysis for revealing cues about illegal transactions tracking and the construction of a source network (that includes multi-level information for every source as well as the interconnections/interrelations among the identified sources).

Big Data NN-Based Analysis Box: Having identified and collected vast amounts of multimedia material related to illegal trafficking, ANITA applies a set of sophisticated Big Data analytic services for efficiently manipulating the acquired information and robustly detecting meaningful events. Below the list of the provided set of analysis.

- Text analysis services, delivered through the usage of a semantic based engine and capable of automatic categorization and entity extraction of the contents coming from Social, Surface/Deep/Dark Web, and other sources.
- Visual content analysis in order to identify potentially interesting pieces of information or evidence in the formed databases. For addressing the particular challenge deep hashing approaches are developed to recognise semantic entities at multiple scales.
- For supporting the processing of documents written in different languages a multilingual translation service is developed in order to automatic translate segments of speech to another language, audio streams, speech-to-text methodologies to perform the transformation of a speech segment to the form of a written document.
- Illegal trafficking trend analysis in order to extract information about specific trends, analytics and actionable insights on buying habits and user behaviours.

Knowledge Management and Reasoning Box: Apart from the inevitable large-scale data-driven analysis, the ANITA system is grounded on appropriate semantic knowledge structures that summarize explicit domain expert knowledge regarding the application field and which enable the realization of high-level semantic inference tasks (e.g. inconsistency checking, reasoning, outlier detection, etc.). The collected knowledge (i.e. application domain expertise) renders feasible the realization of complex and highly demanding tasks, like criminal network construction, illegal shops tracking and knowledge-based search and retrieval that are of vital for analysing different aspects of the illegal trafficking incidents.

Investigation Application Box: all the above-mentioned system functionalities drive the design and support the operation of a set of novel investigative applications to be delivered to the project stakeholders. In particular, the ANITA system is based on the design and implementation of a scalable and Big Data oriented infrastructure, able to analyse large volumes of data in near real time and to summarize analysis results to provide LEAs with relevant insights on illegal trafficking related phenomena.

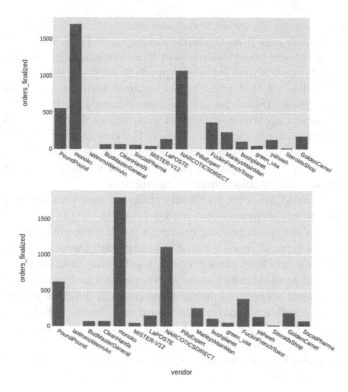

Fig. 2. Trend analysis on orders done in the Berlusconi market by different vendors in two different snapshots.

Integration of Human Factor in the Analysis Loop Box: overall, the fundamental consideration of the ANITA system to integrate the human user in the analysis pipeline serves the following two fundamental project goals (and simultaneously main outputs of the system): a) To significantly boost the efficiency of the investigation process, by continuously improving the robustness of the feature detectors through the incorporation of the explicit and implicit user feedback, while also updating and expanding the knowledge infrastructure for the selected application domain. b) To remarkably speed up the training process of new/novice investigators, practitioners and officers for the application domain at hand, by re-using and transferring knowledge that has been collected and combined from multiple expert users.

3 Big Data Services and Analytics

As described in Fig. 1 in the box of *Big Data NN-based analysis* the services computing part reflects mostly the large scale trend analysis. Our research approach in this direction focuses on developing services, methods, techniques, and approaches to extract useful information from Social, Surface, Deep, and Dark Web in order to develop a classification tool and a trend analysis tool.

On the one hand, the following text summarises the approach we followed to classify any given web page from the Surface, Deep, and Dark Web to give a clear insight of its content and being independent from the language constraint. First, using a random forest machine learning approach we were able to predict with an accuracy 81.664%, whether a web page contains illegal activities, making use of the 3 activity classes (Suspicious, Unknown, Normal) as dependent variable. Second, our proposed approach showed an accuracy of 66.251% on 26 different classes of a specific activity type (i.e., Drugs, Hacking, Forum, Social-Network, Violence, Fraud, Counterfeit-Money, etc.). Finally, we rank recommendations to provide the best approach to predict the content of a web page is to use both website appearance and software quality parameters.

On the other hand, in order to classify different web sites we developed an architecture to collect, preprocess and model data. On top of that, we conducted a trend analysis on the classifications, in order to see if there are relations between observable factors (e.g., if more cocaine is being sold, there is less hash being sold). The process starts from the information gathering from different pages, in order to extract all possible information about vendors and products of different markets. This process is executed on the same pages in different interval of time. In this way, it is possible to analyze the trend of different variable, as price or number of visualization. The Fig. 2 shows the trend analysis applied on the order finalized by different vendors. The figure shows two snapshots: one related to the order finalized in 2019-09-11 and the other the order finalized in 2019-09-18; even from this single datapoint a trend in the time-series is evident.

3.1 Trend Analysis Module Architecture

The scraping tool consists of four consecutive steps. These steps will globally be discussed to give an overview of the design of the tool. In the next chapter will discuss each part in a little more depth. The overview is given in Fig. 3.

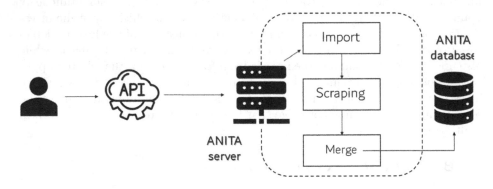

Fig. 3. General overview of the scraping part of the tool.

The goal of the complete tool is to extract features from darknet market and to structurally store this information to be able to find changes and trends in the pages about vendors or products on these markets. This can be done by manually looking at the information for specific vendors or products or using the accompanying visualization tool.

The input of the tool consists of a dump of a market to be scraped in a ZIP format or as a simple folder. The tool can take the information of the market by the user himself or it can automatically extract the information inside the web pages included in the ZIP file.

1. **Import.** The first phase imports and filters the useful files out of the provided dump of the market. The tool takes the HTML files and checks whether the HTML file is a page about a vendor or product. At the end of the entire process, all pages analyzed are removed from the server, except for the ZIP file, that is stored in the system for security purpose.
2. **Scrape.** The second phase is focused on retrieving the features out of the HTML files. While every market is different, every market has a separate file that includes the information what to scrape from the page. In this phase the file simply scrapes this information to save in the database.
3. **Merge.** The third phase focuses on merging the scraped information. While markets usually contain out of different pages that might contain the same information, there will be duplicate values in the data. For example, the profile page of a vendor might have information about the score of the vendor, while the page about feedback also contains this information. The merge step merges the information per page into information per vendor or product.
4. **Export into database.** The last phase saves the information extracted in the scraping step and merged in the merge step into the database.

At the end of the process, the information extracted are saved into the db. In order to give access of those information to the end user, we provide some API services.

4   Conclusion

The ANITA project aims to define a tool for monitoring and fighting illegal trafficking activities on the Dark Web. To support this goal, ANITA provides a pipeline that, after having analyzed the Dark Web to discover different black markets and extract information from them, it applies different approaches to analyse them, from Big Data analysis to Knowledge management, allowing the interaction from all these components to improve results. In our case, we are focusing on the Big Data risks and trends analysis services experimentation and implementation. We implemented two different approaches, one based on the analysis of web pages using software quality, making the entire process language-independent. The other approach, starting from many product and vendor pages, provides a trend analysis among all variables extracted from these pages (e.g. price, order finalized, and trends).

References

1. Lewis, J., Baker, S.: The economic impact of cybercrime and cyber espionage. Technical report, Centre for Strategic and International Studies (2013)
2. Miller, C.H., et al.: Training law enforcement officers to identify reliable deception cues with a serious digital game. IJGBL **9**(3), 1–22 (2019)

Quality Assurance of Heterogeneous Applications: The SODALITE Approach

Indika Kumara[1,2]([✉]), Giovanni Quattrocchi[3], Damian Tamburri[1,2], and Willem-Jan Van Den Heuvel[1,2]

[1] Jheronimus Academy of Data Science (JADS), 's-Hertogenbosch, Netherlands
[2] Eindhoven University of Technology (TUe), Eindhoven, Netherlands
{i.p.k.weerasingha.dewage,d.a.tamburri,W.J.A.M.vdnHeuvel}@tue.nl
[3] Politecnico di Milano, Milan, Italy
giovanni.quattrocchi@polimi.it

Abstract. A key focus of the SODALITE project is to assure the quality and performance of the deployments of applications over heterogeneous Cloud and HPC environments. It offers a set of tools to detect and correct errors, smells, and bugs in the deployment models and their provisioning workflows, and a framework to monitor and refactor deployment model instances at runtime. This paper presents objectives, designs, early results of the quality assurance framework and the refactoring framework.

Keywords: IaC · Cloud · HPC · Quality · Defects · Refactoring

1 Introduction

In recent years the global market has seen a tremendous rise in utility computing, which serves as the back-end for practically any new technology, methodology or advancement from healthcare to aerospace. We are entering a new era of heterogeneous, software-defined, high-performance computing environments. In this context, modern distributed applications should be able to utilize heterogeneous Cloud and HPC (High Performance Computing) infrastructures.

The SODALITE (SOftware Defined AppLication Infrastructures managemenT and Engineering) project aims to support development and operation teams in exploiting heterogeneity. It provides application developers and infrastructure operators with tools that abstract their application and infrastructure requirements to enable simpler and faster development, deployment, operation, and execution of heterogeneous applications.

The SODALITE consortium consists of four academic partners CERTH (Centre for Research and Technology), Jheronimus Academy of Data Science, Polytechnic University of Milan, University of Stuttgart, and five industrial partners ADPT, ATOS, CRAY, XLAB, and IBM. The website and the Github repository of the SODALITE can be found at *sodalite.eu* and *github.com/SODALITE-EU*. The project runs from February 2019 to February 2022.

© Springer Nature Switzerland AG 2021
C. Zirpins et al. (Eds.): ESOCC 2020 Workshops, CCIS 1360, pp. 173–178, 2021.
https://doi.org/10.1007/978-3-030-71906-7_16

A key objective of the SODALITE is to assure quality and performance of heterogeneous applications. To this end, the project builds a taxonomy of errors, bugs, smells, and their resolutions, all pertaining to the deployment of heterogeneous applications (Sect. 3). Based on this taxonomy, the project builds the tools for verifying and validating deployment models, and predicting smells and bugs in them (Sect. 4). Continuously changing workload and infrastructure resources can make a given deployment suboptimal. Thus, the SODALITE also includes a framework that can monitor the application and its infrastructure, and refactor the deployment as appropriate (Sect. 5). This paper presents goals, designs, and early results of the aforementioned project outcomes.

2   The SODALITE Framework: Overview

Figure 1 shows the high level architecture of the SODALITE framework. The heterogeneous target infrastructures are highlighted at the bottom. Currently, we offer support for Openstack, Edge clusters managed by Kubernetes, and HPC clusters managed by the Torque workload manager. All components in the framework rely on the presence of a *Knowledgebase*, which consists of knowledge graphs defining the concepts and the constraints that are relevant to heterogeneous applications as well as the information about the deployed application and the available resources. The IDE and Domain Specific Language (DSL) enable the DevOps teams to model their applications in terms of the components to be deployed and executed. The model-to-model transformation is applied to translate the models defined in the DSL into infrastructural codes in TOSCA (Topology and Orchestration Specification for Cloud Applications) [5] and IaC (Infrastructure as Code) languages [3] such as Ansible, Chef, and Puppet. Orchestrator executes the generated infrastructural codes to deploy the application in its operational environment on multiple infrastructural resources. To enable defect-free, optimized of deployment of applications, SODALITE also offers a set of application and infrastructural code optimizers, which is the focus of this paper.

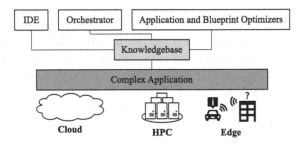

Fig. 1. Overview of the SODALITE Framework

3   Taxonomy of Smells, Bugs, Errors, and Resolutions

A software engineer can inadvertently introduce bugs/smells/errors to the deployment models. A specific result of the SODALITE project is a taxonomy of bugs/smells/errors, and their resolutions for TOSCA and IaC. The taxonomy is to support the development and evaluation of the tools that can predict bugs/smells/errors in heterogeneous application deployments and recommend fixes (see Sect. 4).

- **IaC and TOSCA Smells and Resolutions.** We have identified and categorized the smells and their fixes from a multivocal literature review on the best and bad practices for IaC and TOSCA.
- **IaC and TOSCA Bugs and Resolutions.** A qualitative analysis of commit messages and issue reports is used to derive a taxonomy and data set for IaC bugs and fixes. We are in the latter stages of this study.
- **Cloud and HPC Application Bugs/Errors and Resolutions.** We have started a literature review on the bugs and errors pertaining to deployment, operation, and execution of Cloud and HPC applications.
- **IaC and TOSCA Errors and Resolutions.** We have identified an initial set of IaC and TOSCA errors and their resolutions from the literature. We will create a complete taxonomy of errors and resolutions based on the results of the above three studies.

4   The SODALITE Quality Assurance Framework

We provide the developers with a QA framework to find and correct (verification) errors (e.g., inconsistencies), smells, and bugs in a deployment model and its provisioning workflow/plan specified in TOSCA and IaC (the initial focus is on

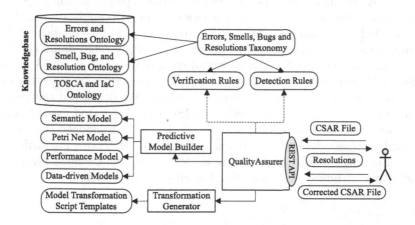

Fig. 2. The SODALITE Quality Assurance Framework

Ansible). The developers can also analyze and validate the performance of an application deployment with our QA framework.

We use the ontological reasoning to verify the constraints over the structures of TOSCA blueprints and IaC scripts. To verify the constraints over the provisioning workflow (e.g., deadlock detection), we use Petri Net models. To detect smells/bugs, we use three main approaches: informal rules, semantic rules, and data-driven approaches. The informal rules are the detection rules supported by the existing linter tools for IaC (e.g., Ansible-Lint). The semantic rules are reasoning rules over the SODALITE ontologies. The data-driven approaches adopt and further extend the existing machine learning based bug prediction methods developed for general purpose languages. The performance modeling employs a combination of benchmarking/profiling and simulation.

Figure 2 provides an overview of our QA framework. *Knowledgebase* consists of TOSCA ontology, IaC ontology, errors and resolutions ontology, and smells/bugs and resolutions ontology. We create the first two ontologies based on the TOSCA standard and IaC specifications, and the last two ontologies using the above taxonomies. We use the taxonomies also for defining verification rules and smells/bugs detection rules. *QualityAssurer* takes as input a CSAR (Cloud Service Archive) file consisting of TOSCA, IaC scripts, and performance goals, and uses *Predictive Model Builder* to build the required prediction models. *Predictive Model Builder* can build different types of models: knowledge-based and data-driven models for smells/bugs prediction, knowledge-based models and Petri net models for verification, and statistical models for performance estimation. *QualityAssurer* uses the created models to predict smells/bugs and identify errors and performance violations. It also queries the *Knowledgebase* to recommend the potential fixes. A software engineer can select the desired fixes from the recommendations, and apply the selected fixes to correct the defective artifacts. To ensure consistency and reduce errors, we use model transformations to automate the correction of defective artifacts. Using a template-based approach, *Transformation Generator* generates the required model transformation scripts.

The early results include the verification of the deployment topologies using semantic reasoning, and the performance modeling of HPC applications using the data collected from running HPC benchmarks (e.g., LINPACK and STREAM Benchmark) and applying regression analysis on the collected data. The initial support for transforming an Ansible workflow into a Petri Net model has been developed. We extended the Ansible-Lint tool by adding rules for detecting smells (implementation, design, and security) in Ansible. We developed the semantic reasoning for detecting security smells in TOSCA [4]. A curated dataset of Ansible has been created to develop and evaluate data-driven models. We have also developed deep learning and NLP based techniques for detecting linguistic smells and module usage issues in IaC [2]. We are extending the CloudSim framework (*cloudbus.org/cloudsim*) for simulating heterogeneous applications.

5   The SODALITE Refactoring Framework

The main objective of the predictive deployment refactoring is to refactor or adapt the deployment model of an application at runtime to prevent the violation of the performance goals of the application. The components of an application can be deployed in different ways using heterogeneous resources (e.g., a small VM and a large VM) and deployment patterns (single node, cluster, with or without cache, with or without firewall), resulting alternative deployment options. A valid selection of deployment options results in a valid deployment model variant for the application. The deployment refactoring requires a model that can estimate the impacts of a given deployment option selection on the performance metrics under different contexts such as different workloads.

Figure 3 provides an overview of the SODALITE refactoring support. At the design time, we profile deployment variants to collect the data required to build the machine-learning based predictive model. At runtime, the *Refactorer* monitors the deployed application to collect the data and to update the learned model. The predictive model enables the *Refactorer* to predict the potential violations of the application goals, and consequently to find alternative deployment model variants. As the deployment environment evolves, the new resources will be added and the existing resources will be removed or updated. The *Refactorer* discovers new deployment options, the changes to the currently used deployment options, and the bugs introduced by the changes (e.g., performance anti-patterns).

Given the performance goals and the deployment model variant selected at runtime by the *Refactorer*, the SODALITE framework employs distributed control-theoretical planners to further refine the resource allocation of running heterogeneous applications [1]. For each component deployed in each node of the deployment model, a dedicated *controller* oversees its execution and reallocates CPU and GPU cores without restarting the actual software (i.e., vertical scalability). In addition to the controllers, a *supervisor* is deployed on each node to manage resource contention scenarios that could occur among components running on the same machine. The supervisor governs the allocation of resources

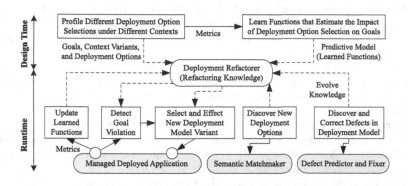

Fig. 3. The SODALITE refactoring framework

according to the actual resources requested (by the controllers), the priority of each component and monitored performance.

We have so far completed the design time part of our framework and implemented the control-theoretical layer. We have developed the methodology to model the deployment variability of heterogeneous applications using the variability modeling techniques. Furthermore, We have developed the approach to profile the different development option selections under different workload ranges, and to use the profiled data to build the machine learning based prediction model. The initial support for semantic matchmaking of deployment options (for discovering new deployment options) also has been developed. The control-theoretical planner can re-configure Kubernetes containers dynamically to maintain response time targets. It currently supports TensorFlow applications that can use both GPUs and CPUs.

6   Conclusion

This paper presented an overview of three key tasks of the SODALITE project. During the second year of the project, we plan to complete the taxonomies and the verification support, and to develop data-driven approaches for predicting IaC bugs and for supporting deployment refactoring. During the last year, we plan to complete the rest of the defect prediction tool and the refactorer, and to validate the project outcomes with the industrial case studies.

Acknowledgement. This paper has been supported by the European Union's Horizon 2020 research and innovation programme under grant agreement no. 825480, SODALITE. We thank all members of the SODALITE consortium for their inputs and feedbacks to the development of this paper.

References

1. Baresi, L., Leva, A., Quattrocchi, G.: Fine-grained dynamic resource allocation for big-data applications. IEEE Trans. Softw. Eng. 1 (2019). https://doi.org/10.1109/TSE.2019.2931537
2. Borovits, N., et al.: DeepiaC: deep learning-based linguistic anti-pattern detection in IaC. In: Proceedings of the 4th ACM SIGSOFT International Workshop on Machine-Learning Techniques for Software-Quality Evaluation, MaLTeSQuE 2020, pp. 7–12. Association for Computing Machinery, New York (2020). https://doi.org/10.1145/3416505.3423564
3. Guerriero, M., Garriga, M., Tamburri, D.A., Palomba, F.: Adoption, support, and challenges of infrastructure-as-code: insights from industry. In: 2019 IEEE International Conference on Software Maintenance and Evolution (ICSME), pp. 580–589. IEEE (2019)
4. Kumara, I., et al.: Towards semantic detection of smells in cloud infrastructure code. In: Proceedings of the 10th International Conference on Web Intelligence, Mining and Semantics, WIMS 2020, pp. 63–67. Association for Computing Machinery, New York (2020). https://doi.org/10.1145/3405962.3405979
5. Lipton, P., Lauwers, C., Rutkowski, M., Lauwers, C., Noshpitz, C., Curescu, C.: Tosca simple profile in YAML version 1.3. OASIS Committee Specification 1 (2020)

FogProtect: Protecting Sensitive Data in the Computing Continuum

Dhouha Ayed[1], Eva Jaho[2], Clemens Lachner[3]([✉]), Zoltán Ádám Mann[4],
Robert Seidl[5], and Mike Surridge[6]

[1] Thales, Paris, France
[2] Athens Technology Center, Athens, Greece
[3] TU Wien, Wien, Austria
`c.lachner@dsg.tuwien.ac.at`
[4] University of Duisburg-Essen, Essen, Germany
[5] Nokia Bell Labs, Munich, Germany
[6] University of Southampton, Southampton, UK

Abstract. Computing resources are being moved towards the edge of
the network, in the form of so-called fog nodes, providing benefits in
terms of reduced latency, increased processing speed, data locality, and
energy savings. Data produced in end devices like smartphones, sensors
or IoT devices can be stored, processed and analysed across a continuum
of computing resources, from end devices via fog nodes to cloud services.
Data related to critical domains, such as healthcare, public surveillance
or home automation, requires tailored data protection mechanisms, spanning the whole computing continuum.

The FogProtect project aims to provide novel advanced technologies
and methodologies to ensure end-to-end protection of such sensitive data.
Our generic solutions facilitate the provisioning and usage of applications
and services in the computing continuum, by combining four technology
innovations: (1) secure data container technology for data portability and
mobility, (2) data-protection-aware adaptive service and resource management, (3) advanced data protection policy management, (4) dynamic
data protection risk management models and tools.

The applicability and impact of those solutions is evaluated and
demonstrated on three complementary real-world use cases in the area
of (1) smart cities, (2) smart manufacturing, and (3) smart media.

Keywords: Fog computing · Edge computing · Data protection ·
Privacy · Computing continuum · Adaptive systems · Policy
management

1 Basic Project Information

The project "FogProtect: Protecting Sensitive Data in the Computing Continuum" is a research and innovation action funded by the European Union's Horizon 2020 programme. The project runs from January 2020 to December 2022.
The project website is at https://fogprotect.eu/.

This project has received funding from the European Union's Horizon 2020 research
and innovation programme under grant agreement No. 871525 (FogProtect).

© Springer Nature Switzerland AG 2021
C. Zirpins et al. (Eds.): ESOCC 2020 Workshops, CCIS 1360, pp. 179–184, 2021.
https://doi.org/10.1007/978-3-030-71906-7_17

The project consortium is led by Ubiwhere LDA (Portugal) and further comprises the following organizations: Athens Technology Center SA (Greece), IBM Israel Science and Technology LTD (Israel), University of Southampton (UK), Nokia Solutions and Networks GmbH & Co. KG (Germany), Thales SIX GTS France SAS (France), Technische Universität Wien (Austria), University of Duisburg-Essen (Germany), De Vlaamse Radio- en Televisieomroeporganisatie nv (Belgium).

2   Project Objectives

Cloud computing is transitioning from few large data centres to a truly decentralized paradigm, where resources are increasingly provided near the network edge, in the form of so-called fog nodes. Data produced in end devices (e.g., smartphones, sensors or other IoT devices) can be processed across a continuum of computing resources, comprising cloud services, fog nodes, and end devices [2]. By distributing data processing functionalities over this computing continuum, an optimal trade-off between conflicting goals – such as low network latency between data sources and data processors, high processing speed and low energy consumption – can be achieved [1].

However, this widely distributed processing of data also introduces new challenges concerning the protection of sensitive data [5, 9, 10]. During our research we identified the following major problems of data protection in the computing continuum [6]:

- Resource limitations of fog nodes and end devices constrain data protection methods
- Heterogeneity of fog nodes and end devices hampers consistent security
- Node connectivity meta-data can leak sensitive information, such as users' location
- Mobility of devices requires compliance with changing data protection policies
- Frequent changes at the edge imply highly dynamic changes of data protection risks
- Lack of transparency about stakeholders may lead to unauthorized data access

To tackle these issues, FogProtect will deliver new and advanced generic technologies, mechanisms, and solutions to ensure end-to-end data protection across the computing continuum. This also involves securing the whole life-cycle of data, taking into account the rights and obligations of data subjects, data controllers, data processors, and data users. In particular, FogProtect will make it easier for data controllers to comply with relevant data protection regulation, such as the EU General Data Protection Regulation (GDPR), and for data subjects to exercise the rights stipulated by the regulation.

As shown in Fig. 1, FogProtect combines four innovation areas to deliver increased management capabilities towards end-to-end data protection. A brief introduction of each innovation area is given in the next subsections.

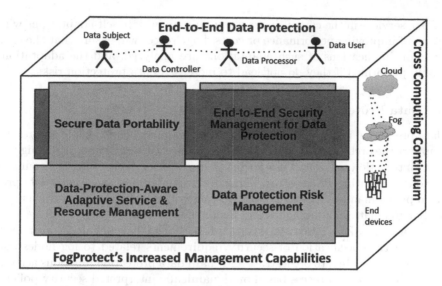

Fig. 1. An overview of FogProtects's four innovation areas.

2.1 Secure Data Portability

Dynamically composable, logical data encapsulation will provide data protection guarantees not only for the storage of data, but also for processing and egress to other sources in conformance with policies regulating the usage of data. To achieve that, FogProtect will create a layered framework, where different pluggable tools and technologies can be used at each layer in accordance with both the nature of the data and purpose of the data processing.

2.2 Data-Protection-Aware Adaptive Service and Resource Management

Based on continuous monitoring and analysis of data protection risks, appropriate adaptations will be carried out automatically. These adaptations will ensure the continued assurance of data protection in spite of changes [6]. For this purpose, FogProtect will create a model-based approach, in which the current system configuration is explicitly modeled in a machine-readable format, and kept up-to-date using monitoring.

For reasoning on possible adaptations to mitigate data protection risks, methods from artificial intelligence (optimization, planning, machine learning) will be used. Adaptations may relate to both the infrastructure of the computing continuum and applications running on that infrastructure. If multiple adaptations are possible to mitigate the found data protection risks, FogProtect will aim to select the best adaptations concerning their impact on other goals like performance and costs.

Also, services in the computing continuum may initiate self-adaptations with the aim of improving performance or costs. FogProtect will ensure that the data protection implications of such adaptations are analyzed, and the adaptations are only performed if they do not lead to increased data protection risks.

2.3 Data Protection Policy Management

A data protection policy management solution requires being flexible and robust to support the orchestration layer of the fog architecture and support the big volume of interaction and data transfer between end-user devices, fog environment and cloud computing data centres. Therefore, we provide an end-to-end data protection policy management framework dealing with the distrusted, multi-tenant, and dynamic nature of fog nodes and instances.

The framework is based on a data protection policy definition formalism supporting the specification of security requirements related to fog nodes and instances and a system to orchestrate and chain data protection functions according to smart decision process based on dynamically interpreted security policies and data protection regulation.

The data protection policy formalism offers the administrators the flexibility to bound data of various subjects to a given application while having the ability to migrate across multiple fog nodes during the data lifecycle with a smart reasoning on policies and a refinement of the implication of data protection policies on various fog nodes and end-user devices.

The orchestrated data protection functions take into account the distributed nature of the environment and could be virtualized enforcement points, enforcement points for constrained environment, attack detection functions, etc. For instance, the best practice for devices that deliver data on demand is to position a Policy Enforcement Point (PEP) closest to the data to protect. Consequently, various PEPs need to be deployed at several devices and nodes of the fog. However, such enforcement requires the knowledge of the current protection policy in force that is generally managed in a centralized point. The services running on constrained devices might not have a constant connectivity to a centralized decision point to enforce the policy. In this case, a lightweight enforcement process is needed. It can for example be based on a standalone access token without permanently relying on a central decision point.

2.4 Data Protection Risk Management

We identify, analyse and control sources of cyber-security risks (i.e., threats) over the lifecycle of applications in the computing continuum. This involves (i) the development of knowledge and inference methods to construct predictive models of potential risks prior to deployment and (ii) the use of information acquired (and mostly only available) after deployment, to diagnose run-time threats and trigger adaptations or policy changes to manage the associated risks. The goal is to use an automated ISO 27005 risk assessment procedure [3,4], embedding it into the autonomic management loop so risk levels can be taken into account.

This will allow trading risk factors near the edge (such as limited physical protection) and near the data centre (such as the aggregation of data), as well as using data protection risk levels to constrain other autonomic management of factors such as cost, performance, energy use, etc.

3   Use Cases

Three complementary real-world use cases evaluate and demonstrate the applicability and impact of the FogProtect solutions introduced in the previous chapter. The use cases are focusing on different industrial sectors spanning multiple contexts: (1) smart cities, (2) smart manufacturing, and (3) smart media. Each use case entails different, specific data protection challenges from these sectors. This will enable being the ideal platform to reflect the whole life-cycle of data, taking into account the rights and obligations of data subjects, data controllers, data processors, and data users by ensuring end-to-end data protection across the computing continuum.

On the one hand, the use cases help the project team to identify requirements and constraints that the solutions developed in the project need to address. On the other hand, the demonstration and validation of the solutions developed in the project will also be carried out in the context of the use cases.

4   Current Project Status

The project has started recently. The focus of the first project phase has been on the elicitation of requirements from different sources (the project's use cases, the relevant literature, relevant standardization activities etc.) and on defining the architectural and technological foundations of the project, based on well established formalization methods, standards and processes [7]. Additionally, the state of the art is analyzed, regarding cutting-edge technology, concepts, and architectures in the area of application and infrastructure orchestration as well as data protection, risk management, and policy management.

The next step is the detailed specification of the technical components of FogProtect and their interfaces. A first prototype – integrated, tested, and validated on the use cases – will be available at month 18 of the project (June 2021). In the second half of the project, the FogProtect solutions will be refined and extended in a second iteration, taking into account the experience with the first prototype as well as new technical developments.

FogProtect leverages knowledge and experience gathered in previous work of project partners in the recently finished RestAssured project [8]. Therefore, we expect to be able to quickly resolve the architectural questions and to start working on the specific innovation areas.

References

1. Bellendorf, J., Mann, Z.Á.: Classification of optimization problems in fog computing. Future Gener. Comput. Syst. **107**, 158–176 (2020)
2. Bonomi, F., Milito, R., Zhu, J., Addepalli, S.: Fog computing and its role in the internet of things. In: Proceedings of the First Edition of the MCC Workshop on Mobile Cloud Computing, pp. 13–16 (2012)
3. Chakravarthy, A., Wiegand, S., Chen, W., Nasser, B., Surridge, M.: Trustworthy systems design using semantic risk modelling. In: Proceedings of 1st International Conference on Cyber Security for Sustainable Society, pp. 49–81 (2015)
4. Goeke, L., Heisel, M., Mohammadi, N., Surridge, M.: Systematic risk assessment of cloud computing systems using a combined model-based approach. In: 22nd International Conference on Enterprise Information Systems, Prague, May 2020. to appear (2020)
5. He, T., Ciftcioglu, E.N., Wang, S., Chan, K.S.: Location privacy in mobile edge clouds: a chaff-based approach. IEEE J. Sel. Areas Commun. **35**(11), 2625–2636 (2017)
6. Mann, Z.Á.: Data protection in fog computing through monitoring and adaptation. KuVS-Fachgespräch Fog Comput. **2018**, 25–28 (2018)
7. Mann, Z.Á.: Notions of architecture in fog computing. Computing. **103**, 51–73 (2021). https://doi.org/10.1007/s00607-020-00848-z
8. Mann, Z.Á., et al.: Secure data processing in the cloud. In: Mann, Z.Á., Stolz, V. (eds.) Advances in Service-Oriented and Cloud Computing: Workshops of ESOCC 2017. CCIS, vol. 824, pp. 149–153. Springer, Cham (2018). https://doi.org/10.1007/978-3-319-79090-9_10
9. Roman, R., Lopez, J., Mambo, M.: Mobile edge computing, Fog et al.: a survey and analysis of security threats and challenges. Future Gener. Comput. Syst. **78**, 680–698 (2018)
10. Stojmenovic, I., Wen, S., Huang, X., Luan, H.: An overview of fog computing and its security issues. Concurrency Comput. Pract. Experience **28**(10), 2991–3005 (2016)

Intelligent Monitoring of Virtualized Services

Thanasis Tziouvaras[1] and Kostas Kolomvatsos[2(✉)]

[1] Department of Electrical and Computer Engineering, University of Thessaly, Volos, Greece
attziouv@uth.gr
[2] Department of Informatics and Telecommunications, University of Thessaly, Lamia, Greece
kostasks@uth.gr

Abstract. Interactive TV applications impose novel requirements in future networks due to the huge volumes of data transferred through the network. ENFORCE provides a framework for the management of such applications targeting to support the real time adaptation on end users needs. The project offers a set of functionalities over virtualized resources as provided by the SoftFIRE platform. Apart from the envisioned functionalities, ENFORCE acts as a benchmarking tool and an extension to the SoftFIRE framework enhancing its monitoring capabilities for the provided virtualized resources and services. Our aim is to pro-actively respond to changes in iTV demand, thus, making the platform fully aligned with the real needs of end users. In ENFORCE, virtual resources are defined for realizing Set top Boxes (STBs) functionalities to be transformed to virtual STBs (vSTBs).

Keywords: Interactive TV services · Intelligent monitoring · Virtualized services

1 Introduction

Future networks are expected to involve numerous heterogeneous devices interconnected to support a variety of applications. Among them, interactive TV (iTV) applications are of great importance. Such applications are characterized by **increased traffic** and **continuous changes** in the service demand. In this respect, intelligent approaches should be investigated to improve efficiency. ENFORCE proposes the adoption of an intelligent framework for the **continuous fulfillment** of iTV application requirements. We deploy a real time intelligent monitoring module capable of proactively detecting changes in demand and performance of iTV services. Reconfiguration, Virtualized Network Functions (VNFs) processing and proactive response to demand changes are subjects where ENFORCE provides solutions in direct combination with the SoftFIRE platform. The proposed monitoring mechanism is combined with the VNFs controller to reconfigure the virtualized resources performing scaling up/down actions on demand. ENFORCE also offers a benchmarking tool that reveals the strengths and weaknesses of the aforementioned solution. In this sense, the evaluation of the monitoring mechanism and the

Project: Intelligent Monitoring of Networking Services (ENFORCE).
Call: SoftFIRE Project Open Call II (June–October 2017).

© Springer Nature Switzerland AG 2021
C. Zirpins et al. (Eds.): ESOCC 2020 Workshops, CCIS 1360, pp. 185–189, 2021.
https://doi.org/10.1007/978-3-030-71906-7_18

platform is conducted over multiple test scenarios where the demand for iTV services and their performance requirements varies.

The following list depicts ENFORCE's contributions:

- The provision of an extension of the SoftFIRE platform (monitoring of iTV services demand) that will issue the adaptation on demand changes through the adoption of forecasting techniques. The extension will be capable of reacting in the case where changes in the demand are identified, thus, the automated scalability could be secured.
- The provision of a tool that enables benchmarking of the platform. ENFORCE simulates iTV services demand and tests the performance of the platform to reveal any possible problems in the management mechanism of the virtualized resources as well as possible pitfalls in the VNF infrastructure manager.
- Support of iTV Services. ENFORCE provides experimentation for two parts of a virtual Set top Box (vSTB), i.e., the vPVR (virtual Personal Video Recorder) and the aggregation of video streams defined in multiple formats. ENFORCE defines a service for manipulating the incoming requests from clients concerning the aforementioned functionalities.

2   Related Work

5G technology is in its infancy, thus, only a few frameworks are already present in the field. In short, some important research projects in the domain are as follows: ACTORS [1] aims to design a methodology that combines virtualization, feedback and actors-based dataflow programming in resource-constrained software-intensive embedded systems. EVANS [2] focuses on the management aspects of the virtualized network resources rather than the virtualization techniques of physical network resources. NUBOMEDIA [3] tries to minimize the complexity of infrastructures by creating a specific purpose Cloud platform bringing all the Cloud advantages to the arena of real-time interactive multimedia. VIDA [4] proposes data virtualization as the basis of design of a query engine and is used to efficiently access, query, and integrate raw data.

3   The ENFORCE Solution

3.1   High Level Description

ENFORCE provides the definition of virtualized STB functions for supporting iTV services. Our solution employs virtualized resources to create the respective services due to the unique opportunity they provide for shifting certain functionalities to the Cloud. The planned activity within **ENFORCE implements a part of a vSTB** which relies on open technologies for delivering improved customer experience applications. Such technologies include but are not limited to personal video recording, WWW-based content enrichment, parental control services and personalized content delivery. The virtualized resources are defined with the adoption of the SoftFIRE components and are fully aligned with the platform's specifications and needs.

The ENFORCE solution provides VNFs and service function chains required to support **two parts of a vSTB** i.e., *the vPVR (virtual Personal Video Recorder) and the aggregation of video streams defined in multiple formats*. For the first functionality, ENFORCE defines a service for storing the available data for future reference while for the second functionality we employ a decoding, an aggregation and an encoding scheme for multiple resource combination and service provisioning in the final video stream. We also deploy a monitoring mechanism that oversees the demand for the afore-mentioned functionalities and triggers the re-configuration process of the services in the form of scaling up / down the available resources. Specifically, *for the first function-ality, ENFORCE upgrades / downgrades the storage of resources while for the second functionality upgrades / downgrades the VNF chains for handling increased / decreased input streams*. The input streams adopted for testing are those that are available on the Web (e.g., Youtube streaming TV service).

The monitoring mechanism amounts to a set of performance metrics that can be considered appropriate for evaluating an invoked VNF in terms of '*quality*'. This con-textual information, aggregated and stored by ENFORCE, forms the ***pattern behavior of a VNF***. ENFORCE further provides efficient mechanisms for supporting intelligent analytics tasks, such as statistical queries over the performance metrics that provide more useful and historical information about VNFs. The historical analysis of behavioral pat-terns of a service in terms of its performance metrics results to a ***rich knowledge*** on the pattern a service is running. In order to encompass the aforementioned functionalities, we design and deploy an intelligent monitoring module as described below.

3.2 Intelligent Monitoring

This module enables ENFORCE to monitor a large number of iTV services and trigger the appropriate modules to take actions related to the services life cycle. This process is performed in real time as the discussed scenario involves a dynamic environment where demand changes continually while ENFORCE aims at maintaining the performance of the system at high levels. To accomplish this, an intelligent monitoring component gath-ers data related to the performance of services. Such information is then utilized to take actions related to service scaling. To this end, a number of ***Key Performance Indicators*** (KPI) is defined which are gathered by a monitoring probe that is configured with the endpoint of the monitoring service. A scaling action is initiated when: (a) the system deduces that the application requirements require higher or lower service performance levels compared to the current setting, or (b) the system observes the performance of services and decides when the application requirements are not fulfilled. We have also deployed forecasting algorithms that are able to cope with the temporal nature of the traffic data. Briefly, we consider a hierarchical structured network in which users issue requests for iTV services. These requests require the reservation of application and net-work resources as they generate network and application traffic respectively. In terms of abstract modeling approaches, we consider such traffic equivalent. In this sense, we treat them as traffic prediction problems and use the same type of learning tools and ideas to address them. In order to evaluate the efficiency of our solution we utilize a benchmarking scheme capable of covering the required scenarios.

4   ENFORCE Implementation Details and KPIs

The setup of our experiment is centered on a client-server scheme in which we are monitoring each node's behavior while also obtaining the necessary metrics during the experiment execution. SoftFIRE uses VNFs to provide the functionality required by the experimenter. In order to reserve, deploy and use the provided VNFs, we adopt **Topology and Orchestration Specification for Cloud Applications** (TOSCA) files which are uploaded directly to the reservation system. We deploy a client and a server VM which are be able to communicate with each other exchange information such as vSTbs requests and video streams. Our aim is to identify whether the involved VMs can efficiently support a high number of clients while serving their requests in parallel. Hence, we use a custom VNF which houses the client-server connection and we instantiate it by having a 16.04 Ubuntu-clean image installed. Moreover, we specify the connection of those two services and we designate each one's flavor key template. Flavor key template is a predetermined hardware profile which is loaded to the VM during the reservation stage. The performance of the platform is evaluated based on three KPIs:

- **Latency**. This KPI aims to provide insights on the latency of invoking the iTV services implemented in the ENFORCE project. The latency was recorded just after the request for invocation of the offered services. Our aim is to maintain the latency values below a pre-defined threshold. When the latency is below the designated threshold (e.g., 5–8 s), the Latency KPI will be fulfilled. For verifying the KPI, ENFORCE created multiple services requests and measured the observed aggregated latency.
- **Service availability**. This KPI deals with the availability of the implemented services. Services should be always available to the requests for iTV functionalities. Service availability was verified by creating multiple requests to the provided services and measuring the number of the correct invocations. After the execution of the experiment, the percentage of the correct invocations was calculated.
- **Storage demand fulfilment**. This KPI deals with the fulfilment percentage of the requests concerning the storage requirements (for streams that are not recorded) as users demand. ENFORCE measures the fulfilment rate based on a number of requests for iPVR functionalities. This KPI was verified by creating multiple requests for iPVR services and measuring the number of the fulfilled requests. After the execution of the experiment, the percentage of the fulfilled requests is calculated.

All the selected KPIs were evaluated in parallel during the experiment execution in order to obtain cumulative insights for the performance achieved by the ENFORCE solution.

5   Conclusions

ENFORCE experiment contributes to the understanding of the minimum requirements that efficiently support video streaming services. Our results exhibit the appropriate characteristics of the hardware required to efficiently support the desired services. The proposed monitoring mechanism can easily assist in scale in / out actions to upgrade

/ downgrade the resources involved in the virtualized environment. In this way, the management of the available physical resources is efficiently handled to maximize the performance and secure the quality of service.

Acknowledgment. This research received funding from the European's Union Horizon 2020 research and innovation programme under the project ENFORCE accepted in the 2nd SoftFIRE Open Call.

References

1. ACTORS: Adaptivity and Control of Resources in Embedded Systems (2008). https://www.actors-project.eu/. Accessed 10 Nov 2014
2. EVANS: End-to-end Virtual Resource Management across Heterogeneous Networks and Services (2011). https://www.fp7-evans.eu/. Accessed 10 Nov 2014
3. NUBOMEDIA: an elastic Platform as a Service (PaaS) Cloud for interactive social multimedia (2013). https://www.nubomedia.eu/. Accessed 10 Nov 2014
4. VIDA: Transforming Raw Data into Information through Virtualization (2014). https://cordis.europa.eu/project/rcn/189848_en.html. Accessed 10 Nov 2014

Author Index

Printed in the United States
by Baker & Taylor Publisher Services

Printed in the United States
by Baker & Taylor Publisher Services